A

Journey

of

New Beginnings

Charlotte Davison

Dedication

As an aspiring author stepping into the world of fictional romance, I would like to express my heartfelt gratitude to my family. Their unwavering support and encouragement have been the guiding light throughout my writing journey. This book is therefore dedicated to them because their love and inspiration fuelled my passion for storytelling. I thank them for standing by me every step of the way.

Table of Contents

About Charlotte

Charlotte lives with her husband in a sleepy English village in Somerset, near the beautiful English Mendip Hills. Its location and superb scenery have always been referred to as their happy place, where life takes on a much steadier pace. They are both retired and love spending as much time as possible with their wonderful family, friends, and adorable cocker spaniel, Marley. They are fortunate to own a beautiful home in Brittany, France, where they enjoy spending holidays with family and friends.

Charlotte's working career spanned many organisations, including printing, construction, and insurance, and finally ended within the Prison Service, where she worked alongside the in-house Senior Probation Officer. This role was challenging, but it certainly gave her insight into how life can be very different on the inside.

During the lockdown in 2020, she finally had the time and inspiration to pursue her lifelong ambition of writing a fictional book. After completing her first novel, she quickly moved on to her second, eager to continue her literary journey. She is excited about the new characters and plot twists she has developed and can hardly wait to see where her imagination takes her.

Writing has become essential to her daily routine, and she is grateful for the opportunity to explore her creativity. She loves the connection with the book's characters and believes they illustrate real life in many ways. With this in mind, Charlotte hopes this novel will appeal to many readers.

With great positivity and determination, she believes that when there is something in life that you want to achieve, you should do it, challenge yourself, and not look back.

Embarking on a journey of new beginnings is like stepping into the unknown with a heart full of hope and anticipation. It's a chance to leave behind the old, embrace the new, and discover new perspectives, opportunities, and experiences. It's a time for growth, for learning, and for transformation.

This journey can take many forms, from starting a new career, moving to a new town, or even beginning a new relationship. No matter the nature of the journey, it's always filled with excitement and anticipation for what lies ahead. While the journey may be challenging, it's important to remember that every step forward is a step towards a better future. We can create a fulfilling and meaningful life by staying committed to our goals, remaining open to new experiences, and learning from our mistakes.

In short, the journey of new beginnings is a transformative experience that has the power to shape lives in unimaginable ways. It requires courage, resilience, and unwavering determination, but the rewards are immeasurable and filled with endless possibilities.

Introduction

In the captivating story "A Journey of New Beginnings," we follow the adventures of Ella, a spirited young woman longing to explore Europe after graduating from university. One fateful day, while browsing a local newspaper, Ella stumbled upon an intriguing advertisement seeking travel companions for an adventurous backpacking expedition across Europe. Eager to seize this opportunity, she promptly responded to the ad and soon discovered that two other like-minded young women shared her aspiration. As they came together, a strong and unbreakable bond quickly formed, igniting their shared passion for exploration as they embarked on their extraordinary journey across Europe.

As they travelled through different countries, they encountered various challenges and experiences that changed their lives forever. They visited famous landmarks, tried new foods, and met people from different walks of life. The trio faced many challenges throughout their travels, from unexpected obstacles to heartache and drama. Despite these hardships, Ella and her friends remained determined to make the most of their journey. They learned to adapt to new environments, confront their fears, and rely on each other for support.

Throughout her journey, Ella realised that life is an intricate web of unpredictable events, constantly throwing new challenges her way. However, instead of letting these obstacles hold her back, she learned to embrace the unexpected and approach every moment with an open mind and an adventurous spirit.

As Ella navigated her path in life, she faced a significant change on the horizon. She had to manage her incredible stroke of luck and good fortune while dealing with the ups and downs of love and emotions, alongside the challenge of running her own business. Through this mindset, she discovered a new beginning—a chance to start over and take control of her life. Little did she know that this decision would ultimately lead her down a path that would change her life forever.

Chapter 1

“Another rainy day in Buckland Ridge,” Ella sighed, gazing out at the mist-shrouded hills and the droplets sliding down the window. “Looks like we’ll be stuck indoors again.”

Her mum, sitting across the room, looked up from her book. “I know, dear. It’s a shame we can’t enjoy the outdoors with this unpredictable weather.”

“Yeah, I miss the days when we could explore the hills and hiking trails,” Ella said, her voice tinged with longing and a hint of sadness.

“I remember when this place used to be bustling with tourists,” her mum added. “But it seems like the weather has driven them away.”

Ella nodded, thinking about the declining popularity of the Yorkshire Dales. “It’s a shame because the natural beauty here is stunning. The rolling hills, the lush greenery, and the serene tranquillity—it’s all so breathtaking,” she said, a hint of reverence in her voice.

Suddenly, Sammy, their black-and-white cocker spaniel, jumped up, tail wagging.

Ella laughed. “I think someone still wants to go for a walk, rain or shine.”

Her mum smiled. “Well, a little rain never hurt anyone. Just be careful out there.”

Ella quickly put on her raincoat and called Sammy, ready to brave the wet and windy weather outside. Their determination to enjoy the outdoors despite the rain was truly inspiring.

An alert suddenly caught Ella’s attention on her phone. It notified her about a flood warning for the nearby River Felling due to the expected rainfall in the area. This unexpected event made her ponder the consequences of climate change on weather patterns, which have become increasingly unpredictable locally and globally.

Ella then turned her thoughts to how much she missed her sister Lauren, who had travelled to Melbourne, Australia, along with her best friend after completing nursing college. It had been 18 months since Lauren left the UK after qualifying as a senior nurse, and despite regular virtual communication, Ella and her mum still missed her terribly.

As the days turned into months, the possibility of Lauren's permanent stay in Australia seemed more likely. However, Ella and her mum held on to hope for her potential return, which kept their spirits high. The future was uncertain, but they remained optimistic.

Constantly imagining how wonderful life would be in the sun, Ella couldn't help but feel envious of her sister's new life. Lauren's life was absolute bliss. She soaked up the sun, rode the waves, and indulged in beach barbecues. She often shared photos of her adventures, making them feel like they were with her.

Ella often daydreamed about visiting her beloved sister someday, perhaps bringing their dear mother along if funds allowed. Despite the tragic loss of their father in a work accident, Ella's mother, on a modest income, raised both her and Lauren. This early hardship only fuelled Ella's determination to succeed.

Thankfully, the compensation from the accident allowed her mother to pay off the mortgage, a significant relief, and even left some extra money for emergencies. Ella's mother worked as a dinner lady and cleaner at a local junior school, doing her best to make ends meet. Being a single-parent family, they didn't have the same luxuries as others, but this never deterred Ella's spirit.

At 18, Ella was fortunate to be granted a scholarship to pursue her university education. This scholarship, a testament to her mother's unwavering support, lifted the heavy financial burden her mother would have had to bear, allowing Ella to focus entirely on her academic pursuits. After three years of tireless dedication and hard work, Ella was awarded a Bachelor of Science in Food and Nutritional Science.

As Ella and Sammy made their way through the village, their footsteps sloshed through puddles created by the relentless rain that had turned the ground into a treacherous, slippery surface. Even though the downpour made the journey difficult, Ella couldn't shake off the unease as she meticulously picked her way along the precarious footpaths leading to the village.

Approaching the village newsagent, she noticed a pile of complimentary local newspapers outside. She quickly grabbed one and tucked it under her raincoat to shield it from the rain. Ella hurriedly made a U-turn and returned home after finding the newsagent deserted due to the bad weather.

Upon entering the house, her mother noticed her shivering and promptly served her hot tea and biscuits. As Ella settled into the cosy living room and began reading the newspaper, her mother asked if she found anything interesting. Ella replied casually, and her mother responded, "Just the same old stuff then."

While reading, Ella came across an advertisement inviting someone to join two girls on a backpacking trip across Europe. Intrigued, she decided to pursue the opportunity and impulsively dialled the number. She was greeted by a girl named Tilly, who appeared warm and cheerful, easing Ella's nerves.

During the call, Tilly shared her plans for a European adventure with her friend Jo and suggested meeting at a local pub in person. Excited but cautious, Ella agreed, grappling with the decision to meet for such a significant opportunity.

The following evening, Ella arrived promptly at the Stags Head pub, where they had arranged to meet. She wanted to ensure they had a comfortable place to discuss their plans, so she arrived early to secure a table. The pub buzzed with cheerful conversations, clinking glasses, and background music. Amidst the lively atmosphere, Ella saw two girls walking in through the door. She couldn't help but look at their appearance—one had strikingly pink hair, while the other had a sleek bob cut. Tilly and Jo were utterly different in looks and personality.

Tilly's pink hair and nose piercing made her stand out, while Jo, with natural hair and a petite frame, had a more understated appearance.

With her heart pounding, Ella stood at a distance and waved her arms wildly, hoping to catch the attention of the two girls. After introducing themselves, Tilly pulled out a chair and began discussing their travel plans, explaining that they would likely need to find work to finance the trip. The conversation flowed smoothly as they discussed the upcoming journey, which included taking the Eurostar to Paris and continuing from there—a prospect that filled Ella with a sense of adventure and intrigue.

Ella's mind raced with a flurry of emotions—a mix of thrill, trepidation, and excitement. The thought of embarking on a new adventure had her heart beating fast with anticipation, but the nagging sense of apprehension was hard to shake off. Despite her doubts, Ella was resolute in her decision to take this leap of faith if chosen for the journey, a testament to her determination and courage.

Ella inquired about the expected duration of the journey, to which Tilly responded that their budget and any unforeseen circumstances would determine it. The timing of their departure was flexible. Ella felt optimistic about travelling with Tilly and Jo, as it was clear that the three of them had connected instantly.

Upon departing from the pub, Ella promised to make her decision promptly. Tilly mentioned they had received substantial interest from potential applicants after posting their advertisement. When selecting potential applicants for a journey such as this, it was necessary to prioritise those who possessed a strong sense of humour, were trustworthy, and exhibited a friendly demeanour. They were also looking for people who were open-minded, adaptable and passionate about travel.

Ella now faced the daunting task of telling her mother about her possible plans to embark on a backpacking journey across Europe if the girls approved of her joining them. She knew that her mother would be apprehensive and concerned about her safety. However, Ella was determined to convince her that this trip was an opportunity she could not afford to miss. She was confident that with detailed planning and the companionship of her new friends, she could overcome any obstacles that came her way.

Chapter 2

"Ella, have you really thought this through? Are you sure you've saved enough money for this trip?" her mother asked, raising her eyebrows.

"Yes, Mum," Ella replied. "I've saved a little from working at the café in the village and helping out in their kitchen."

Understanding her mother's concerns, Ella explained that at 20, she wanted to experience something thrilling before committing to a career in Food and Nutritional Science or perhaps something entirely different.

Ella reassured her mother that she would proceed cautiously and take good care of herself.

They sat together in the living room, discussing the upcoming adventure, knowing their funds would eventually run out. Ella's mother had a hint of sadness on her face, but there was also a twinkle in her eye as she gave her daughter her blessing to follow her dream.

Ella felt a wave of gratitude wash over her, and she smiled and said, "Thanks, Mum."

As they continued talking, Ella's mother couldn't help but comment on how much she would miss her daughter's untidy ways and who would care for Sammy, but she said it all in a light-hearted tone, masking her underlying emotion.

Despite feeling sad, her mum understood the significance of this adventure to her daughter.

Ella wasted no time contacting Tilly and Jo, expressing her strong desire to join them on their European trip. They quickly started planning, which involved updating their passports and work permits and obtaining European rail passes. They were relieved that the only vaccination required was for hepatitis, a relief for Ella, who disliked injections. After verifying Ella's passport's validity and converting money into Euros at the bank, Tilly booked accommodation and obtained all necessary documents. A friend from Uni offered Ella a large rucksack and sleeping bag, so everything was in place for the big day. The trio of backpackers was eager to embark on the journey of a lifetime and was determined to stick together through thick and thin.

However, life sometimes goes differently than planned! The day of their adventure arrived, and with a mix of apprehension and excitement, the trio set off on their journey. As Ella stepped onto the train bound for London, she turned around to take one final glimpse at the picturesque Dales. The rolling hills were carpeted with lush green grass, dotted with fluffy white sheep and their lambs. The vibrant colours of the spring flowers added a joyful touch to the already stunning scenery. The air was crisp and fresh, carrying the sweet fragrance of blooming flowers. As Ella gazed at the beautiful landscape surrounding her, she couldn't help but feel a deep sadness. This place had been her forever home and held a special place in her heart, surrounded by the beauty of nature and the unparalleled warmth of her community.

Tears welled up in her eyes as she thought about her mother, who had always been her anchor, a source of unwavering strength and comfort.

Ella's mother had always been her strongest advocate and source of encouragement, constantly pushing her to pursue her aspirations. Despite her mother's unwavering support, the prospect of travelling afar lingered in Ella's thoughts.

With a heavy heart, she waved goodbye to the only home she had ever known and set off on her new adventure.

Three hours later, they arrived at St Pancras and saw the sign leading them to Eurostar.

As the girls walked through the station among the crowds, they noticed some with similar backpacks while others were dressed in professional business clothes.

Some just relish the lively atmosphere of the capital.

Tilly assumed command, confidently leading the group and instructing her friends, "Just follow me!"

As they boarded the train, Ella felt a surge of excitement for the opportunity to explore a new city. She was hopeful for the new memories she would create with her two newly bonded friends.

As she settled into her seat, ready for the journey ahead, she was filled with anticipation, eager to see what adventures lay ahead.

After a few hours and a brief rest, Ella awakened with a start, her heart racing with the anticipation of their arrival at Paris Gare du Nord. She excitedly informed her friends, and the girls hastily gathered their belongings in preparation for disembarking.

Tilly took the lead, stepping off the train and onto the platform, with Ella and Jo following closely behind. Navigating Paris can be overwhelming, with numerous transportation options, such as metros, taxis, minibuses, and coaches, available to passengers. Opting for the more affordable bus option, they quickly found their pre-booked hostel in the historic Latin Quarter. They were overjoyed finally reaching their first destination and proudly checked Paris off their list.

As they raised their arms in celebration, they exclaimed, "We made it to Paris; what a fantastic city!" With hunger and weariness setting in, their main goal was to find a comforting and substantial meal. Their quest led them to a charming local restaurant adjacent to their hostel—a delightful discovery in the heart of Paris. There, they indulged in various heart-warming dishes and, after a satisfying meal, retired for a good night's sleep at their pre-booked hostel.

Feeling refreshed the next day, they set out to explore Paris. Their first stop was a Patisserie where they savoured warm croissants and freshly made ham baguettes. Sitting in a quaint café in Paris, Tilly admired the city. "That's why everyone comes to France," she exclaimed, savouring every bite of her flaky croissant smothered in rich chocolate. The girls spent the morning exploring the sights of Paris, from the iconic Eiffel Tower to the charming streets of Montmartre. While basking in the beauty of Paris, Ella and Jo were struck by the city's vibrant energy and rich cultural experiences despite the constant noise and heavy traffic pollution. The city's charm and allure made them wonder as they strolled along.

During their stroll, Jo opened up to Ella about a troubling matter, a personal issue weighing heavily on her mind. Jo continued, mentioning that Tilly had opened up about her challenging upbringing while they were both together at university.

Tilly had confided in Jo about her tumultuous childhood, bravely disclosing the hardships of living with an abusive father.

Jo and Ella had a lengthy conversation about Tilly's past. It was heart-wrenching for both girls to contemplate that someone they cared about had gone through so much pain and suffering during her young life. Jo shared how Tilly's father prevented her from enjoying a typical childhood and experiencing teenage activities. He would confine her to her bedroom for days, using fear and intimidation to maintain control over her, leaving Tilly feeling like a prisoner. Ella couldn't understand how a father could treat his daughter this way.

As Jo continued to talk about Tilly, Ella was overwhelmed with shock and sadness at the thought of how fearful and isolated Tilly must have been. Jo recounted how Tilly would seek refuge in a cupboard whenever her father returned home intoxicated, his violent and unpredictable behaviour leaving her scared and vulnerable. Ella couldn't fathom the emotions Tilly experienced during those times, but she recognised that such fear and anxiety could have impacted her mental well-being. It now made sense to Ella why Tilly seemed easily frightened by small things, like a tap on the shoulder, and sometimes appeared afraid of physical contact.

Jo also expressed her concern about Tilly's desire to visit Europe, wondering if her interest in backpacking through Europe was something she wanted to do or a way to escape her fears. Tilly's decision to dye her hair pink also worries Jo, who fears it may be a sign of rebellion against her father rather than a statement to others.

Despite facing multiple challenges, Tilly displays remarkable resilience. She keeps her past to herself without confiding in anyone, making navigating through them tricky, but she continues to move forward. Tilly desperately needs the empathy and support of those around her. She must manage her circumstances and discover a path that works for her.

They finally left Paris by train and headed to Belgium. Although the train was delayed by an hour, Ella managed to call home to reassure her mother that she was safe. After a 90-minute train ride, they arrived at the central square, where it started raining heavily. Ella was reminded of the rainy days back home and couldn't help but smile. They searched for their raincoats in their backpacks, and luckily, Ella found hers in an outside pocket. After getting dressed for the wet weather, they took a bus directly to the hostel.

Despite feeling tired, they found their way to Rue de Midi, a charming street lined with quaint cafes and boutique shops and asked for directions to the pre-booked hostel. When they arrived, the receptionist greeted them warmly and escorted them to their room. The manager understood their extended stay in Paris and agreed with their admiration for the city's beauty and attractions.

He then suggested some things to do in Brussels and gave the girls brochures to carry in their haversacks.

When they asked where they could get some food, he kindly informed them that a hot meal was already prepared and waiting for them.

The girls, showing their thoughtful and considerate nature, ventured down to the dining room, appreciating the hospitality of the hostel owner.

During dinner, the hostel owner poured them a glass of wine and served delicious waffles with cream, a famous Belgian dessert.

The hostel staff went above and beyond to ensure their guests had an enjoyable and comfortable stay.

The girls were grateful for the exceptional service and warm hospitality they received at the hostel, a testament to the staff's commitment to guest satisfaction.

Although tired after the day's travelling, Tilly was excited to immerse herself in the vibrant nightlife scene of Brussels, known for its lively music and energetic dancing, and suggested to Ella and Jo that they venture into the city and experience everything it offers.

Ella and Jo were exhausted but still agreed to accompany Tilly, knowing that sticking together in an unfamiliar place was the best way to ensure everyone's safety.

As they ventured out into the night, Tilly started dancing with a couple of strangers, enjoying drinks and singing along with the music, much to the concern of Jo and Ella.

As the evening progressed, Tilly's behaviour became more erratic, and Ella and Jo increasingly worried about her safety. They noticed one man taking a particular interest in Tilly, prompting Jo to suggest they stay close to her, but the rowdy crowd made it difficult.

As it got later, Tilly continued to drink heavily. When they approached her and urged her to leave with them, Tilly remained stubborn, caught up in the moment with a reckless glint in her eyes, adding tension to the situation.

Ella and Jo knew they couldn't force her to leave, but they couldn't bear the thought of leaving her alone in that state. They decided to stay close by, watching from a distance, hoping Tilly would come to her senses soon.

Despite their best efforts, Tilly remained determined not to leave with the girls. They tried talking to Tilly, reminding her of the dangers of staying out too late and caring for herself, especially in unfamiliar places, but their attempts were unsuccessful. Tilly had decided to stay and have fun, which is precisely what she did, leaving Ella and Jo to wander back to the hostel alone and without her.

Chapter 3

I t was early morning when Ella glanced over and saw that Tilly's bed had not been slept in.

"Jo, wake up," Ella announced in a demanding voice.

"What is it?" Jo muttered.

Tilly didn't sleep in her bed last night!

They were now both distraught and apprehensive and couldn't begin to think about what to do.

Ella saw her rucksack lying on the floor beside her bed and looked inside to see if any clues could help her find her.

Her mobile phone was missing, so both girls assumed she had it with her.

Ella tried to ring the number.

It went straight to voicemail, so she left a message, hoping she would pick up.

Jo frantically asked if they should call the police.

Before doing that, Ella suggested they return to where they last saw her and try to piece together their last sighting of her.

"Good idea," Jo said.

They hurried down to breakfast, trying to figure out what to say to the hostel owner, just in case he started asking questions about Tilly's whereabouts.

Fortunately, he was out at the local market, and his wife was the only person in the building.

The girls hastily ate breakfast and told the Manager's wife they needed to return to town. They decided to keep Tilly's disappearance a secret until they had any positive updates to share.

Ella mentioned that they would come back later to collect their bags.

"Have a good day", she replied.

As they began to retrace their steps to where they had been the previous night, they were hopeful that Tilly could be found.

However, the language barrier proved challenging, as not everyone they encountered spoke English.

This made it incredibly difficult to communicate with the locals and passers-by.

They tried describing Tilly's unique appearance, which included her striking pink hair, but unfortunately, this led to some comical misunderstandings.

Despite these setbacks, they persevered and searched the side streets by the riverbank, even venturing into an abandoned building, but to no avail.

Their search seemed fruitless, and they were growing increasingly worried about Tilly's whereabouts.

As they walked down the street, their eyes scanned the pavement for any sign of Tilly's whereabouts. Then, something caught their attention - an old train ticket lying on the ground. The ticket was for the express train between Paris and Brussels Central, making them wonder if it could belong to Tilly.

Although they were unsure, Ella carefully picked it up and put it in her pocket for safekeeping. After examining the ticket more closely, they discovered it had the same ticket number as theirs, leading them to believe it must belong to Tilly.

Despite their best efforts, they could still not contact Tilly, as her phone went straight to voicemail.

Growing increasingly worried and unsure about what to do next, they decided to take a break and came across a small café overlooking the main market square.

As they sat outside the café, a man who appeared to be a tourist approached them. His face was filled with curiosity as he came closer to them.

He then politely inquired if the two girls had been sitting at the café last night.

Ella quickly confirmed that he was correct.

The man smiled and explained that he was taking photos of the lively atmosphere in the area last night.

Ella's heart pounded as she frantically asked the man if he had caught sight of their friend Tilly, who appeared to have gone missing.

Her voice quivered with fear as she described Tilly's unique appearance - her long, vivid pink hair was hard to miss.

She implored the man to think hard and recall any sightings of her friend.

The man furrowed his brow, deep in thought, as he tried to remember.

Suddenly, his eyes lit up with recognition, and he remembered seeing someone who matched Tilly's description.

He recalled seeing her talking to a man before they both disappeared.

The man's words sent a chill down Ella's spine, and both girls immediately knew they needed to act fast to find Tilly and ensure her safety.

The man apologised for being unable to offer more assistance and wished them good luck in their search.

Both girls expressed gratitude for his help and began their search for Tilly towards the nearby park.

They knew they had to find Tilly as soon as possible.

Upon entering the park through two metal gates, they were astonished to find Tilly fast asleep on a park bench.

They rushed over to her and attempted to arouse her from an unconscious state.

Tilly appeared lifeless but shouted to her, "Wake up, Tilly, it's Jo and Ella."

She stirred slightly and looked up at them with glazed eyes.

Uncertain of what happened, Jo asked nervously, "Do you think she has taken drugs?"

Ella removed her coat and placed it around Tilly, who was cold and disoriented.

Eventually, Tilly regained composure and remembered some of the events from the previous night.

She had met a so-called charming man on the street who had invited her to dance.

They talked briefly and then decided to drink at a nearby bar.

As she drank with the man, Tilly remarked that she began to feel increasingly disoriented.

The last drink was particularly strong, and it made her feel dizzy and confused. It soon became apparent that something was wrong.

Tilly had concluded that her drink may have been spiked without her knowledge.

Suddenly, her heart began to race frantically as she searched her pockets for her phone and realised that some money was missing, causing her to panic.

She couldn't believe that someone had stolen some of her hard-earned cash.

More importantly, Tilly couldn't help but worry about where her phone could be.

Ella noticed her distress and quickly tried to calm her down, promising they would sort everything out once they returned to the hostel.

While standing next to Tilly, Ella noticed something shiny out of the corner of her eye and found Tilly's phone lying under the bench.

Tilly was grateful when Ella picked up the phone because it had become essential to her life.

Tilly's social circle was relatively small, confined to the familiar and cherished names in her contacts list. Among these contacts, Tilly cherished the presence of her brother and friends Jo and Ella, as they were the only people she trusted wholeheartedly. They represented an essential and irreplaceable part of her life, offering her the warmth of companionship, solace in times of need, and unwavering support.

After finding her phone, she felt a massive sense of relief. Although she had gone through a stressful experience and lost some money, she was extremely thankful to have her phone back. This served as a reminder of how even the small things in life can have a significant impact.

The occurrence was a stark reminder of the dangers that can exist in everyday situations.

She promised herself to be more cautious in the future and always be mindful of her surroundings.

With her friends by her side, Tilly slowly but surely began to calm down and feel more like herself.

It is possible that Tilly was lucky, and the stranger left before causing her any further harm.

Upon returning to the hostel, they took her to their room, where she enjoyed a relaxing hot bath.

They asked the Manager's wife to prepare breakfast for Tilly, and she graciously agreed.

Shortly after, she knocked on their door with a warm serving of porridge, toast, jam, and a large pot of tea.

Chapter 4

It has been two weeks since they began their journey, and during this time, they had the chance to explore France and Belgium, immersing themselves in each place's rich culture and traditions. Along the way, they experienced many unforgettable moments, some filled with joy and others unpleasant.

As they prepared for the next leg of their journey, they stumbled upon a charming little café and decided to take a break.

Lost in their thoughts, they reminisced about their childhood memories while enjoying the aroma of freshly brewed coffee and delicious cakes.

Jo had given Ella a somewhat detailed account of Tilly's upbringing, and they both wondered if Tilly would be willing to share her personal experiences with them a little further and open up about her life.

After something a little stronger than coffee, Tilly finally felt comfortable enough to share some of the pain she had gone through.

It was a poignant moment, and they were grateful for the opportunity to get to know each other better.

As they engaged in lively conversations, they shared hearty laughs. They expressed a wide range of emotions that would become treasured memories, lasting forever, even beyond their journey.

Tilly began her story by lighting a cigarette and saying her home life was not like a normal childhood. She had been abused physically and mentally by her father.

Ella, in a state of disbelief, turned to Tilly and asked, "Can it really be true that she had a father who abused her?" Tilly, with a heavy heart, confirmed that it was indeed true. She added that he was an evil man who mistreated not only her but also her brother, Stephen.

On occasions, he would shut them both away in their bedrooms without food, and they would be there all day and sometimes all night, too.

He would come home drunk, push Mum around, smash up everything in sight, and flop down wherever he fell.

So, everything Jo had told Ella was true, and what she had said was now falling into place.

Tilly expressed that the mere mention of her father still evoked a sense of confusion in her, leaving her struggling to comprehend why this domestic abuse had happened to her and her brother. The fear that she had been carrying with her for so long continued to grip her tightly, even after all this time.

There was a time when her brother came home late from a school football match; Dad was waiting at the front door, belt in hand, striking him so hard the welts on his back bled, which got infected and lasted for days, leaving him scarred forever.

Mum wasn't a strong lady. Although she loved her children dearly, she was afraid and would always believe in him rather than us.

Mum lived a short life, and Tilly could only think that the abusive way Dad treated his family added to her sudden death when she was only in her early 50s.

It devastated Tilly when she lost her mother, but she knew life could be very unpredictable.

While Tilly's brother maintains occasional contact with their father, neither Tilly nor her brother has any affection or respect for him, and he is now a lonely old man who seeks forgiveness, but it's far too late, as he has caused them permanent physical and psychological damage which can never be restored.

Despite experiencing immense emotional pain and heartbreak, Tilly refused to waver in her resolve. She was fully aware of the challenges and obstacles that awaited her on the path to happiness and fulfilment, but she remained steadfast in her determination to pursue it.

Despite her numerous adversities, Tilly drew comfort and found inner strength in her capabilities and unyielding passion for life.

As time passed, Tilly realised that she would have to attain it actively if she wanted to experience compassion and companionship.

Through relentless hard work and determination, Tilly secured a place at Manchester University and earned a degree in Fashion and Design.

Tilly knew she had been leading a solitary life for far too long and needed to break out of her shell and connect with the world around her.

She realised that travelling would be the perfect way to do just that and was excited at the prospect of exploring new places, experiencing different cultures, and making unforgettable memories.

Upon hearing Tilly's story, Ella and Jo were utterly amazed. They found it hard to believe what she had told them and struggled to understand how two young people could be treated and abused in such a manner. It was becoming increasingly difficult to comprehend the severity of the situation.

Jo felt a wave of emotions as she listened to the heart-breaking story of the young girl she had recently befriended at university. It was difficult for Jo to fathom the depth of pain and sorrow that Tilly had already endured in her short life.

Ella and Jo offered comfort to her by expressing their sympathy towards her.

Tilly acknowledged that her anger was a symptom of something much deeper, and it would remain with her for the rest of her life.

They hugged Tilly, reassuring her that it's okay not to be okay sometimes.

They were proud of how she overcame the crisis that affected both her and her brother's lives.

Suddenly, Tilly mentioned she needed to share something with Jo and Tilly.

The two friends exchanged a strange glance at each other and listened attentively.

Tilly revealed that she realised she was attracted to women at a young age but never spoke about it to anyone due to her upbringing.

She had always felt a stronger connection with women than men, and recently, she had come out to her friends about her identity. Ella praised Tilly's bravery and encouraged her to speak out more.

Despite her efforts to move on from her past, it was evident that Tilly's traumatic childhood had deeply affected her. The constant abuse had left her with feelings of being unwanted, rejected, and unloved, which made her crave companionship and love even more.

As Tilly lighted up another cigarette, she hesitated to answer Ella's question about how her past experiences had influenced her current emotions.

However, Ella reminded her that friends should always support each other's choices in life. Jo further affirmed that everyone has the right to choose their path, irrespective of their past experiences. Tilly was touched and thanked both girls for being good listeners and letting her share her story.

Next, it was Jo who wanted to share her story.

Jo opened up about her childhood experiences during the girls' storytelling session.

She revealed that she was born and raised in Chelsea, within the bustling city of London and was an only child.

Her father was a Chartered Accountant, and her mother worked as a Financial Advisor in the city.

Despite their successful careers, their hectic work schedules often left little time for family bonding.

However, she always managed to keep herself occupied with books and other hobbies, which helped her cope with the loneliness.

Jo was fortunate to have a nanny she cared for and respected, who became like a mother to her in many ways. This relationship gave Jo a sense of normalcy and someone she could trust and love deeply.

During her childhood, Jo's upbringing was quite different from what most would consider typical.

Between the ages of seven and fourteen, she was sent to boarding school, which proved to be a challenging experience for her.

Being separated from her parents during this time made things even more complicated, and Jo reflected on just how tough those years were for her.

Despite her privileged upbringing, Jo often felt isolated and secluded, which was evident in the bitterness and sadness in her tone as she shared her story.

Ella couldn't shake the feeling that Jo's parents' excessive wealth had created an isolating and lonely environment for Jo.

However, tragedy struck when Jo's dad suffered a heart attack five years ago.

After his recovery, the family decided to move away and live a simpler life.

They retired early and settled in Riverdale, some 10 miles outside Buckland Ridge, where they purchased a smallholding.

Jo is the proud owner of two black Labradors, Mollie and Monty, who never fail to bring joy and calmness to her life.

Jo's farm is a haven for various animals, including a beautiful horse whom Jo has named Jellybean.

Jo and her mother ensure that every animal is well-looked after while enjoying the outdoor lifestyle of living on a farm.

Her father oversees everything, ensuring everything runs smoothly without enduring too much heavy work due to his past illness.

Moving from London to the countryside has brought many changes to their lives, and Jo and her family wouldn't have it any other way.

Jellybean holds a special place in her heart and considers him her soul mate.

They have a unique bond that is hard to explain, but Jo finds talking to animals preferable to communicating with humans at times, as she said rather amusingly, "They cannot always answer back."

Riding Jellybean through the moors is a fantastic adventure that offers stunning panoramic views that extend beyond the visible horizon.

Regardless of the weather, there is nothing like exploring the muddy grasslands in solitude, surrounded by nature and its wonders.

The current situation has changed quite a bit since Mum and Dad have distanced themselves from the hustle and bustle of city life and their social circle. Their main aim is to focus on spending quality time together as a family, such as embarking on holidays, visiting their villa in the scenic South of France, and creating beautiful memories. Jo's face radiated with unmistakable joy as she expressed her happiness about reuniting with her parents after years of separation and loneliness. She also conveyed a deep sense of contentment with how things unfolded.

Meanwhile, Ella listened intently to Tilly and Jo's accounts of their childhood and felt it was the perfect time to share her own story.

She leaned forward, ready to speak, and began to tell her own experiences, eager to connect with her friends.

Ella now shares her story.

Ella began her story by saying that although her real name is Melanie, she has always been known as Ella because, for whatever reason, she wasn't sure.

After attending York University, Ella earned a Food & Nutritional Science BSc degree.

While Ella was telling her story, Jo suddenly saw a tear trickle down Ella's cheek as she told them that her father passed away when she was just two years old, leaving her Mum to bring up two children, herself and her sister Lauren.

Her father worked as a scaffolder, and one winter morning, he went to work on a school building and began to set up scaffolding.

Unfortunately, while working on the top level of the structure, he lost his balance and fell from a significant height.

The impact of the fall caused him to sustain multiple injuries, and he was immediately rushed to the hospital for treatment.

Despite the best efforts of the medical staff, his injuries were too severe, and he passed away a few hours later. The sudden and tragic loss of her father has left a profound impact on Ella and her family.

Mum often speaks about Dad, especially on special occasions such as his birthday and during the festive season.

He was a devoted husband and father, and his untimely death left a deep void in family life.

Ella's memories of her father are distant and hazy, as he passed away when she was very young.

Still, Lauren remembers his infectious laughter and the unwavering love he gave to his family.

Ella has had to face the challenges of growing up without a father figure in her life. This has left her with an unresolved void that she finds challenging. Her father's absence has left her with a lingering sense of curiosity about the kind of person he was and how he would have influenced her life.

She spends a lot of time imagining what her father would have been like and what kind of relationship they would have had. His absence has affected her in many ways, and at times, she struggles to come to terms with the reality of growing up without a father.

Without a husband and father in our lives, the bond of love between my mother and sister Lauren is genuinely remarkable. Despite the ups and downs of life, the three of us always made sure to give each other as much love and support as possible.

However, as fate would have it, Lauren began to feel restless after she had completed her nursing college education. With a school friend, she decided to explore new opportunities beyond the UK, particularly in the field of Nursing. She thought the UK's NHS system was failing, so she took a bold step towards her career by seeking what Melbourne, Australia, had to offer.

Even though Lauren's relocation to Australia is not intended to be permanent, there is every possibility that she could return home to the UK. However, Ella and her mother are sceptical about this prospect, as Australia offers Lauren a lot, including employment prospects, favourable weather, and numerous other benefits that are important to her.

Ella then began speaking fondly of her beloved dog, Sammy. She vividly described how she always carries a photo of him in her purse, constantly reminding herself of their cherished bond.

When Ella's mood falters, Sammy's playful antics and unwavering devotion lift her spirits and make him an essential part of her life.

Ella was excited as she shared her aspirations to embark on a journey of adventure and exploration. With an unshakable spirit and a sense of wonder, Ella appeared eager to embrace all of life's possibilities and was ready to take the next step in her journey with open arms.

After each person shared their stories, Ella gazed away and pondered how different everyone was. "Our lives are so very different," she thought.

Tilly came from an abusive family with hurt and sadness, her brother being the only person she could turn to for help and advice when needed.

Her mother was very meek and mild, standing by her husband, not leaving him because of the fear he had injected into her. How awful this must be for Tilly, not giving or receiving her parents' love and then losing her mother at a young age, with nobody she could love and trust except her brother.

Jo's story is unique and different from others in many ways. She yearns for quality time with her family and desires to feel loved and appreciated.

However, this aspect seems missing from her young life, leaving her isolated.

Jo's Nanny had been the only person she could turn to for friendship, comfort, and perhaps even love.

Jo grew up without many essential elements necessary for a loving childhood, yet she consistently showed remarkable thoughtfulness and consideration toward others.

After years of loneliness, Jo has reunited with her parents, which gives her hope that they can remain a united family despite the lost years that lie behind them.

As Ella reflected on her life, she realised that one of her biggest desires was to have a father who could have been there to love and support their family.

Unfortunately, he was young when the accident caused his tragic death, leaving behind a devastated family.

Still, Ella knew that it brought the family closer together, which was what her dad would have wanted.

Despite her father's absence, Ella's mother always reminded them that his love would remain forever, and they would always be a family, no matter what.

Ella has come to understand that while wealth can buy many things, the love of a family is truly priceless, and it cannot be replaced or bought with any amount of money.

The memories and love that her father left behind have stayed with the family throughout the years, helping them through tough times.

Listening to Jo and Tilly's fascinating stories, Ella felt that an everlasting bond of friendship had formed between them, knowing that this was a journey of new beginnings for all of them.

Chapter 5

Having covered a considerable distance, Holland was their next stop.

The capital, Amsterdam, was unforgettable.

It is known for its artistic heritage, elaborate canal system, and narrow houses, and the Museum District houses the Van Gogh Museum and works by Rembrandt.

To see these works of art up close was unbelievable and fascinating.

Cycling was key to the city's character, and there were numerous bike paths.

During their trip to Amsterdam, they had a few hurdles to overcome. One such instance saw them losing their sense of direction, exploring parts of the city not considered safe for women and young girls known as the 'red light area'; however, despite these obstacles, they thoroughly enjoyed their time in Amsterdam, discovering hidden gems and marvelling at the city's beauty. Ella, in particular, was surprised by the flat terrain of Holland, which made cycling less strenuous and allowed them to cover more ground while enjoying the picturesque landscape.

Stopping for refreshments, Ella and Jo noticed that Tilly seemed distant and preoccupied, which caused them to wonder about her thoughts and actions.

It was unclear if she was fully engaged in the adventure or if something was troubling her.

Out of nowhere, Jo proposed a fantastic plan for the three of them to take the train to her family villa in the South of France.

Both Ella and Tilly warmly received Jo's proposal. They appreciated the idea because they saw it as a way to unwind, take their time to explore this beautiful part of the French Riviera with its warm climate, and enjoy each other's company without the pressure of searching for employment to sustain themselves. It was also a chance for Tilly to leave the distressing experience she had gone through in Brussels firmly in the past.

The girls were excited at the prospect, especially Tilly, who was utterly dazzled by the offer of staying at a luxurious villa on the French Riviera.

"Done deal!" declared Jo.

"Our next destination is Antibes!"

They managed to secure seats on a night train bound for Nice, but it cost a considerable chunk of their travel budget,105 euros each, to be precise.

Despite the setback, they were confident about recouping some of their expenses by taking advantage of the rare opportunity to stay at the villa for free, an offer they couldn't turn down.

The girls arrived at the bustling train station in nice feeling tired and excited.

From there, they hopped on a local bus to Antibes, a journey lasting around 36 minutes.

Upon arriving, Ella found herself in awe of the stunning surroundings.

She struggled to describe the beauty of the place—the warm sunshine, swaying palm trees, crashing waves against the promenade wall, and pristine white marble-like walkway made it feel like paradise.

Jo sent a message to her mother at home, informing her that they would be staying at the villa and inquiring about the location of the spare house key.

Suddenly, Jo began to blush, announcing that her mother had generously paid for their shopping, transferring 1000 Euros into Jo's bank account to help with food and small luxuries during their stay.

Although Jo appreciated her mother's kindness, she politely declined further funding for their travels. She didn't want to feel indebted to her mother and preferred maintaining her independence.

Jo hoped that her mother would understand her perspective and respect her decision.

Ella couldn't help but wonder if Jo's parents were trying to make up for missing out on her childhood by buying their way into her life. Having prioritised their careers and social life over her upbringing, it would appear that they were trying their best to support her now as much as possible.

After a long and tiring journey, the girls were exhausted and hungry. Jo had thought ahead, so on their way to the villa, they stopped at a nearby supermarket to stock up on food and other essentials.

As the sun set over Antibes's stunning coastal town, they finally arrived at the villa's gates.

As Ella approached the villa, the long, imposing gates surrounding the property caught her attention, giving the impression of something out of a Hollywood movie and a sense of exclusivity.

The driveway, a winding path of gravel and stone, led them up to the entrance, adorned by superbly maintained gardens filled with the delicate fragrance of lavender and the vibrant splendour of bougainvillaea, its cascading pink blossoms creating a stunning display around the villa's entrance. Citrus trees dotted the grounds, adding their bountiful foliage to the already enchanting charm of the place.

Tilly stood in awe; eyes wide as she took in the beautiful sight before her.

The villa that would be her home for the next few weeks was beyond her wildest dreams—a place she had never even imagined visiting, a beautiful place that could only have been made in heaven.

As Jo entered the house with the shopping bags, she felt the weight of the groceries in her arms. She placed them on the floor and let out a sigh of relief.

Ella noticed her exhaustion and offered to prepare the evening meal to show her gratitude for the fantastic kindness shown to both her and Tilly.

Ella's kindness touched Jo, who expressed gratitude for the offer. Ella suggested a quick and easy Spaghetti Bolognese, which delighted Jo.

Everyone agreed, and the aroma of the food filled the air. The girls eagerly consumed their meals, savouring each bite.

Ella received compliments on her cooking, causing her to turn a shade of pink as she modestly accepted the praise for her culinary skills.

As the evening unfolded, the group not only uncorked one bottle of wine but two and proceeded to savour every moment, engrossed in animated discussions and contagious laughter that filled the air around the table.

Exhausted from their long journey, the girls could feel their eyes getting heavy. Their sleepy faces made it clear that it was time to go to bed. They bid each other goodnight and went to their respective rooms.

Once their heads hit their pillows, they fell into a deep and peaceful sleep.

Ella woke up the following morning feeling refreshed and full of energy. She walked towards the French doors and pulled them open, revealing a fantastic view of the coastline. The sun had just started to rise, casting a warm golden glow over the water, making it sparkle like diamonds. The soothing melody of the waves crashing against the shore filled the air, creating a peaceful atmosphere.

The azure-blue Mediterranean ocean was silently rippling, creating a sense of serenity.

In the distance, the snow-capped French Alps stood tall and majestic, forming a perfect backdrop to the tranquil scenery. The sun cascaded down from the blue skies, painting the sky with a beautiful array of orange and pink hues, creating a stunning sunrise.

Ella was lost in the moment, feeling deeply grateful for witnessing such a beautiful sight. She couldn't help but think, "I never want to leave this place." The view was like a dream come true; she knew it would be etched in her memory forever.

Walking along the mezzanine floor towards the kitchen, she noticed Tilly and Jo were already busy cooking breakfast.

As Ella entered the kitchen, the delicious aroma of poached eggs and a little luxury of smoked salmon wafted toward her. Tilly turned around, revealing that both she and Jo were cooking up a breakfast fit for royalty.

Ella couldn't resist the urge to comment sarcastically, jokingly inquiring whether they would be dining on caviar for lunch.

Jo chuckled and replied that their next destination the mountainous Chamonix, would likely mean simpler meals such as porridge, pasta, stews, and perhaps a pizza.

Tilly wrinkled her nose and twisted her mouth in disgust. "Ugh, Porridge!" she exclaimed, feeling put off by the mere thought of it, remembering the days when her mother had always insisted that porridge was the ultimate breakfast and could help her grow more robust.

As Tilly served breakfast, they sat on the balcony, admiring the stunning view. They indulged in freshly percolated coffee and contemplated swimming in the pool.

Ella joked about waiting before jumping in the pool just in case she sank due to all the food she had eaten.

While Ella was checking her phone for messages, she suddenly looked up and noticed Tilly chatting with the next-door neighbour.

Jo informed Ella that Tilly was talking with Maddie, a highly skilled artist Jo had met on her last visit with her parents.

Suddenly, Jo's face lit up with a friendly "Hi" and a warm smile as she approached Maddie.

At that moment, Maddie's eyes lit up with genuine warmth as she welcomed Jo and asked about the duration of her visit. Jo shared that they were embarking on a backpacking adventure across Europe, immersing themselves in the stunning natural scenery and rich, diverse cultures.

They had decided to take a well-deserved break and recharge their batteries before embarking on their next adventure, filled with anticipation and excitement.

Out of nowhere, Tilly's gaze locked onto Maddie's artwork as she approached with great interest. Walking closer to Maddie, she exclaimed, "You're incredibly talented!"

Maddie looked up, surprised, and smiled as she thanked Tilly for her kind words.

Preparing to set up her easel, Tilly kindly offered assistance stabilising it to prevent it from toppling over.

Maddie expressed her gratitude for Tilly's thoughtfulness, and they worked together to steady the easel in a more secure position.

Maddie was immediately struck by Tilly's comforting and welcoming demeanour. She began to share her perspective on the difficulties of being outdoors when the temperature climbs to 35 degrees or higher during the summer. Maddie then expressed her genuine fondness for savouring the outdoor ambience in the early morning when the gentle breeze offers a revitalizing and refreshing experience.

For Maddie, this tranquil setting provides the ideal environment for a leisurely breakfast before the day's heat sets in.

She relishes the tranquillity of the morning, listening to the birds chirping, and watching the sun rising, painting the sky with various colours.

As Tilly looked inside Maddie's apartment she saw paintings everywhere, some on the floor, others against the walls.

Tilly was impressed by the exquisite artwork on show.

She couldn't help but admire the beautiful landscapes painted by hand, using different techniques such as watercolours and oils. The colours used in each painting were vibrant and captivating, making the artwork even more stunning. Maddie's talent genuinely amazed Tilly; she couldn't wait to see more of her work.

As they chatted away, Maddie opened up about her life before relocating to Antibes.

Having moved away from Brighton a few years ago after ending a somewhat unhappy relationship, she purchased this beautiful ground-floor apartment surrounded by Bougainvillea, the perfect place to pursue her passion for painting.

Tilly carefully inquired about Maddie's past relationship, and she confirmed they were together for ten years but drifted apart over time, saying Sarah wasn't the person she once knew.

Tilly was stunned when she heard that the love of her life was a girl called Sarah.

Maddie said she had known many women over the years, some just as friends and others in more serious relationships.

There was something special about Sarah; we had planned to spend the rest of our lives together, even get married, but unfortunately, life didn't work out that way.

Tilly and Maddie chatted happily, enjoying each other's company, laughing and joking.

Ella watched with interest over the garden fence that Tilly was enjoying her time getting to know Maddie.

As Ella lounged by the poolside, basking in the sun's warmth, she felt a wave of relaxation. The sight of the inviting pool beckoned her to take a refreshing dip and challenge herself to swim a few laps. With a sense of anticipation, she mused to herself, "Why not give it a try? It's the perfect opportunity to test my swimming skills."

On the other hand, Jo was busy taking photos of the beautiful scenery around them, informing Ella that she would join her in the pool later.

Suddenly, Tilly excitedly revealed that she had been asked to join Maddie on a visit to the promenade, where she planned to display and perhaps even sell some of her stunning artwork. Her creations featured a captivating mix of lively hues and a wide range of subjects, encompassing everything from picturesque landscapes to thought-provoking abstract designs a charming fusion of vivid colours. Tilly helped Maddie display her beautiful artwork by positioning her paintings alongside the promenade wall and other exhibitors. They made just enough room for Maddie to showcase her landscapes, which she had arranged with Tilly's help.

It was late into the evening when Tilly returned with Maddie, and Ella couldn't help but notice an improvement in Tilly's attitude.

Gone was the air of melancholy that had previously hung over her, replaced by a sense of calm and ease.

Tilly couldn't wait to tell Ella and Jo that Maddie had sold two of her treasured paintings.

Expressing their delight at the sale of Maddie's artwork, Jo invited her over to join them for a meal.

The evening air was warm enough to enjoy dinner outside, surrounded by the sweet scent of lavender.

The girls had been at the villa for almost two weeks, enjoying the beautiful scenery and each other's company.

While strolling along the elegant marble patio, Ella's thoughts mingled with the rich aroma of her wine. She immersed herself in contemplation about the deep bond between Tilly and Maddie. Tilly had entrusted Ella with the knowledge of Maddie's recovery from a previous relationship with another woman, and Ella couldn't help but notice the growing closeness between the two friends. Despite the warmth of their current connection, Ella couldn't shake off the lingering awareness of the potential difficulties that might surface when the time came for them to part ways. and embark on the next chapter of their lives.

The impending trip to the mountains weighed heavily on their minds, and they knew they needed to leave soon to reach their destination before Christmas.

Despite the rapidly approaching deadline to carry on with their backpacking journey, the girls began reminiscing about the incredible time they had spent together in such a beautiful location. They were overcome with gratitude towards Jo, who had made their stay an unforgettable experience.

As they sat and chatted, Tilly couldn't help but feel a sense of deep appreciation for the bond she had formed with Ella and Jo. The memories they had shared had left an indelible mark on her heart, and she knew that this adventure would forever be one of the most cherished experiences of her life.

As the girls began to pack up and prepare for the next leg of their journey, Tilly asked Jo and Ella to join her in her room.

They were surprised by her sudden request, but they could sense that she had something important to share with them.

As the girls gathered around, Tilly sat on the edge of her bed and began to speak.

With a calm and confident tone, she explained her reasoning for bringing them all together. She wanted to share something with them that was incredibly important to her and could change her life forever.

Tilly's heart was pounding with anticipation as she prepared to reveal her decision to her friends.

She had kept it to herself for so long, but now she felt ready to share it with those closest to her.

As she began to speak, her eyes shone bright, filled with the passion and conviction building up inside her.

Shaking slightly, Tilly explained that when she first decided to journey around Europe, she always thought that if she found something or someone that made her feel happy and secure, she might leave the group and go her own way.

It had troubled her for some time, and she knew it was now the time to follow her heart.

Tilly's life had been lonely, devoid of meaningful connections, with so much hurt and companionship.

However, all that changed when she met Maddie.

The moment they met, there was an instant connection—a spark that ignited a friendship and possibly love that Tilly had never experienced.

Maddie was everything Tilly had ever wanted in a friend and more. She was kind, understanding, and always there to listen.

With Maddie, Tilly opened up in ways she never had before, sharing her deepest fears, hopes, and aspirations.

As their friendship grew stronger, Tilly realised that Maddie was the missing piece in her life—the one person who had filled the void that had long existed in her heart.

For once, Tilly felt like a person, knowing that Maddie was the reason for it.

Tilly knew this decision would bring her a level of happiness she had never experienced before, and she was determined to hold on to that feeling and cherish it forever.

She hoped that her friends would be able to understand and support her, knowing that this was a path she needed to take for her well-being.

Ella reminded Tilly that the ultimate decision was hers and that they would stand by her no matter what.

Tilly's face broke into a grateful smile, and her eyes sparkled with contentment and peace as she looked forward to a new chapter in her friendship with Maddie.

Despite this, they felt sad, knowing that Tilly wouldn't be accompanying them on the next stage of their journey.

However, Tilly reassured them she would be fine and advised them not to be concerned about her.

Tilly embraced them and conveyed how much she cherished their friendship throughout the previous few months.

Her facial expression showed that she had made up her mind, and nothing could change it.

Ella said she would rather see her enjoying a new life in the South of France than being back home with all those bad memories and that awful hurt she had been carrying all those years.

Tilly expressed gratitude to Ella for her kind words.

The night before their departure to Chamonix, Maddie hosted a farewell gathering in her apartment's beautiful flower garden, where emotions ran high.

Despite some initial reservations, Tilly ultimately felt confident in her decision, and there was an increase in her overall happiness and contentment.

So far, the journey has brought about significant changes in Tilly because Jo had always envisioned that they would start and end the journey together. However, Tilly quickly reassured Jo that she was a responsible and independent adult capable of making wise and significant decisions.

Chapter 6

It's strange how things have turned out.

The backpacking journey began with three, but only two girls remained.

Ella hoped her backpacking journey might include nights outdoors in her one-person tent on a beach or field, trying a more rural experience, but it hasn't been like that.

Despite this, their budget is holding well, thanks to Jo's parents' contribution. They had the opportunity to stay in their holiday home, which was terrific. However, the trip to the mountains will be costly, with everything in Chamonix being expensive, from food and accommodation to alcohol, especially cocktails.

While Ella initially considered their journey an extended holiday, she realises that good things don't last forever.

They placed their rucksacks in the hallway before heading to see Tilly to say a final farewell.

As Tilly said her goodbyes, she kissed the girls quickly and reminded them to stay in touch.

Speaking softly, Maddie assured them that she would take care of Tilly and hoped for a more profound friendship to develop.

Jo acknowledged Maddie's promise but expressed concern for Tilly, knowing that she had faced so many challenges in her upbringing with the abuse she and her brother had endured at the hands of their father.

Despite the troubling events of her childhood, it was a relief to see Tilly happy and contented in every way.

It shows she is now beginning to get much stronger and cope with her feelings, which is good.

Encouraging her to express herself and discuss her problems can positively impact her mental well-being.

Tilly, after years of searching, finally found the peace and happiness she had yearned for when she met Maddie.

The surprise of their close friendship amazed Tilly, as initially it seemed unlikely due to their differing interests and personalities.

However, they somehow clicked and formed a deep and supportive bond filled with genuine love and care for each other.

Their friendship is a beautiful reminder that sometimes, the most unexpected connections can blossom into the strongest and most meaningful relationships.

As they bid Tilly and Maddie farewell at their doorstep, they couldn't help but notice Tilly's slight melancholy.

Perhaps she was sad to see them go, or was she contemplating the changes this unexpected friendship with Maddie had brought into her life?

Despite her momentary sadness, Ella and Jo were confident that Tilly would be alright. After all, she had shown herself to be resilient and adaptable in the face of many.

Turning and walking away, Ella and Jo set off on the next part of their journey.

Somewhat nervous but very excited, they began their journey towards the mountains.

Their stay at the villa gave them the energy to carry on.

Goodbye, Antibes!

 We are on our way, Chamonix!" they exclaimed, ready to embrace the new experiences that awaited them.

After a few days of trekking and taking breaks, followed by a train journey, they finally arrived at Chamonix - a French ski resort in the Alps, well before heavy snowfall was expected later in the month.

Now, in early October, the daylight was fading fast, and almost complete darkness had set in by late afternoon.

The two girls arrived at the ski resort feeling exhausted and hungry.

They quickly made their way to the check-in area.

Along the cobbled pathway, they met a friendly couple who appeared to be in their early 60s and were introduced to Eric, the Resort Manager, and his wife, Maria.

Although they were both French, their English was excellent.

The girls asked if there were any available jobs, and they were happy to hear a positive response.

Eric informed them there was plenty of work for those with good social skills, energy, and the right documents.

Eric then asked to see their passports and temporary work permits.

After searching through their backpacks, they handed their documents to Eric's wife, who examined them on the computer.

She confirmed that everything was in order and inquired if they intended to stay for the winter season.

Jo eagerly replied, saying they were, and expressed interest in possibly becoming chalet hosts, working with childcare, or even working at the resort's foodie bar.

Maria told them they would receive free lodging and meals and be allowed to keep any tips they earned.

Also, a bonus of 75 euros will be paid to them at the end of the month as a gesture of goodwill for their hard work and courteous treatment of guests.

Ella was more than happy and gave Jo a high-five in disbelief.

Maria kindly offered to go over everything with them the next day, including the weekly schedule, when they felt more rested and less hungry.

After handing the key to their chalet, Maria left them to settle in.

All Jo and Ella could think about was a warm meal, a refreshing shower, and a comfortable bed.

Excitedly, they climbed up a steep slope to their temporary home for the next few months.

Jo exclaimed to Ella as they opened the door, "We made it! Amazingly, we're finally here together."

As they entered their chalet, they were delighted to find it was cozy and welcoming.

A wood burner was glowing brightly, a red check tablecloth covered the dining table, and a small bouquet of delicate white flowers resembling Edelweiss adorned it.

The girls were amazed by the thick duvets covering the beds in their apartment.

The chalet also offered a fantastic view of the ski slopes.

Looking out the window, they saw many cable cars carrying enthusiastic tourists up and down the slopes.

Some of the tourists seemed highly excited, with their faces beaming with joy and anticipation, while others appeared to be a little nervous, with their eyes fixed on the steep and winding slopes ahead.

Leaving the warmth of Antibes, they were caught off guard by the sudden chill of the night breeze.

Their next challenge was to prepare for the winter climate.

While rummaging through their rucksacks for warm clothing, they suddenly realised they hadn't packed snow boots. Jo suggested they purchase a pair without hesitation, stressing the importance of proper footwear for navigating icy and snowy conditions.

After showering and dressing in warmer clothes, they explored the resort.

Ella and Jo were taken back by the majestic Mont Blanc Mountain, which rises over 4,000 meters high and is situated on the border of France and Italy.

The snowy peak was stunning despite its imposing appearance, leaving them speechless.

Ella felt compelled to capture the moment on her phone. As they watched the skiers getting ready to take on the slopes, it was evident that there would be some falls and broken bones during the season.

Nonetheless, seeing the experienced skiers confidently taking the mountain was impressive.

Jo and Ella chatted about their upcoming days off and the possibility of renting skis.

Jo suggested they visit the slopes to see the various levels marked by coloured signs: blue for easy, red for intermediate, and black for expert.

However, Ella was hesitant and didn't want to commit to anything because she felt intimidated.

Jo empathised with her friend's complex array of emotions.

After carefully considering her friend's state of mind, Jo proposed they take a moment to relax and enjoy a delicious meal at the charming café down the street.

The café seemed like a popular spot for everyone to hang out, making it the resort's central gathering place for people of all ages.

"I have a feeling we'll enjoy it here," Jo remarked.

"Fingers crossed," Ella responded.

As they felt their stomachs rumble, they eagerly ordered juicy, sizzling burgers and a generous serving of crispy golden fries. They also opted for velvety hot chocolate topped with fluffy marshmallows to warm themselves up.

As they savoured every bite and sip, they immersed themselves in the lively atmosphere of the resort, taking in the lively conversations and laughter that filled the air.

Feeling exhausted and needing rest, they returned to their chalet just before 10:30 pm.

They unpacked their night clothes and climbed into the spacious and cozy bed.

They quickly fell asleep and slept like babies until the morning.

Ella was first to awake to the sound of activity outside.

Tourists were bustling, picking up their skis and ordering hot drinks on the go.

Despite the noise, Ella felt energised after a good night's sleep and urged Jo to wake up as they had a busy day ahead.

They both admired the beautiful view of the sunrise over the mountains, with its blend of yellow and red shades.

After swigging down a half-cold cup of coffee, they decided to stroll to the office to chat with Eric and finalise any outstanding matters.

It wasn't long before Eric joined them and inquired if they had decided what position they would be interested in.

Without any hesitation, they both expressed interest in becoming Chalet Hosts.

Eric then informed them that the resort had recently constructed ten new chalets and required as many Chalet Hosts as possible.

The job entailed several duties, such as good housekeeping, laundry, and assisting the guests with help and advice when required.

Eric informed them they would be responsible for one chalet, possibly two, during peak times, ensuring guests had an enjoyable stay. They may also be responsible for caring for young children if their parents decide to go skiing without them.

The girls were okay with these responsibilities, and Eric prepared temporary agreements for them to sign and date before starting their work.

They both thanked him for his help and guidance, and he said, "Good luck, girls," hoping they would enjoy their stay at the resort.

The rest of the day was spent relaxing and getting used to their new surroundings, so they decided to visit the mountain store, which sold various items for those wanting to explore the outdoors.

Both girls needed new snow boots because their old walking boots weren't suitable for the snowy and icy conditions. They went to a store and found an extensive collection of boots in different styles, colours, and sizes. They chose two pairs of brightly coloured snow boots that caught their eye.

While taking a look around, Ella and Jo ran into some Ski Reps who were about their age. The Ski Reps were friendly and offered helpful advice on skiing dos and don'ts.

They all decided to meet up later at the bar to hang out, exchange stories, and get to know each other better.

The resort was filling up with more people arriving for the weekend, but they didn't mind.

They relished the opportunity to meet new people and make some new friends.

Thanks to the snow boots, walking around the resort was a breeze.

The boots were so comfortable that they hardly noticed the snow crunching underfoot.

Spirits were high, and they were looking forward to the rest of their stay and all the exciting adventures that awaited them.

Ella and Jo were excited to explore the charming town of Chamonix, nestled among the snow-capped mountains, offering a magnificent view.

While strolling down the meandering alleys, they couldn't help but notice a chic discotheque bustling with young people and an array of restaurants boasting an extensive menu of delectable food.

After some deliberation, they decided to eat at one of the restaurants, which served mouth-watering pizzas.

Aside from the delicious food, the warm and inviting atmosphere of the town added to their overall experience, hoping to make their journey exciting and memorable.

Chapter 7

That evening, casually dressed, the girls headed to the bar to meet with some holiday reps for a drink at the 'Get to Know Evening.'

Some boys were ordering yards of ale, which held almost two pints, appearing to be a very popular way to order beer at the resort.

Ella remarked that she would rather have a glass of wine than making several trips to the loo all night.

Everyone seemed to be hitting it off, conversing and laughing, and the girls began feeling part of the group, discussing their roles at the resort.

Like Ella and Jo, most of the other reps had backpacked to Chamonix and were from many different countries.

Some took time out after leaving college or university and travelled straight to Chamonix to find work before deciding their next move.

The staff's get-to-know evening is certainly a team-building exercise to build much-needed relationships for those working together at the ski resort.

The girls showed a genuine curiosity when hearing different stories and experiences shared by others.

During the evening, they got acquainted with Ryan, a young man from Banff, Canada.

Ryan had just finished his law studies and was travelling with his friend Tyler, who was studying medicine.

Ryan and Tyler met at university and have remained friends since.

Tyler's girlfriend decided not to join them on their European trip because she felt uncomfortable being away from home for an extended period. Despite her absence, Tyler was thrilled about the prospect of embarking on an adventure across Europe, eager to immerse himself in new cultures and expand his perspectives.

Ella began to reveal their experiences, mentioning that they had started with three girls: herself, Jo, and Tilly.

On their backpacking journey, the girls visited France, Belgium, and Holland, each offering its unique charm and character.

During their journey, they had the privilege of staying at Jo's parents' villa in the South of France to enjoy a relaxing break before venturing onwards.

Ella informed the boys that Tilly, the other group member, decided not to continue the journey to the mountains with them.

Ella began to explain, revealing that Tilly had a troubled upbringing where she suffered physical and mental abuse up until her recent years.

Feeling extremely shocked by what Ryan and Tyler heard, they couldn't believe how someone could be treated this way.

While staying at the villa, Tilly formed a close friendship with Maddie, a neighbouring artist. They connected well, and Tilly finally found some much-needed happiness that had never existed in her life before.

Tilly did not for a single moment imagine that she would find the love and happiness she deserved so quickly.

It was a joy to see the strong connection she had with Maddie, who had become a close confidant and brought joy to Tilly's life.

However, the decision to continue the journey to the mountains rested solely on Tilly's shoulders, and she knew that whatever choice she made would significantly impact her future.

After much contemplation, Tilly ultimately decided not to continue the journey to the mountains.

It was a difficult choice, but Tilly felt that staying with Maddie was the right decision for her at this moment.

It was agreed that Tilly would keep in touch and continue to follow their journey on social media.

Although Tilly's decision may have been tough, she made it with the best intentions and has remained true to herself.

She is grateful for the time she spent with Ella and Jo and cherishes the memories they made together.

Ryan and Tyler listened with great concern to Ella's description of Tilly's childhood, understanding the seriousness of the situation.

Tilly's story had touched them all.

After a short while and a few more drinks, the boys mentioned that the ski training here was beneficial, which undoubtedly cemented their decision to become Holiday Reps and thus make the long journey from Canada.

Ryan and Tyler explained that they loved being surrounded by nature.

They relished the fresh air and the opportunity to explore the great outdoors.

Furthermore, they mentioned they had some skiing experience and were interested in hitting the slopes whenever possible.

The boys had a strong passion for adventure and were constantly excited to experience new things.

As the night ended, they bid each other farewell and made plans to meet up very soon.

Let's catch up on the practice slopes Ryan casually remarked.

Jo replied with a tentative "maybe," while Ella was very unsure.

The following day was designated as Training Day.

They were thrilled to receive their instructions and itinerary for the week.

It was a jam-packed schedule, with plenty of responsibilities to keep them busy.

They discovered they were assigned to different chalets, with Ella in Chalet No. 17 and Jo in Chalet 26.

After completing their training, Ella and Jo felt confident in fulfilling their roles.

They were determined to create a welcoming environment for their guests, and with each passing day, they became more comfortable with their duties and established a structured routine.

Their ultimate goal was to make their guests feel at home.

The stunning views of the mountains and the refreshing air made their job even more appealing, creating an unforgettable experience. Despite unexpected challenges, the girls remained optimistic and viewed their workplace as their temporary home. They were provided with uniforms and walkie-talkies, which they tested to ensure they knew how they worked.

Guests of many different nationalities were arriving at the resort, and Eric had arranged for English hosts to take care of English guests, making communication easier.

Similarly, German and French guests had the same arrangement of hosts from their respective countries.

'What a brilliant idea,' Ella thought.

After completing their respective work shifts, Ella and Jo took a well-deserved break. Jo convinced Ella to join her on the slopes for some beginner skiing.

Despite Ella's initial hesitation, Jo's persuasion skills ultimately won her over, and the two girls were soon on their way to the mountain slopes.

They excitedly headed towards the rental centre to secure their ski gear, eager to embark on the adventure that awaited them.

Jo was eager to guide Ella through the experience, and Ella appreciated her friend's encouragement, having acknowledged Ella's worries but knowing that trying something new could be a great experience.

Jo recommended that Ella start by tackling the most accessible slopes and sticking to the beginner areas if she felt unsure or wasn't ready to challenge herself further. This way, Ella could gradually build her confidence and skills before taking on more challenging terrain.

They soon arrived at the beginner's summit, and it was time for Ella to try it.

The snow-covered slopes seemed more intimidating than ever.

Her heart raced as she pushed off from the top, but to her surprise, she found she was enjoying herself.

The rush of wind in her hair and the snow under her skis made her feel alive, and she couldn't help but smile.

Ella's nerves were fading, and Jo's encouraging words kept her going.

Jo and Ella laughed and cheered each other on as they made their way down the slope.

Ella felt renewed energy and excitement despite her initial fears and concerns.

As Ella's exhilarating skiing lesson ended, she turned to Jo with a smile beaming across her face. "That was fun," she said breathlessly.

Jo smiled back at her, delighted to see her friend had enjoyed herself.

The girls' hearts were still racing with excitement as they went to the cozy little café that had become their favourite place to unwind.

They eagerly ordered drinks and settled into a quiet corner, enveloped by the warm atmosphere and the sounds of laughter all around them. As they sipped their drinks, they couldn't contain their excitement as they relived every thrilling moment of Ella's eventful and exhilarating ski lesson.

As they talked, Ella eagerly shared the thrilling news of her first skiing lesson with her mother over the phone. "I didn't fall or bump into anything, Mum! I think I did well for a beginner," she exclaimed.

Jo listened attentively, feeling immensely proud of her friend's accomplishment.

Overall, it had been a wonderful day, filled with excitement, friendship, and the joy of trying something new.

As Ella and Jo trudged through the snow on their way back to their apartment, Ella suddenly turned to Jo and asked if she remembered to lock the front door before they left.

Jo raised her brow, trying to remember, suddenly noticing the door was slightly ajar.

Panic set in as the two girls quickly made their way up to their chalet, their hearts racing with fear and trepidation.

As they cautiously opened the door, their worst fears had been confirmed – someone had broken into their chalet while they were out.

The room was in a total mess, with drawers flung open and clothes and personal items carelessly strewn about.

Upon closer inspection, it appeared someone had rifled through Jo's underwear drawer and made off with some loose cash. Clearly, the thieves had been solely focused on finding money, as nothing else seemed to be missing.

Fortunately, they found solace in knowing their cherished possessions, including Jo's Apple watch, credit cards, and student passes, were safe.

This peace of mind was a direct result of Jo's thoughtful choice to entrust their belongings to a secure locker at the ski shop while they enjoyed the slopes.

As they reflected on their experience, it became increasingly clear how crucial it is to safeguard their valuables when travelling.

Ella was the first to suggest they report the incident to Eric and involve the police. After all, they needed to find out why this had happened and who was responsible.

They were both hesitant about involving the authorities as it made them feel uneasy. They were concerned about getting caught up in a potential criminal investigation. Despite their reservations, they knew that reporting the incident was the right thing to do.

As they discussed their options, Ella reminded Jo not to touch anything for fear of compromising potential fingerprints.

Overall, it was a nerve-wracking and unsettling experience.

The girls were obviously in a state of panic when they discovered that their room had been robbed.

Ella couldn't help but think about having someone in their room without their knowledge, which can be extremely uncomfortable and unsettling.

In a hurry, they swiftly made their way to the office to inform Eric about the incident. Eric, aware of the situation and confident in his ability to handle it, assured them that he would take care of everything.

Unfortunately, this was not the first time such an incident had occurred at the resort.

Within an hour, the Police arrived at the scene to investigate their room.

He warned the girls that when everyone is out skiing, it is easy for thieves to target and enter rooms unnoticed.

Sometimes, they even dress like the skiers themselves and blend in, making it difficult to identify them.

As they spoke with the Police Inspector, they learned this was not an isolated incident; a gang of thieves had been targeting the resort. They suspected that more than one person was involved, making it even more challenging to catch them.

In the meantime, Eric and members of his staff took extra precautions to ensure the safety of their guests.

They increased security measures and ensured all guests were aware of the situation.

Despite the unfortunate incident, Ella and Jo were grateful for the quick response of the Police and the support of those helping, feeling reassured and safe, knowing they were in good hands,

Ella struggled with a tough decision about telling her mother about the theft. She knew that her mother would worry a lot if she found out. After thinking it over, Ella and Jo decided not to tell their parents about the theft.

Ella and Jo anxiously awaited updates from the police about the theft the day after it happened. However, they didn't receive any news. They had taken essential precautions to protect important documents, such as passports, by securing them in the office safe to prevent further loss.

Eric informed the girls that he believed the gang responsible for the theft had left the area. However, the police had now received crucial evidence that could lead to their arrest and were monitoring their movements to catch them in the act.

Despite the unfortunate event, they refused to let it dampen their Christmas spirit as the festive season approached.

They received an invitation to the Christmas Eve party for all the staff at the local bar, which delighted them and made them forget their bad luck over the past couple of days.

The streets of Chamonix were aglow with Christmas trees, creating a magical atmosphere with their colourful lights: the snow-covered rooftops and cable cars transporting skiers to the slopes added to the picturesque scene.

However, an eerie sound lingered in the distance and didn't seem to fade away.

At first, they assumed it might be the sound of rolling thunder approaching, causing them to worry about the possibility of an impending storm.

Was it thunder or something more ominous lurking among the peaks?

The thought was beginning to send shivers down their spines.

Walking back to their chalet, they began to quicken their pace, trying to ignore the noise, but it grew louder.

Despite their best efforts to brush it off, the sense of unease continued to gnaw at them, and they couldn't help but feel that something wasn't quite right.

While Ella was tidying up Chalet 17, an elderly couple who had been frequent visitors to Chamonix for many years entered the room. The couple, both in their early 80s, inquired of Ella whether she had heard an unusual booming sound emanating from the mountaintop.

Ella acknowledged that she had heard the sound, and the couple were surprised because they had never experienced anything like it before during their previous visits to Chamonix.

Ella tried to ease the elderly couple's fears by reassuring them that there was probably no need to worry.

As Ella attentively carried out her daily cleaning duties, ensuring everything was spotless, the gentle elderly lady approached her with a warm smile, asking if she would like a cup of English tea.

Grateful for the thoughtful gesture, Ella responded with heartfelt appreciation, "How kind of you. Thank you very much."

The couple appeared genuinely eager to engage in conversation.

Ella began speaking about her journey so far, recounting in vivid detail the stunning cities she had visited, the friendships she had made along the way and the myriads of experiences she had encountered.

As the discussion deepened, Ella shared with the couple that she had grown up without a father. Yet, amid this absence, she cherished the love and support of her mother and sister above all else. After completing her university degree, Ella deliberately chose to embark on a path of self-discovery, recognizing the need to cultivate a deeper understanding of herself and others.

She found that embracing independence and seeking new horizons was essential to realizing this objective.

For Ella, backpacking emerged as the perfect vehicle to navigate this journey.

The couple appeared deeply moved and inspired by her story, feeling a surge of admiration and respect for her courage and determination.

They listened attentively to her story and nodded in agreement as she spoke of the importance of family.

They also acknowledged Ella's impressive accomplishments since leaving England and expressed hope for a bright future.

It was heartening to see that Ella's unwavering commitment to kindness and helpfulness had not gone unnoticed.

Her friendly demeanour and warm personality had impacted this lovely couple, and she couldn't help but feel proud of herself.

As Ella was about to leave the couple's chalet, the lady had placed two 50 euro notes in her unbuttoned overall pocket, a kind gesture that left her overwhelmed with gratitude but unsure how to express her thanks.

Ella was completely taken aback, feeling a mix of overwhelming gratitude and bewilderment as she tried to find the right words to thank this incredibly generous couple. They insisted that she join in and embrace the joy of the Christmas festivities along with the entire resort staff.

As she approached the chalet door, Ella's gaze fell upon the lady's husband, seated in a cozy armchair, peering thoughtfully out the window. When he turned to acknowledge her, he offered a kind smile and a subtle wink.

In response, Ella returned his warm smile, her eyes reflecting her profound appreciation for their exceptionally kind gesture.

Ella decided to take a stroll to the café for a hot drink, feeling grateful for the kindness shown by this lovely couple.

As Ella stepped into the café, she was embraced by the enchanting fragrance of freshly brewed coffee and rich, velvety chocolate. The air, in stark contrast to the chilly snow outside, was filled with a comforting warmth, drawing her in with an irresistible allure.

Finding a peaceful place to sit by the window, Ella settled at a table where she could gaze outside and witness the graceful descent of snowflakes falling graciously, gently blanketing the ground in a pristine layer of white.

As Ella sipped her hot drink, she overheard a group of people chatting nearby about recent burglaries in the area, saying that the police had arrested two men and a woman involved in the crimes.

She found herself unable to shake the nagging thought of whether they would ever be able to recover the money that was stolen from them. The chances seemed slim, and it wasn't easy to hold out much hope. Nevertheless, Ella remained optimistic, telling herself they might receive some news shortly.

Lost in thought, Ella peered out the misty window when she saw Jo finishing her shift at Chalet 26.

Her excitement surged and beckoned Jo to join her.

With careful steps, Jo crossed the slippery road to the cafe, where Ella was eagerly, almost impatiently, awaiting her.

Sitting down together, Ella couldn't contain her enthusiasm as she recounted the generous monetary gift that she had received from the elderly couple staying in Chalet 17.

Chapter 8

The resort was alive on Christmas Eve with a festive atmosphere as everyone came together to celebrate. Skiers adorned themselves with Santa hats and slid down the snow-covered slopes with remarkable skill and finesse. They were cheerful and greeted onlookers with warm wishes of "Merry Christmas!".

Ella, who had also participated in skiing, shared some photos of her skiing efforts on the Family Group Chat. These photos were taken by Jo, who had accompanied her on the slopes. Ella was proud of herself for having tried skiing and enjoying the experience.

After completing their tasks for the day, which included giving each bed fresh linens and ensuring the chalets were thoroughly cleaned, Ella and Jo finally had the chance to immerse themselves in the joyful Christmas celebrations.

Ella began to notice that Jo seemed sad and asked her how she felt.

Jo said everything was okay, but Ella could tell something was bothering Jo.

Eventually, Jo shared that her mother had texted, saying her father was sick and might have to spend Christmas in the hospital. Ella felt sorry for Jo and offered her support.

The news had undoubtedly damaged Jo's holiday spirit, and Ella couldn't help but feel empathetic towards her.

To ease Jo's concerns and fears and distract her from her father's declining health, they ventured into town and immersed themselves in the Christmas celebrations as best they could.

They had heard that Eric and Maria had organised some fantastic Christmas fun, and they couldn't wait to be a part of the celebrations.

As soon as they arrived, Ryan and Tyler welcomed them and offered to buy them a drink.

With a warm and approachable demeanour, Ryan promptly engages in conversation with Ella and displays a noticeable fascination with Jo, evident from the sparkle in his eye.

He enquired about Ella's skiing journey, to which she responded that she is still navigating the learning curve and has a considerable way to progress before attaining expert status.

Jo, being the supportive friend that she is, told Ryan that Ella had the potential to progress to the blue slopes in no time.

However, Ella preferred to play it safe and stay on the ground for now.

Ryan and Tyler laughed loudly, predicting that Ella would soon easily conquer the blue slopes.

Overall, the evening was enjoyable, and everyone had a great time. The atmosphere was alive with laughter, dancing and music, providing a perfect distraction from Jo's worries and anxieties.

As Ryan sat calmly with the girls, he asked them if they had heard any unusual sounds coming from the mountain.

Ella quickly responded, confirming that they had heard something and began asking Ryan for his thoughts.

In a calm and urgent tone, Ryan explained that when snow accumulates on the mountaintops, it can sometimes shift downwards, producing a loud sound that reverberates like thunder. He elaborated that, in some cases, it could even trigger a ferocious and unstoppable avalanche of loose snow. However, he stressed that our seasoned staff members were tirelessly monitoring the situation and painstakingly preparing warning notices for the imminent guests visiting the resort in the next week, leaving no stone unturned to ensure everyone's safety.

The authorities assured him that they would take immediate and decisive measures if the situation worsened, promising to swiftly relocate the guests to another resort in case of an emergency.

The mere thought of a potential avalanche made Ella's knees tremble with fear.

She was keenly aware of the mountains' capricious nature, and the realisation that a sudden shift in the snow could unleash a calamity filled her with an overwhelming sense of dread. Despite her inner turmoil, she made a concerted effort to conceal her mounting anxiety from those nearby, determined not to instigate unnecessary panic.

Ella took a deep breath and tried to steady herself, even though her heart was still racing, knowing that she had to remain calm and focused, no matter what.

Ella made a snap decision to call her Mum and Lauren via Facetime and found a quiet spot outside the bar.

It was a great feeling to see and hear them even though they were miles apart. Ella, being a considerate person, decided not to mention the possibility of an avalanche as it might cause unnecessary worry. The three of them had a conversation for at least 30 minutes, and everyone seemed to be in good spirits. During the chat, Ella mentioned that she was enjoying skiing but was still a beginner. However, her experience so far had been pleasant, if not invigorating.

Ella's mother admired the photos of her daughter on the slopes and was amazed at how professional she looked.

"Not sure about that, Mum," but it was good fun.

Lauren had been eagerly looking forward to Christmas day and had made plans to celebrate it with her friends by organizing a barbeque on the beach.

As Lauren held up her laptop, Ella and her mother could see the stunning view of the crystal-clear waters of the vast ocean stretching out across Australia's beautiful coastline.

The bright sun shone, and you just saw a gentle breeze of the Palm Trees, making the atmosphere calm and tranquil.

While Lauren basked in the warm Australian sun during Christmas, Ella had a different experience venturing into the frosty winter wonderland, braving the biting cold with her snug ski jacket and sturdy snow boots.

Despite the biting cold on that wintry night, she couldn't help but be captivated by the breathtaking sight of the snow-capped mountains encircling her. Their majestic peaks shimmered and sparkled under the soft, silvery glow of the moon, casting a spellbinding aura over the landscape.

The stark contrast between the two countries couldn't have been more pronounced.

Despite the distance, Ella's mum held a perfectly chilled gin and tonic, exchanging warm greetings, surrounded by the joyous ambiance of the holiday season, wishing each other a Merry Christmas and a Happy New Year.

As the conversation drew close, they promised to stay in touch and catch up more in the New Year.

Ella placed her laptop on the table and started to feel somewhat homesick and sad about saying goodbye to her Mum and sister without knowing when she would see them next.

However, she knew she had to pull herself together, not just for her own sake, but for Jo also.

She ambled back into the bar, feeling slightly cold and confused after hearing Ryan speak of a potential snow avalanche at the resort.

Walking between those dancing and having fun, Ella ordered herself a gin and tonic.

Moments later, she was approached by a friendly young man who introduced himself as Hugo Monet.

He quickly remarked that he was not related to the famous French painter Monet.

Ella chuckled at his amused tone and extended a warm greeting, expressing her pleasure in meeting him.

During the conversation, Hugo shared that he had just arrived for the Christmas holidays and planned to stay with his Uncle Eric and Aunt Maria, who run the resort.

Ella appeared surprised by this revelation and began engaging in a lengthy conversation with this tall, handsome, fair-haired young man.

She couldn't help but notice his well-toned physique, which hinted at his regular gym workouts.

He revealed that he used to be a professional downhill skier until two years ago. Unfortunately, his career ended due to receiving two severe leg breaks during a skiing accident.

He decided to retire from the sport to prevent further harm to his body. He explained to Ella that being a top athlete requires intense fitness training, often involving twice-daily sessions.

Downhill skiers can reach speeds of up to 120km faster than some vehicles on the road.

Participants must know their physical limitations as this sport can be dangerous.

As they continued to talk, Hugo talked more about his life.

He had grown up in Dijon and had always loved skiing.

His parents had supported his passion for skiing from a young age and had driven him to all his competitions.

Now that he was no longer a professional skier, he worked as a ski instructor at a local centre for novices and intermediates.

It must have been such a difficult decision to give up something he loved, Ella thought to herself.

When asked about coaching younger athletes, he nodded and explained that sharing his knowledge and experience with the next generation gave him a sense of fulfilment. Ella was pleased to hear that he had found a way to stay connected to his passion.

At the same time, he was also experiencing a difficult time in his personal life, and Ella could see by the expression on his face that he was trying very hard to avoid the subject.

Did he have something to hide, or was it something very painful for him that he did not want to discuss?

As they sat down for a chat, Hugo excitedly told Ella that his uncle had recently mentioned two new girls had joined the resort staff: Ella and Jo.

In response, Ella's voice filled with excitement as she exclaimed, "That's me!" and gestured towards her friend Jo, who was engrossed in a conversation with Ryan across the room.

While Ella recounted their adventurous backpacking journey, he marvelled at their unwavering determination, physical strength, and remarkable strides they had made together.

As Hugo spoke, Ella's mind then wandered to a previous conversation with Ryan, who mentioned the word "avalanche."

Would there be any warning if the worst happens?

Should she speak with Eric to learn more or wait for the situation to develop?

It was now getting quite late, so she said goodbye to Hugo and walked over to where Jo was enjoying a joke or two with Ryan and Tyler.

Feeling somewhat tired, Ella decided to return to the chalet and hoped Jo didn't mind. She had remarked not to rush her drink and that she would see her back at the chalet.

As Ella cautiously made her way through the treacherous icy pathways on her journey home, once again, the thunderous, violent noise in the distance intensified, echoing across the snowy landscape. Startled, she looked up to behold an avalanche of snow hurtling down from the face of a menacing, dark mountain, the raw power and force of nature on full display.

An avalanche, oh no, it cannot be!

Ella gasped in fear, her heart racing as she looked up at the massive wall of snow hurtling towards her.

She knew she had to move fast to survive, but her legs felt like lead, and her mind was a blur of confusion and panic.

Ella's chest heaved with each breath as she tried hard to race through the snow, desperately attempting to find Jo. The biting wind whipped against her face, causing her eyes to water and her skin to sting. Fear bubbled up inside her, threatening to overwhelm her completely.

As Ella pushed through the crowds of people, the screams of panic grew louder, making her more agitated.

Despite the chaos unfolding around her, Ella refused to give up. She had to find Jo, no matter what. She scanned the crowd, searching for any sign of her friend.

Amidst the relentless chaos, when Ella was on the brink of losing all hope, a profound sense of relief engulfed her as she caught sight of a familiar face amid the tumultuous crowd. It was Jo. With a revitalised sense of purpose, Ella forged ahead, unwavering in her resolve to push through the crowd and reach Jo before it was too late.

Together, they ran towards safety, and as they emerged from the chaos of the avalanche, Ella knew that they had been lucky to escape with their lives.

The police stopped people from entering the town and directed them to a safe location.

The Medical Centre and office had been designated safe areas for those seeking refuge.

Ella observed the snow rapidly descending onto the village with more snow gathering behind it, creating a blizzard-like condition that made it difficult to see anything beyond a few feet in front of her.

Jo turned around to face Ella, her expression serious. She knew that the snowstorm outside was rapidly becoming worse by the minute, and the people inside the town's bar were in grave danger.

Without hesitation, she informed Ella that she would return to warn the others and assist them in finding a safe place to take shelter.

However, Jo also knew there would be people seeking safety at the Medical Centre, and she asked Ella to stay back there to assist them if needed.

Ella's heart raced as she nodded in agreement, feeling the weight of responsibility on her shoulders.

She knew that every little bit of help counted in times of crisis.

As she looked up, she could see and hear the sound of the search and rescue helicopters in the air, beaming down their searchlights, looking to find anyone trapped in the snow. The howling winds made it difficult to hear anything else, but Ella could sense the urgency in the pilot's voice as they communicated with the ground team.

Trees began crashing down the rugged mountainside with a deafening roar, their mighty forms splintering like fragile matchsticks as they tumbled, casting a shroud of chaos and panic over the unsuspecting village below.

A sense of terror crept over her, but she held onto her resolve, knowing she had to focus on providing crucial assistance to those in dire need amid the unfolding disaster.

An emergency worker rushed by, telling her to take shelter quickly because of the danger of falling debris along its path.

Her only thought was for Jo and if she was safe.

Rescuers began searching for anyone who could be lost in the mountains. With spiked shoes and ropes slung around their waists, around a dozen mountain volunteers took to the slopes in the hope of finding life because, as one rescuer told me, one life saved is better than none at all.

As usual in times like this, a thorough roll call is of the utmost importance to ensure the safety and security of all visitors and resort staff.

Providing detailed information about their whereabouts can be time-consuming, but it is essential in times of emergency.

Despite feeling helpless, Ella knew that she had to do her part, if only to distract herself from the gravity of the situation.

Amid the chaos, she couldn't help but wonder whether Jo made it back to the town's bar safely.

Her heart sank when a faint voice from the back of the Centre informed her that the bar had been severely hit by the sliding snow, blocking the entrance. Fortunately, there were no reported injuries so far, and everyone was safe inside.

Ella sighed in relief as she realised that her worst fears had not come true. However, she felt a strong urge to find out if Jo was safe and was determined to do everything to ensure her friend's well-being.

As she walked through the Medical Centre, she noticed Eric and Maria looking distraught, and Ella could see they were struggling to keep it together.

Eric then called out, asking Ella to stand at the centre's entrance and collect names and chalet numbers.

He warned her not to stray towards the slopes in any way, as it was hazardous out there.

They needed to stay local to the Medical Centre until they received the all-clear from the Rescue Unit.

Ella promptly agreed, determined to do her part to help.

Maria tapped her shoulder, telling her she was heading inside the Centre to help the locals serve hot soup and drinks.

Anyone returning from the mountain feeling exceptionally cold and bedraggled would welcome a hot drink, especially those rescuers braving the elements.

Ella thought it was a great idea and shouted her approval.

At least four staff members took names and chalet numbers, and so far, everyone had been accounted for and appeared safe.

It was a relief to know that nobody was missing or injured, or so she thought.

However, Ella reminded Eric that the town bar had many resort staff celebrating at the Christmas Eve Party in town, and some were trapped inside by massive snow drifts.

It was a worrying situation, and Eric knew he had to act fast.

About ten minutes later, Eric decided to take a chance and use his walkie-talkie to try to communicate with anyone who may be inside the bar.

Fortunately, a security officer at the bar responded to Eric's call and assured everyone was unharmed. There were no serious injuries, but it was evident that many people were making the most of the alcoholic drinks available at the bar, particularly the brandy and whisky. The supply of wine bottles was quickly diminishing, and everyone appeared to be enjoying themselves, oblivious to the severe situation unfolding outside.

Eric believed everyone inside the bar was better off staying there until help came, and that he would check the drinks tab later when he knew everyone was safe, but in the meantime, there were more urgent matters to take care of.

Ella stood at the doorway of the bustling office, scanning the room for someone who might need assistance.

Amid the busy atmosphere, she noticed two people approaching, and she recognised them as the lovely couple of Chalet number 17.

With a concerned expression, she asked, "Is everything alright?"

As Ella engaged in conversation with the couple, she observed that the woman's husband had sustained a head injury.

The woman shared the harrowing details of the incident, describing how her husband had slipped and fallen inside the chalet, his head making forceful contact with the corner of a wooden table.

The injury had left him disoriented and in urgent need of help.

Recognizing the severity of the situation, Ella compassionately offered to accompany them to the Medical Centre, where the elderly gentleman could promptly receive the necessary medical care for his injury.

Ella stayed by their side throughout the entirety of their visit to the Medical Centre. She made sure that the gentleman received the best attention for his head wound. She continued to offer her support and comfort until she was satisfied that they were okay.

After enjoying a steaming cup of sweet tea, the couple expressed their heartfelt gratitude to Ella for her unwavering support and assistance.

They were especially thankful for the brave and selfless young man who fearlessly came to their rescue during the fierce snowstorm.

The elderly couple detailed how the snowstorm had severely damaged the chalet, leaving them trapped inside. It was the stranger's remarkable display of strength and determination that freed them from the snow and debris blocking the doorway. The couple were deeply moved by his actions and assured Ella that they would forever be thankful for the young man's extraordinary kindness.

After he ensured they were safe, he left to respond to a call for help from someone in need higher up on the mountain.

His bravery in risking his own life was commendable.

Ella's mind was filled with curiosity as she pondered the courageous young man's identity. She found herself in awe of his fearlessness and marvelled at his willingness to put his life on the line in such a selfless and brave way.

Ella then recommended to the couple that the Centre was the most secure location to be at that time. She kindly asked them to stay there until all the required safety measures had been put in place to guarantee their safe return to their Chalet.

Inside the Medical Centre were plenty of people walking around; some looked very dazed, others in complete shock at what had just happened, but hopefully, they were all safe now, for the moment at least.

Chapter 9

The snow outside still fell heavily, and the winds were getting stronger by the minute.

Looking down at her watch, Ella saw that it had passed midnight, and it was now Christmas Day.

Never had she spent Christmas like this before, and it was starting to feel like it would never end.

Ella spotted Eric passing by the Medical Centre and immediately caught his attention.

She inquired about any updates concerning those stranded in the town bar.

He told her that the snowploughs were preparing to handle the large snow drifts around the entrance and assured her that everyone was completely safe, for the moment anyway.

He also mentioned that the mood inside the bar was positive, with people in high spirits despite the ordeal.

Ella was relieved to hear this news, as Jo was among those who were inside and safe. His words conveyed a sense of solidarity and resilience, giving Ella hope that everything would turn out alright in the end.

As she carefully scanned through the list of names of those who had made it to safety, a deep sense of worry and anxiety began to creep up on her. Her eyes darted back and forth, searching fervently for the name of the man she had encountered at the Christmas Eve Party, Hugo Monet. Despite her persistent efforts, his name was nowhere to be found on the list.

Could it be possible that he was the same young man who had been seen courageously attempting to rescue people amidst the chaos and destruction up on the mountain?

The mere thought sent shivers down her spine and made her heart skip a beat.

She hoped and prayed that if Hugo was stranded on the mountain, he would be okay and not lying hurt somewhere.

Suddenly, she heard someone calling her name.

It was Jo!

Immediately, Ella rushed over and gave her a tight hug, feeling relieved that she was alive and safe.

Ella then began walking with Jo into the Medical Centre, where she was given food and a hot drink.

As they sat down beside a warm heater and indulged in some hot food, Jo explained that upon returning to the bar, she noticed they were in deep trouble and that they needed more help.

Determined to reach safety, they all worked together to dig themselves out with shovels and whatever was available.

Despite the snowplough arriving late, the group did not lose hope and decided to take matters into their own hands.

With unwavering determination, everyone worked tirelessly to create a path for as many people as possible to pass through the narrow doorway.

Ella immediately asked about Ryan and Tyler's well-being and was told that both were okay and had been actively involved in the rescue operation to save those trapped inside the bar.

They were determined to evacuate everyone as quickly as possible despite the challenge of the small gap in the doorway.

It was evident that success in their mission would allow the snowploughs to shift their focus to other areas that urgently needed assistance.

Once the girls had made themselves warm and eagerly eaten much-needed food, Ella and Jo emerged into the frigid air outside, their boots crushing the freshly fallen snow beneath them.

Standing silently, they gazed at the still and serene landscape, taking in the gravity of what had happened a few hours earlier.

The snowflakes had ceased their gentle fall, leaving an eerie silence on the mountain. It was unimaginable that danger had just passed, as they had never thought they would have to fight for survival, especially on Christmas Day! But now, as they stood there in the stillness, they couldn't help but be grateful for the peace that had settled over the mountain.

Eric began updating everyone on the effects of the recent storm. He reassured them that the storm had caused minimal damage to the ski resort's buildings and overall infrastructure.

Nevertheless, some repairs were necessary to ensure the safety and comfort of the guests. The slopes had railings that needed fixing, and a few chalets required roof repairs. Additionally, the wooden steps leading up to the rental store were damaged and needed immediate replacement.

The good news was that the damage was not severe and could be fixed quickly, but the storm had caused significant snow melting, which posed a risk of flooding.

Once the sun started shining at the bottom of the valley, sandbags would need to be placed strategically to block doorways and prevent floodwater from entering buildings. Proactive measures were essential to ensure the guests' safety and avoid damage to the property.

The darkness of the night was beginning to show daylight as dawn was fast approaching.

Once a sanctuary, the Centre was now bustling with activity as visitors and staff emerged from safety in the hope that life would return to normal and that danger had passed.

It was mid-morning when Ella's eyes fell upon numerous reporters and their cameras setting up their equipment just outside the local bar.

The reporters were unyielding in their quest for the latest scoop, undeterred by the slippery, wet roads. Their sole focus was gathering the most recent news, leaving no obstacle in their path.

On the other hand, Ella was resolute in her decision not to be interviewed, and quickly returned to the Centre, hoping to avoid any unwanted attention.

Shortly after, Eric's voice rang out, announcing the successful rescue of everyone from the Town bar. This news was met with a sigh of relief as many people began their journey back to the Medical Centre, still the safest place to be at the moment.

Those trapped at the Town Bar were still struggling to come to terms with the lasting effects of their terrifying ordeal, contemplating whether the copious amounts of alcohol they had drank had played a role in affecting their emotional well-being. On the other hand, the most important thing was that they were safe and out of harm's way.

It seemed ages since the deafening roar of the avalanche, a force of nature that had swept through the resort, had subsided.

Suddenly, a calm appeared, as if the world was taking a deep breath.

The serene beauty of the natural surroundings did little to alleviate the mounting concern that gripped everyone.

Hugo's uncertain fate cast a veil of unease over the once-idyllic resort. The fact that he was the only person missing from the attendance list only intensified everyone's worry, redirecting the rescue team's efforts toward locating him.

As Ella looked at Eric, she could feel his anxiety intensify with each passing moment, his eyes fixated on the mesmerizing yet ominous sight before him and hoping beyond hope that Hugo would emerge unscathed from the devastation.

Eric couldn't shake the feeling that Hugo was stranded somewhere or, even worse, that he may not have made it to safety in time.

It was now midday, and the snow began slowly settling in the valley below, leaving a thick, white blanket enveloping everything on its path and creating a peaceful and quiet stillness.

Suddenly, and without warning, a loud siren sounded.

It was a sound that someone or something had been found in the mountains, and help was urgently needed.

Within no time, a team had been put together, and immediate action was implemented.

Everyone knew that time was of the essence, and they had to act fast.

Even a couple of rescue dogs had joined the team, their keen sense of smell and hearing making them invaluable in the search for whatever or whoever was in the mountains.

Fully trained rescue dogs can find trapped humans under deep snow in a matter of minutes. They are constantly trained to sniff scents and can keep going a lot longer than humans in the coldness of wild winter storms.

Like their human counterparts, these dogs are fearless and recognised worldwide for their courage and bravery.

A group of people gathered outside the Medical Centre; their eyes fixed on the mountain before them.

They watched with admiration as a team of brave men, women, and dogs attempted a tricky rescue operation.

The mission, spanning a vast area, was of such a scale that onlookers found it overwhelming to fully witness the ongoing events. Nevertheless, they took comfort in knowing help was coming for those in need. The sound of a helicopter filled the air, its powerful blades slicing through the atmosphere as it swiftly maneuverer in all directions, generating a whirl of activity above.

Eric informed everyone that the rescuers would continue their search throughout the night, refusing to give up until they found whoever was missing.

Maria shared Eric's concern and also appeared worried about the situation.

Despite the intense search and rescue operation on the mountain, everyone who had been accounted for at ground level could safely return to their chalets, providing some relief.

Both Ella and Jo decided that they would need to get a message back home to their parents, just in case they saw any reports on the news channels about the disaster at the ski resort.

Ella knew that her mother would be out of her mind with worry, while Jo also needed to know her father's condition after his health scare and if he had been admitted to hospital.

However, Ella, feeling uneasy, suggested calling her mum immediately to update her on the situation.

Jo agreed and decided to call her parents, too.

Back at the chalet, Ella found a quiet corner where she could get a signal. Unfortunately, there was no electricity, so generators were temporarily used to provide power.

Nonetheless, Ella managed somehow to get through.

Ella's worried mother picked up the phone as she heard her daughter's voice on the other end. "Hello, Mum," Ella said, her mother's concern intense as she asked if her daughter was okay.

Ella knew her mother had been following the news bulletins about the avalanche and had probably been worried sick since she could not contact her due to the bad weather conditions causing the loss of phone signals.

Although her Mum sounded very concerned and anxious, Ella tried her best to reassure her that there was no need to worry.

However, she wasn't entirely sure if she was successful in doing so.

In a soft and gentle tone, Ella's mother asked her when she hoped to return home. Ella replied that they planned to stay until the end of March when the winter season ends.

"That long?" her mother asked, expressing her concern.

After a brief pause on the other end of the phone, Ella's mother's voice came through. In a gentle tone, she said, 'I love you, Ella, my beautiful daughter. Please just stay safe.'

Ella felt a wave of warmth wash over her as she replied, "I love you too, Mum!"

With a sense of contentment, she said goodbye and ended the call.

Shortly afterward, Ella's heart sank as she noticed the distress in Jo's eyes. Her friend was sitting on the edge of her bed, deep in conversation with her mother.

With a gentle nod, Ella silently conveyed her readiness to listen, providing a comforting presence as she waited to hear Jo's news.

After a while, Jo hung up the phone, and Ella asked if everything was okay.

"Not sure," she replied. "Dad was taken to hospital last night by an ambulance, and Mum is with him.

He's hooked up to a heart machine, and everything appears stable for the moment, but they are waiting for the rest of the results to come back.

Feeling somewhat anxious and uneasy, Ella muttered,' What a day!

Is there anything else that could go wrong.?

Suddenly, there was a knock on the window. "Hello, is anybody there?"

Ryan was at the door, and Jo rushed to greet him.

He told her everyone was out of the bar safely and the building had minimal damage.

Jo was thanked for her efforts in rescuing those stranded in the bar, saying she was happy to help and asking if he was ok.

I'm a little sore, but nothing serious.

Tyler has had some butterfly stitches put in his knee because he slipped and fell on some broken glass, and the cut was rather deep, but other than that, we have all come away without any severe injuries.

After a tough day, Jo felt immense gratitude toward Ryan and Tyler. They had played a crucial role in rescuing those stranded in the bar, and their assistance had undoubtedly prevented the situation from escalating into something far worse.

As Ryan was about to leave, he asked Jo if she would like to meet for a drink sometime, giving her time to recover from the day's ordeal fully.

Jo had a big smile and, feeling excited, looked forward to meeting Ryan again.

Ella, who overheard their conversation, noticed Jo blushing before shutting the door.

Curious, she asked Jo if she was going to accept Ryan's invitation, to which Jo replied politely, "Of course."

Could this be more than just a friendship, Ella thought?

The next morning, after a somewhat disturbed night and with little sleep, Ella found herself gazing out of her bedroom window, lost in thought.

Suddenly, she noticed a helicopter circling a specific area nearby, and her curiosity attracted interest.

However, her mind was all over the place, and she needed to clear her head. Without thinking, she decided to go for a walk.

As she strolled through the quiet streets, she bumped into Eric, who appeared pale and visibly distressed.

Concerned, she approached him and asked if he was okay.

Eric then revealed that he had just heard from one of the rescuers that Hugo was indeed stranded on the mountain.

Ella was stunned by the news, placing her hands over her head. "Oh, Eric, let's hope they find him safe and well," she said, her voice trembling with worry.

As Ella listened intently, Eric, after a long and anxious wait for news about his nephew, finally began to explain everything the rescue team had told him so far.

Apparently, they were told that Hugo had helped a young family who appeared trapped and unable to get off the mountain, requiring assistance and much-needed help.

He then walked them back towards the safety of the resort, unhurt and in good spirits.

But, instead of returning home, Hugo decided to go back up the mountain to see if anyone else needed help.

He started his descent after ensuring everyone had safely returned from the mountain, but the slippery snow made it difficult for him to maintain his balance, and he eventually lost his footing.

Struggling to regain his balance, he stumbled and tumbled down a small ravine in the ice.

The fall left him injured and unable to move.

Concerned, Ella asked if he was severely hurt.

Eric could only tell Ella what he knew so far, knowing that acting quickly and getting him to safety was imperative to avoid potential risks.

The temperature up there was recorded at minus 20 degrees and getting colder, making it highly likely that he could suffer from hypothermia if he stayed there for a prolonged period. Therefore, it was crucial to take immediate action and ensure his safety.

Could you please keep me updated, Eric?

"Of course, my dear," he said.

As Ella opened the door to their chalet, she could see Jo, laid out on the bed, with a towel wrapped around her wet hair, checking her phone and sipping a hot cup of tea. "Everything alright," Ella asked.

"Yes," Jo replied with a smile. "I'm just catching up on my messages and enjoying a little relaxation time."

Jo also had some good news regarding her father's recent health scare.

She revealed that his test results had returned clear, allowing him to return home in time to enjoy some Christmas celebrations with Mum and the rest of the family. Ella sighed, relieved upon hearing the news and commented on how much relief it must have been for her.

Jo nodded and confirmed that it had been a stressful time for all involved, especially with the added stress of the snow disaster. However, Jo was overjoyed to have her father back home safe and sound.

As the two girls continued to chat, they relished the comfortable warmth of the room, grateful to be together on such a cold, wintry day.

There were plenty of eggs in the fridge, so Ella asked Jo if she would like one of her cheeky omelettes.

"Sounds delicious, Ella! Yes please".

Suddenly, Jo heard her phone receive a text message. It was from Tilly, who wanted to ensure both of them were safe after hearing about the storm's severity on the news. Tilly sounded very worried about them.

Ella felt a sense of urgency as she turned to Jo, emphasizing the importance of reassuring Tilly that there was no need to worry excessively about their safety. Both girls consciously tried to engage with Tilly, using humour and laughter to create a joyful atmosphere and provide a sense of security, ensuring that Ella and Jo remained free from harm.

After ending the call with Tilly, Jo noticed that Ella was panicking.

She told Jo she was highly concerned about Hugo and the lack of updates on his rescue.

As Ella's thoughts raced, she couldn't help but imagine the worst-case scenario. She pictured him shivering in the bitter cold, possibly injured and stranded on the treacherous mountainside. The snowfall had been relentless, making the rescue operation all the more difficult for those trying to help.

The hazardous conditions were adding to the mounting sense of urgency and anxiety.

Jo asked Ella if she was beginning to have feelings for Hugo due to her emotional state.

Ella's response was immediate, and her expression clearly indicated that she was just very concerned for his safety.

She spoke with empathy and warmth, stating that the idea of someone being in danger and without support was distressing.

Despite having only met Hugo once before, she remembered him as happy-go-lucky and exceptionally interesting to talk to,

She could only think that Hugo was the person who risked his life for others, attempting to reach them in treacherous conditions and acknowledging his bravery in climbing the mountain multiple times to save others.

While attentively observing Ella as she spoke, Jo couldn't help but notice the gentle and kind expression in her eyes. This sight filled Jo with a deep respect and admiration for Ella, prompting her to reflect on the many times Ella had shown her compassion and care.

At that moment, Jo felt grateful to have such a compassionate and caring friend like Ella.

It had been two days since the awful snow slide when a loud noise was suddenly heard outside. The sound of a church bell rang out loudly, and Ella later learned that when someone is found on the mountain, a bell rings to let the villagers know that a lost person, whether alive or sadly deceased, has been found.

Passing by the window, she could see several people, mostly emergency workers, carrying a stretcher down the mountain, heading straight towards a waiting ambulance.

Ella quickly got dressed and rushed out of the door towards the Centre.

As she arrived, she instantly saw that Hugo was wrapped in silver foil, with only his head visible.

She leaned over him and asked about his condition.

Thankfully, he spoke rationally and informed her that the paramedics thought he had a suspected broken collarbone, some minor leg injuries, and was experiencing mild hyperthermia.

Although initially worried, seeing him look up at her made her feel much better.

He then went on to say that they were taking him to the hospital for scans and treatment.

They laughed when he mentioned that the thought of a hot cup of English tea would keep him going. Ella promised to make him tea when he returned from the hospital.

As the ambulance waited by the Centre entrance, it became apparent that Hugo was the person saving stranded and injured people on the mountainside.

She then told him that she looked forward to meeting him again after his recovery from the ordeal.

Hugo turned his head slightly, raised his hand from underneath the covered foil, and gave a thumbs-up and a friendly wink.

Ella was so pleased he was okay and that his injuries weren't serious, although a broken collarbone can be painful!

Eric went with him in the ambulance and told Maria to shut the office up for the rest of the day. Hopefully, everyone now had been found and had returned to their accommodation.

Indeed, this had to be a Christmas nobody would ever forget.

Maria had arranged for a pizza van to be set up at the resort's entrance for anyone wanting some hot food because the restaurant was again closed for another night.

Once the word got around, a long queue formed in no time, and the strong aroma of freshly cooked pizzas lured Ella to the van, where she decided that Pizza was on the menu for both her and Jo tonight.

Jo took some time to tidy up their chalet after a long day when Ella suddenly appeared, carrying a tray with two piping hot Cheese, Ham and Chorizo pizzas. Jo's face lit up as she thanked Ella for the unexpected treat. They settled in, enjoying the delicious pizzas with a well-deserved glass of wine, while Ella shared the latest updates on Hugo's recovery. Jo's heart filled with joy upon hearing that he had bravely overcome the terrible incident with relatively minor injuries.

Chapter 10

After nearly a week of being under medical care, Hugo was finally discharged from the hospital, relieved to have survived the accident with nothing more than a fractured collarbone, scratches and some bruising. Meanwhile, Ella had resumed her duties as a chalet cleaner, working diligently to restore the chalets to pristine condition after the busy Christmas season.

As the days passed, the resort began to come back to life, with skiers and hikers excitedly hitting the slopes and trails after being given the green light by those in charge.

The sight of people enjoying themselves on the mountain brought a sense of relief and joy to everyone, as they were grateful to see the resort returning to some semblance of normality after the recent turmoil.

Whilst Ella was getting some provisions at the store, the lady and gentleman in Chalet 17 approached her.

They both wanted to say goodbye because their holiday in the Alps had come to an end.

Standing in the store doorway, the elderly lady told her that although things didn't turn out exactly how they had planned due to the snowstorm, they enjoyed meeting such lovely and caring people.

The couple expressed gratitude towards the many friendly faces who had shown them kindness during their stay in Chamonix.

They especially appreciated Ella's help in getting treatment for the deep head wound her husband incurred.

Due to their age, it was apparent they didn't come to Chamonix for skiing but rather for the natural beauty, the local community, and the scenery. They had been visiting this area for the past eight years and had grown to love it dearly.

They also told Ella that they didn't have any family; it was just the two of them.

If their health permits, they always take a break at this time of year, hoping to return the following year.

Although Ella knew their full names because they were printed on her list, she still wanted to call them the lovely couple in Chalet 17.

Having said their goodbyes, she told them that because she was backpacking with another friend, it would be unlikely their paths would cross again, so she hugged them and wished them a safe journey home.

Looking down at her phone, she could see a text message from Hugo asking if she would like to meet him for a drink at the bar.

She took a moment to collect her thoughts before replying.

It didn't take her long to type out a response, almost thirty seconds, possibly even quicker if she hadn't made a few typos.

She told him she would meet him once she finished her shift.

A thumb emoji appeared on her phone alongside a little red heart. She couldn't help but wonder if the use of this emoji had any special meaning or if it was just his way of signing off.

Ella was getting so excited at the thought of seeing him that she began to tremble with slight uneasiness but couldn't understand why, was Jo right? Did she have feelings for him?

Eric and Maria have returned to the office and are diligently preparing for the busy weeks ahead. They are overseeing repairs to address the storm damage, ensuring that everything is in optimal condition for the upcoming winter snow season, which spans from now until the end of March. Bookings for the next few months have been pouring in, indicating a high level of demand.

The snow-covered landscape has been restored to its previous panoramic setting, and the cool mountain air is crisp and abundant with beauty, creating a sense of calmness.

How could anyone imagine they had undergone such awful conditions on the mountain a couple of weeks ago, with many people fearing for their lives?

Finishing her shift somewhat quicker than usual, Ella ran back to the apartment, changed into something more presentable, and brushed through her unruly hair. She wanted to make sure she looked her best for her meeting with Hugo and was longing to hear about his recent ordeal in the mountain.

When she arrived at the bar, she could see Hugo's arm was in a sling, but other than that, he looked in very good shape.

He told her he was fortunate not to have had worse injuries and couldn't thank the rescue team enough.

They found him just before any further symptoms of hyperthermia set in, and he was lucky to get to the hospital in time before his temperature dropped even lower.

"You saved so many people's lives, Hugo," Ella said admiringly.

"Your attempts to conquer the mountain repeatedly, despite the risks to your safety, prove that you are a true hero. The people here speak of you with so much respect."

"I just did what needed to be done," Hugo replied modestly. "Anyone in my position would have done the same."

He didn't see himself as a hero, just someone in the right place at the right time."

Ella saw that Hugo didn't want to draw attention to himself for his heroic actions.

He explained to her that he knew the mountain better than anyone. While it was the most beautiful place on earth, it could also be incredibly dangerous, knowing how quickly the mountain could change from calm to treacherous, and he was glad to have been able to use his knowledge to help save lives.

Ella couldn't help but admire Hugo's bravery and determination as they chatted. She was grateful for his safe return and the chance to spend time with him.

Hugo's experience gained over the years on the slopes prompted him to attempt to save those unfamiliar with the rugged mountain.

As the evening wore on and three glasses of wine later, Ella found herself feeling pleasantly lightheaded. It was becoming effortless to talk to Hugo. It almost felt as if she had known him all her life, and she couldn't help but be fascinated by his charming French accent.

During their conversation, Hugo expressed that he, too, found it surprisingly easy to talk to Ella. He noted that the key was being able to have a meaningful conversation with someone who genuinely listens, something he hadn't been able to do for a long time. His words hinted at a deep longing for connection and understanding.

In a moment of vulnerability, Hugo confided in Ella his desperate need for a friend to confide in. Could Ella be the friend he was searching for?

She then rewound her thoughts and remembered when they first met.

He couldn't or wouldn't talk about his personal life because he had to find answers to so many questions.

As she observed him, she began to believe that perhaps it was the perfect moment for her to offer her support.

She comforted herself with the thought that if he ever needed someone to talk to, she would be there to offer a listening ear and support him through whatever challenges he was facing.

She wondered whether he was interested in more than friendship, but she quickly pushed that thought aside.

She didn't want to ruin their newly formed friendship by making assumptions or misreading his intentions.

Then suddenly, Hugo asked if she would care to have dinner with him the following evening.

Showing great excitement, she couldn't hold back and said, 'Yes, yes, I would like that very much'.

That's settled, telling her to be ready at 7.30 pm.

A very excited Ella told him she was looking forward to their dinner date.

Walking back to her chalet, Ella couldn't help but feel a sense of happiness and warmth inside. For the first time in a long time, she felt like she had a genuine connection with someone, which was exhilarating.

It could start a new chapter in her life; who knows!

Then panic began to rage inside her as she realised that she didn't have anything appropriate to wear for the upcoming dinner date.

She had only packed casual clothes like jeans, tee shirts, jumpers, and a shabby anorak for her backpacking journey, and the thought of impressing someone as charming as Hugo had never crossed her mind.

Regardless of this, she knew that she had to look her best.

Looking around, she saw Jo and Ryan conversing in the distance.

Tyler was standing next to Ryan, smiling and leaning over a partly damaged fence while observing a group of girls passing by.

Jo and Ryan appeared engrossed in a serious discussion, with his arm resting on her shoulder.

Eventually, the boys left, and Ella caught up with Jo.

"Are you okay?" Ella inquired.

"Yes, Ryan invited me out for a drink tonight, so I have to hurry up and get ready,"

"Wow, that makes two of us."

Jo stopped talking and took a moment to think. She placed two fingers on her lips and pressed them together, lost in thought. After a few seconds, she spoke up. "Could it be Hugo?" she asked in a casual tone. Ella's face lit up with excitement as she replied, "Yes, that's right!" She then explained that Hugo was just a friend and nothing more at the moment.

However, he had invited her to dinner the following evening, and she had accepted the invitation.

It was early evening, and Jo had arranged to meet Ryan, so Ella decided to pamper herself with a hot bath, face mask, plenty of bubbles, and a manicure—all the things you do when you know you are soon to be going on a date with a charming person.

The bath was running, so she poured a glass of wine and took it into the bathroom, lit a couple of candles when suddenly there was a knock on the door.

To her sheer amazement, Tilly was standing in the doorway, giving out a huge grin but also looking worried and concerned.

'Tilly, what are you doing here?' Ella gasped, surprised to see her friend unexpectedly.

Tilly informed Ella that she and Maddie had been watching the news regarding the storm and had grown worried about their safety.

Maddie noticed Tilly's concern, and they both agreed that Tilly would make the trip to Chamonix to ensure the girls were okay.

Tilly felt responsible for suggesting the backpacking trip in the beginning and wanted to ease her worries by ensuring the safety of her friends.

Tilly's concern touched Ella, and she immediately welcomed her inside, out of the cold. "It's so good to see you," Ella said, hugging her friend. "But you shouldn't have travelled all this way."

Tilly nodded, looking relieved to be out of the cold night air. "I know, but I just had to know in my heart that you were both okay."

Ella smiled gratefully and asked, "Have you eaten yet?"

Tilly nodded, "Yes, I stopped at the pizza restaurant in town before coming to the resort."

Eric, the Manager, kindly informed me of your location and welcomed me warmly.

Ella inquired about the duration of her stay, to which she replied that she would only be here for 24 hours as the return train to Nice departs tomorrow evening.

She then proceeded to ask about Jo.

Ella told her that she was out on a date that evening with a very handsome Canadian ski rep named Ryan.

During their conversation, Ella mentioned that she, too, had a date. His name is Hugo, and she began telling her how he had rescued many people during the avalanche. He was now considered a hero in the area.

"How long do you intend to stay here?" Tilly asked.

Hopefully, until the winter season ends, which would be towards the end of March, the plan is to head back home sometime around Easter.

What about you? Ella asked.

Tilly said that both she and Maddie have become more than good friends and are now in a permanent relationship.

We love each other's company and enjoy life together.

Tilly told her she had a job in the town, and the money earned helped with the food and other expenses, so everything was good, especially the weather; Tilly chuckled.

Ella was so happy for Tilly, knowing that everything had turned out well for her, but she said, in all seriousness, "You deserve to be happy."

"Thank you, Ella".

With compassion, she said that her focus now is on finding someone who genuinely cares for and loves her for who she is, and that's all that matters, and Maddie is that person.

Tilly shared that she stays in touch with her brother but has discovered her true sense of belonging with Maddie. She expressed that she couldn't imagine going back to her old life in England and conveyed her joy in living in the moment, cherishing each and every moment with Maddie. "I feel like I have a whole new life now, and it's absolutely amazing," she exclaimed.

She wakes up every morning feeling grateful for her life surrounded by love and happiness. She spends her days exploring new places, trying fresh foods, and creating memories with Maddie that she will cherish forever.

Tilly often reminds herself how far she has come and how much she has grown since leaving England.

She couldn't be happier with her choices and knows she has found her true home with Maddie.

Tilly asked quietly if she could spend the night at the chalet, mentioning that she would be fine sleeping on the sofa. In response, Ella assured her that she was welcome to stay and was told that there were plenty of blankets and pillows available for her to snuggle up with next to the warm wood burner.

"It's very cozy," Tilly remarked with a smile.

When Jo arrived home, it was almost 10:30 pm, and she was filled with excitement after meeting Ryan. Anxious to share her evening and the fun she had, Jo called out, "Hi, Ella, it's only me." To her surprise, Tilly responded, "It's not Ella, it's me."

Jo was taken aback and exclaimed, "Tilly, how on earth did you manage to get here?" She said jokingly that she had found a generous millionaire with his own private jet, and he graciously landed me on your doorstep.

Both girls embraced each other tightly, sat down, and talked for hours while Ella was taking a much-needed relaxing bath.

They talked about the future, with Tilly encouraging Jo to pursue her love for travel and adventure, just like they had dreamed of whilst at university together before their backpacking idea became a reality.

Jo reflected on the importance of having true friends in life as the conversation ended.

Tilly was especially interested in learning about Ryan and Tyler and wanted to know everything about them.

At that point, Ella gracefully entered the room clad in a soft and cozy towelling bathrobe.

Her complexion revealed a tender, radiant flush, evidence of the serene, enveloping warmth she had experienced during her leisurely bath.

With so much laughter and talking filling the room, the girls poured themselves another glass of wine and uncovered a box of tempting partially eaten Christmas chocolates. Tilly once again expressed her deep appreciation for the enjoyable evening spent in the company of her friends.

It was apparent that the evening had left a lasting impression on them before they retired for the night.

"Goodnight. Sleep tight," Jo murmured as she turned out the lights, bringing a gentle end to the memorable evening.

Chapter 11

The alarm rang loudly, causing Ella to stir from the warmth of her bed. Slowly, she began to wake up and move her body, noticing the intricate ice formations on the outside windows, an incredible sight in the dawn sunshine. As she lay there, Ella couldn't help but feel excited about her plans for the evening dinner with Hugo.

She got out of bed and went to the kitchenette, where she found Tilly preparing toast and coffee. "Good morning," she said, smiling warmly. "Would you like breakfast?"

"That's very kind, Tilly; thank you," Ella replied, grateful for the offer.

Just like the time in Antibes, she thought to herself.

Jo had left earlier that morning, wanting to be ready for work in case any guests left a tip before they departed. "We do depend on our tips," Ella said, her voice clear and confident. "Some are good, some not so good, but we must always remember that we have our lodgings and food provided for us, and we can also use the ski slopes with free passes if we want to."

"Can't be bad," Tilly remarked with a chuckle, causing Ella to smile.

Tilly expressed her immense relief and gratitude that everything had ultimately ended well. She also hoped that the avalanche did not cause them too much distress, although acknowledging that there must have been moments when their lives were hanging in the balance.

"We are safe now, and that's all that matters," Ella said with an emotional tone, her voice reflecting the intense experience they had gone through.

Despite the excitement of the evening ahead, Ella knew that she had other things to take care of first.

She needed to check out Chalet 17, but she wasn't in any rush since her guests would not arrive for a few days.

It was apparent that Ella was beginning to get extremely excited about her forthcoming dinner date with Hugo but unsure about what to wear.

Luckily, Tilly had a lovely white silk blouse that she had packed in a hurry without considering the climate in the Alps. She immediately offered it to Ella.

"Thank you so much, Tilly. This blouse is beautiful," exclaimed Ella. "But are you sure?" she asked. "Keep it. You never know when it might come in handy again," replied Tilly generously.

Tilly eagerly shared with Ella that the blouse was a labour of love, meticulously crafted by her hands.

Seeing Ella's eyes light up with joy, Tilly felt a surge of happiness, knowing that the blouse would soon belong to someone who cherished it just as much as she did. Overwhelmed by Tilly's thoughtfulness, Ella couldn't contain her excitement as she admired the blouse's intricate details and lovely craftsmanship.

The blouse was the perfect choice for Ella's date with Hugo—the delicate fabric and flattering cut made her feel confident and beautiful.

Tilly offered a pair of almost-new jeans and a stunning pair of heels in the hope they would fit her perfectly, and to Ella's surprise, they did!

However, Ella found it puzzling that Tilly had packed a pair of high heels for her mountain trip.

Tilly laughed and shared with Ella that she has a habit of packing for every possible occasion, no matter how unlikely it may seem. She also made a point to mention her ability to make quick decisions, emphasizing that it's an essential skill based on her previous experiences.

Ella felt an immense wave of thankfulness that seemed to spill over as she passionately conveyed how Tilly's exceptional kindness in loaning her a beautiful outfit had played a crucial part in boosting her confidence for the much-awaited dinner date.

"That's what friends are for," she said jokingly.

As Tilly stood by the window, her gaze fixed on the snow-capped mountains before her.

She couldn't stop thinking about leaving later that day. With a hint of sadness in her eyes, she turned to Ella and asked, "Will we have a chance to say goodbye before I leave?" Tilly asked sadly.

Ella, with a comforting grin, offered her reassurance. "Both Jo and I will ensure that we finish cleaning on time so that we can bid you a proper goodbye." After all, Tilly had travelled a long way to make sure they were safe after the snowstorm.

Ella left Tilly alone in the apartment and made her way to Chalet 17 to ensure everything was in good order for the guests arriving shortly.

She kept looking at her watch, not wanting to miss Tilly's departure.

Ella sent a message to Jo, unaware that she had just finished her shift and was relaxing with Ryan over a hot drink at the café.

"Hey, don't forget that we need to make sure we say goodbye to Tilly before she leaves for Nice later this afternoon. It's important to express our gratitude for her thoughtfulness and concern, especially after she made the effort to travel so far to meet up with us."

"Agreed," Jo said. "Meet you at the chalet at lunchtime."

At approximately one o'clock in the afternoon, after Ella had finished work, she made her way back to the apartment.

As she entered, Ella swiftly discarded her sweaty top and somewhat grimy apron, trading them for fresh, presentable clothing.

Tilly and Jo were engaged in a lively conversation as they sat on the steps outside the chalet, laughing together.

While they were chatting, Ella asked Tilly if she had taken a relaxing walk around the resort.

Tilly responded affirmatively and went on to eloquently depict the awe-inspiring magnificence of the imposing yet spectacular Mont Blanc.

As Tilly sat there, she couldn't help but be mesmerised by the sight of the cable cars gracefully ascending and descending the towering mountain. The view was nothing short of magnificent, and she found herself completely at ease, her stress melting away in the face of such natural splendour.

Ella went on to explain the panoramic vistas that awaited at the mountain's summit, spanning from Switzerland to Italy, painting a picture of unparalleled beauty and grandeur.

Ella had planned to make the trip up Mont Blanc to see the magnificent views from the top before leaving for home after the winter season ended and her work at the resort had finished.

Tilly was impressed by the mountain's geography, saying that perhaps one day, she would journey up the mountain to see its beauty for herself.

At 4 o'clock, the taxi arrived to take Tilly to the station.

Ella and Jo were sorry to see Tilly leave, but they told her that it might be possible for them to meet up with her and Maddie in Antibes before heading back home to the UK. However, this would only happen if they had enough money left over at the end of their stay here.

Tilly was overjoyed to hear this and hoped that she and Maddie would have the chance to meet the girls again.

Walking down to the waiting taxi with Tilly, they both thanked her for thinking of them, and they gently kissed her on the cheek before saying goodbye.

Ella shouted, 'Don't forget to text us when you return to Antibes.'

Tilly's arm was hanging out of the window, waving goodbye as the taxi sped along the wet road to the train station.

"Love you both!" Tilly yelled.

As they strolled back to their chalet, a sense of melancholy crept over them as they pondered Tilly's departure. They couldn't help but feel uncertain about the possibility of meeting her again. However, they held onto a glimmer of hope that, if their finances permitted, they might have the chance to visit her once their work in Chamonix came to an end.

Ella checked her watch and suddenly exclaimed, "Jo, look at the time! I need to start getting ready."

Jo asked how much time she needed, and they both laughed.

Ella remarked that this was her first date in a long time, and she wanted to look her best.

Ella then asked Jo if she thought she would see Ryan again since their relationship seemed to have progressed beyond friendship.

Jo replied that she liked Ryan and found him pleasant, friendly, and funny.

Being with him made her happy, but she was uncertain about the future of their friendship at that moment and decided to enjoy each day they spent together.

A thrilled Ella eagerly requested Jo's help creating a stylish hairstyle to complement her casual outfit. The silk blouse paired beautifully with her jeans and black strappy heels. Ella couldn't help but feel immense thanks to Tilly, who had helped her in a time of need.

Feeling elegant and confident, she was ready to head out for a fun evening in town with Hugo. It's amazing how a pair of heels can transform a look!

Right on time, at 7.30 pm, Hugo knocked on the door, and she was shocked to see that the sling supporting his arm had been removed, and the bruises and scratches on his face had disappeared. They both smiled at each other, feeling excited for the night ahead.

He told her she looked great but said the shoes she was wearing didn't seem very practical in the snow.

Ella looked down at the black strappy heels and had to admit what he said was right.

She felt her face go redder and redder with total embarrassment.

Putting on snow boots was going to ruin the look of her outfit, but there was no way she wanted to fall, slip, and break a leg, so she ran inside, fetched her snow boots, put the fancy shoes in a bag, and took them with her.

Very sensible, Hugo said with a chuckle in his voice.

Well, that was a good start, Ella thought to herself.

They chatted and laughed as they walked to the restaurant, enjoying the crisp evening air.

As they arrived at 'On the Grapevine Ristorante,' an Italian restaurant in the heart of town, Hugo had taken great care to secure a cozy table for two with a captivating view of the majestic mountains. Wishing to create a truly memorable experience, he gestured for the waiter and made a special request-a bottle of the finest champagne. This gesture was his way of expressing heartfelt gratitude for the overwhelming kindness and support he had received from Ella during the recent avalanche.

Her heart skipped a beat when he began describing her as kind and affectionate. As she reflected on his words, she couldn't help feeling a flutter of excitement at the possibility of a romantic connection. However, she quickly dismissed those thoughts, not wanting to rush to conclusions.

The meal was exceptional, and of course, the champagne was too.

Hugo's choice of wine perfectly complemented their meal, and Ella couldn't help but feel somewhat light-headed with so much wine and champagne.

Their conversation was so smooth and engaging that time seemed to fly by.

As the evening progressed, they became so engrossed in each other's stories that they lost track of time. The night was still young, and they both wished it would never end.

As they left the restaurant, Hugo said, 'Don't forget your snow boots. ' At that point, she couldn't have cared less whether she put them on or not, but sensible Hugo said it was very icy on the pathways.

He was right; it was very slippery, and as they walked side by side, he put his arm around her, not because of the slippery paths or perhaps the fact that she had too much to drink but more of a loving and tender way.

Walking along the beautiful moonlit streets, talking and laughing, they eventually reached Ella's chalet.

As they bid each other goodnight, they both knew without a doubt that they wanted to see each other again.

Hugo said he had the most beautiful evening and hoped they could do it again.

It was lovely, Ella replied. Thank you very much for your company.

Suddenly, he bent over and kissed her, followed by another more passionate kiss. She, too, responded in the same way, both standing in complete silence, looking towards each other with such tenderness.

It was a spontaneous reaction, but she couldn't help feeling such deep affection between them as they said goodnight.

Ella began to sense nervousness in Hugo's mood as they parted ways. He then suggested that they could meet at the café the next day.

She promptly told him it was her day off, so anytime would suit her.

'Perfect', he said with a smile.

He told her he wouldn't bore her with the details because they had such a lovely evening together, but he needed to speak with her about something troubling him.

She couldn't shake off the uncertainty as she went to bed that night, wondering what Hugo wanted to talk to her about.

Chapter 12

The following day, Tilly contacted Ella to inform her that she had arrived safely back in Antibes. She couldn't contain her joy at having met them and expressed her immense relief that they had both made it through the recent snowstorm unharmed.

Maddie, who was also present, conveyed her best wishes to them for their safe onward travels.

Tilly was keen to know how Ella's date with Hugo had gone.

Ella replied that they had a lovely evening together and planned to see each other again.

With her keen intuition, Tilly picked up on some subtle clues that hinted at a deeper connection between Ella and Hugo.

Eager to learn more, Tilly gently encouraged Ella to say more but noticed that Ella's tone had shifted to a quieter, more subdued one.

Ella seemed cautious about discussing her connection with Hugo, expressing the desire not to rush things despite their strong friendship blossoming.

Sensing Ella's hesitation, Tilly decided not to push for more details.

As they chatted, the conversation gradually shifted towards Jo and Ryan. Tilly, intrigued by their connection, inquired whether they had started dating.

Ella, feeling uncomfortable discussing Jo's romantic life, chose not to share any details.

Despite her curiosity, Tilly opted not to delve deeper into the topic and resolved to let things unfold naturally for Jo and Ryan.

As the phone call ended, Ella felt optimistic. She noticed a remarkable improvement in Tilly's state of mind. Tilly sounded much more cheerful and confident, which filled Ella with joy.

It was evident that she had undergone a significant transformation in her attitude and overall outlook on life.

The Tilly that Ella saw before now appeared to be a completely different person, more self-assured, confident, and at peace with herself.

It was as if a weight had been lifted off her shoulders, and she was now free to embrace the world with open arms.

This transformation was a testament to Tilly's resilience and determination, and it left Ella feeling inspired and grateful to have been a part of her journey.

Upon returning to work, Ella was pleasantly surprised by how many tips she had received.

She had saved 400 euros, and Jo received generous tips, collectively saving over 720 euros. Together, their budget was looking very good—so good, in fact, that a journey to Antibes before heading back home was very likely, which filled the girls with excitement.

As Ella glanced at her watch, she realised it was almost time to meet Hugo. However, she felt nervous about their meeting and wondered why it was so urgent.

Arriving at the café, Hugo called out to her and politely pulled out a chair, apologising for his behaviour last night, explaining that he didn't mean to embarrass her with a kiss.

Ella reassured him there was no need to apologise as it had been a beautiful end to a wonderful evening.

As they spoke, Hugo sensed a growing affection from her and reached across the table and touched her hand.

He then revealed that something had been weighing heavily on his mind, and he wanted to share it with her.

"That's perfectly fine," she reassured him. "Go ahead. There's no better moment than the present."

With that, Hugo began to tell his story.

Feeling very apprehensive, Ella remained composed and listened carefully to what he had to say.

In a calm yet apprehensive tone, he then started confiding in Ella about a girl he had met three years ago while skiing in the Alps.

Her name was Julienne.

She was exceptionally skilled at snowboarding and loved spending her days on the slopes, loving everything about the mountains and outdoors, like me.

As we became closer, our relationship developed beyond friendship.

During the first summer of our relationship, we decided to take time away with friends and visit Annecy's beautiful lakes.

We stayed at a picturesque camping site offering stunning views of the location during our stay.

Unfortunately, things did not go as planned, and the rest of the group ended up indulging in excessive drinking. At this point, I noticed a significant change in Julienne's behaviour, and it began to concern me.

The following day, I woke up with a severe hangover and decided to skip the sightseeing they had arranged.

Feeling quite unwell, Julienne informed me that she would be exploring Annecy with the others from the group and that I should try to get some sleep to try and shake off the awful headache. However, after several hours, Julienne and her friends were still missing, and I became increasingly worried.

Looking out from my tent, I couldn't help but capture the beauty around me. The rhythmic strides of evening joggers, a group of daring hang gliders who had descended from the towering mountain, their colourful wings painting the sky in a spectacular display as they spiralled down, adding exciting and adventurous energy to the peaceful setting of Annecy. It was a sight beyond measure.

As the sun began to dip below the horizon, casting a warm orange glow over the campsite, I found myself standing alone, surveying the surroundings in search of any trace of Julienne. The evening was edging towards eight, and a sense of unease was settling in. I couldn't shake the lingering worry about her well-being. As twilight descended, the once serene lake beside the campsite seemed to come alive, its waters flowing with an almost urgent energy, amplifying the feeling of apprehension and saturating the air with a tangible sense of tension.

After feeling a bit better, I decided to walk along the edge of the lake when I noticed a pair of trainers left on the bank. Against the dark night, they looked like Julienne's bright pink trainers.

Did everyone decide to go for a late-night swim in the lake, or could something more sinister have happened?

As I continued my walk, a growing sense of unease began to envelop me, leaving me on edge and increasingly anxious.

Suddenly, someone shouted, asking me if I had seen Julienne.

It was a lad from the group, his face a mix of confusion and concern, looking very troubled and bewildered.

I hurried over, and he told me that Julienne had been walking with them, talking and laughing, and had expressed a desire to swim in the lake.

The young lad told me that most of the group drank a lot of alcohol during the day and advised Julienne she should walk back to the campsite and get some rest, but she insisted on staying, saying she wanted to feel the gentle caress of the lake's ripples against her body.

At that point, there was no way she was listening to what anyone was saying.

Hugo said that he was feeling a mixture of terror and uncertainty and stood frozen, all alone, desperately trying to piece together the alarming events.

With a heavy heart and a mind filled with conflicting emotions, I began the journey back to our campsite.

However, my attention was soon drawn to a group of young men and girls, some of whom were part of our group, huddled together in a secluded spot at the far end of the campsite.

Upon closer inspection, I realised that they were deeply engaged in a drug-related activity, and the gravity of the situation hit me like a ton of bricks.

As I approached the group, they greeted me with worried expressions and inquired about Julienne.

I told them that I had not seen her and that if she didn't return soon, I would have to call the Police.

As we conversed, I couldn't help but notice the group who were using drugs hastily packing up their belongings and scurrying away from the campsite. Their nervous energy and furtive glances spoke volumes about their anxiety regarding potential police involvement. The urgency of the situation was intense, but amidst it all, my focus remained unwaveringly fixed on locating Julienne.

As I sat there, panic slowly creeping in, my mind began to race. The anxiety was overwhelming, but I had to stay focused.

I began to search for any clues that could help me understand what had happened.

Memories of the early days of our relationship came flooding back as I tried to recall if there were any signs that something was wrong.

I couldn't help but wonder what was happening inside Julienne's mind and deeply regretted that I couldn't understand her better.

There always seemed to be an impenetrable barrier preventing me from truly understanding her.

Ella listened intently, seeing the concern on his face, but she showed a glimmer of hope that maybe he wasn't alone in this after all.

As Ella watched Hugo, it was evident that he had been struggling with a significant burden for some time.

However, when he finally opened up to someone who would listen, his manner showed a visible sense of relief.

Ella was the one person who had gained his trust.

He seemed to be entirely comfortable confiding in her, and it was apparent that he was grateful for her support.

Nevertheless, he was ready to face whatever came his way, so long as it meant discovering the truth about Julienne's disappearance.

He needed answers, so in the midst of a harrowing situation, he made a brave decision and fearlessly sought assistance from the Police.

Feeling unsure about what to say, he expressed his urgent need for their assistance locating Julienne.

As Hugo opened up to Ella and recounted his experiences, it was clear to him that he had chosen the perfect confidante in Ella.

What made her the right person to confide in were her attentive listening skills and remarkable empathy.

Hugo stood up and ordered two more cups of coffee, but Ella wondered if something stronger would have been more appropriate for the situation.

Perhaps a Gin and Tonic or two!

Placing the two cups of coffee on the wooden but somewhat wonky table, he continued his story.

The Police had told him to stay at the campsite while they continued their investigation, and the only clue so far was a pair of trainers left by the edge of the lake.

Very early the following day, there was a shout outside the tent.

'Can you hear me?' a voice shouted.

Inspector Claude Vidal introduced himself and informed me that a discovery had been made in the lake, prompting an extensive investigation by the diving team.

I promptly dressed and prepared to offer my assistance in any capacity needed. Inspector Vidal elaborated on the lake's depth, revealing that it reaches nearly 41 meters in some places. He also expressed the slim likelihood of finding Julienne alive unless she happened to be a strong swimmer.

Despite the grim possibility, I was determined to do everything to help with the search.

Later that day, a diver emerged from the lake with both thumbs up, stating that he had found a body.

As the news hit me my entire body went numb with shock. I felt my legs give way beneath me, and I sank to the ground, desperately hoping that what I feared hadn't come true.

After a few moments, a body emerged from the lake.

It was indeed Julienne.

She appeared pale as she was lifted from the murky water, and her hair was entangled with weeds and algae from the lake.

Her clothes were torn, possibly from striking the stony water while the lake flowed swiftly.

The sight that met my eyes was heart-breaking and has left an indelible impression forever. I prayed that I would never have to witness something so tragic again.

I couldn't provide the police with any information regarding Julienne's next of kin because I knew nothing about her close family.

I did, however, give the police my forwarding address in Lyon.

The police assured me they would let me know of any developments regarding the tragic death of Julienne, promising to use their resources to locate Julienne's relatives and perform a detailed post-mortem examination to ascertain the cause of her death.

At that point, I assumed that the matter had ended.

It must have been a couple of weeks later when I had a phone call from the Police in Annecy giving me the results of the post-mortem.

The findings are that from the evidence given, Julienne had died from drowning, but also, there was a large quantity of alcohol and drugs in her body.

It would appear she went for a swim in the lake, leaving her trainers on the bank alongside the lake and entering the lake fully clothed.

With the amount of alcohol and drugs in her body, she was not in total control of her actions.

It was therefore concluded that her death was accidental due to drowning, with no devious intentions, and that no other person was involved.

It took some time to get in touch with her parents, but once they were notified, they swiftly made their way to Annecy to formally identify their daughter's body without delay.

My state of mind was shattered for quite some time, but I knew that I had to try and get back to some normality in my life. But realised that wouldn't be easy.

Ella's curiosity got the best of her as she inquired about the other members of the group who were using drugs at the campsite. She was eager to know what had happened to them.

Hugo confessed to her that he had no solid information about their whereabouts. Still, he couldn't shake off his suspicion that Julienne might have been involved in drug-related issues. He found it perplexing and somewhat upsetting that despite knowing his adamant disapproval of drug use, Julienne had extended an invitation for him to join the party in Annecy.

The whole situation felt like something out of a movie, and he found it challenging to comprehend everything that had happened.

Looking back, someone may well have spiked my drink the night before, making me feel the way I did with a tremendous hangover, giving the group an excuse to carry on with their drug-taking and heavy consumption of alcohol—possibly wanting me out of the way.

I'm unsure, but it puzzles me somewhat, and perhaps I will never know.

Was there a hidden meaning behind it, or was it simply a random occurrence without explanation?

Regardless, I have decided to focus on my future and put the past behind me.

My mental health began to worry me, and I knew I needed to take a step back and reorganise my life.

Ella was curious and asked, "How did you manage to do that?"

At times like this, some people drink and become dependent on alcohol.

I have always loved a drink, just like many people, but more importantly, my aim was to focus on work, taking my mind off everything that had happened over the past months.

Ella quietly asked, "Are you enjoying your work now, Hugo?"

You appear to have put your life back on track because you seem in such a much better place.

Yes, to both questions, he said with such certainty.

However, Hugo mentioned that he recently had the opportunity of working as a Ski Coach near Lyon, getting involved with a group of young people wanting to learn snowboarding, skiing, downhill, slalom, or any other winter sport that appeals to them.

Seeing so many young children entering, enjoying, and competing in the sport gave me great satisfaction.

My love for skiing never waned.

I always wanted to remain involved with the sport, as it had become a part of my identity over the years.

Hugo then squeezed Ella's hand tightly, and they bent over and kissed each other.

Hugo's face looked relieved, and Ella could tell his story was something he had wanted to share with someone for a very long time.

He believed Ella was the one person that made him feel at ease.

He was right; she was a good listener.

Chapter 13

Later that evening, and after a long but interesting conversation with Hugo Ella arrived at her chalet, exhausted and ready for much-needed sleep.

Upon entering, she heard faint giggling voices coming from one of the rooms. Suddenly, Ryan emerged from Jo's room, half-naked and looking uncomfortable with a reddened face.

Jo quickly followed, also only partially dressed and appearing very nervous.

"Let me explain, Ella," Jo said, her voice trembling with worry.

Ella, sensing the tension, calmly reassured Jo that it was not her concern and that she just needed a shower before heading straight to bed as she was completely exhausted.

The following day, Jo seemed hesitant to approach Ella after the events of the previous night. However, Ella made it clear that she respected Jo's need for personal space and that she was always available to chat whenever Jo wanted.

Despite the initial awkwardness, Ella was relieved that they could still connect despite the uncomfortable situation from the night before.

Jo and Ryan continued to spend more time together, relishing in each other's company whenever they could steal a moment away from their working days.

Their connection grew stronger with each passing day.

She had noticed how Jo was constantly seeking Ryan's attention and how Ryan seemed to reciprocate the attention with warmth and loving kindness.

It was evident that Jo was smitten with Ryan, but Ella couldn't shake off the feeling that it was all too sudden.

In spite of this, Ella acknowledged that it wasn't her place to intervene in Jo's personal life, especially since she was currently grappling with her own similar experiences with Hugo.

As Jo spent more time with Ryan, she realised she enjoyed his company more than she ever thought. She looked forward to their time together and may have developed strong feelings for him. It was a new and surprising experience for her. She felt she had missed out on much-needed love and companionship during her young life, so she couldn't deny the joy his friendship brought her.

As Ella walked down the hallway towards the office to collect clean bedding and towels for the chalet, she was lost in thought about the day ahead.

Suddenly, she came face to face with Hugo, who was in deep conversation with Eric.

The unexpected encounter caught Ella off guard, but nevertheless, she exchanged pleasantries with them before continuing on her way.

Then Hugo shouted out, asking if they could meet up that evening for a chat.

Ella readily agreed, and they settled on a time and place.

The thought of it caused her heart to race and her palms to sweat once again.

She knew that there was an unexplainable connection between her and Hugo that she couldn't quite grasp.

Ella felt a mix of emotions as she got ready to meet Hugo that evening.

Even though she was a bit nervous, there was a strong feeling of excitement that was difficult to conceal and hard to understand.

She had spent countless hours remembering their last conversation, reliving every moment with vivid detail, hoping she had helped Hugo by just sitting and listening to his extremely sad story.

She knew that sometimes, all a person needed was someone to talk to, listen to, and care for.

Despite feeling uncertain, Ella was hopeful that she could be that person once again.

Her intense attraction towards this charming young man was undeniable as she eagerly awaited to meet him again and hoped tonight would be the start of something special.

As Ella entered the room, her eyes quickly fixed on Jo and Ryan sitting across the other side of the room.

They sat close together, hands entwined and engulfed in their romantic bubble, exchanging loving glances.

Ella tried to get their attention by calling out and waving, but Jo seemed absorbed in Ryan, oblivious to her attempts.

It was unusual behaviour for Jo, leaving Ella to ponder whether her emotions had overshadowed her usual responsiveness.

As Hugo entered the room, Ella immediately noticed a hint of melancholy in his voice and expression.

He told her that he had to leave Chamonix and travel back to the Ski School in Lyon because he had an urgent and crucial meeting to attend but didn't want to leave without saying goodbye to someone who had become very special to him, realizing that their relationship had progressed beyond mere friendship and wanted to maintain in contact with her.

He asked, "Is that possible, Ella?"

Unable to contain her feelings, Ella replied, "Of course."

Despite the geographical distance between them, Ella highlighted the importance of maintaining a solid connection. So, it was decided to keep in touch and take meaningful steps to enrich the depth and strength of their cherished friendship.

As they talked, he revealed that he deeply desired to visit Buckland Ridge someday. He spoke enthusiastically, telling her he longed to explore its scenic beauty, saying that visiting Buckland Ridge would be his dream come true and hoped to make it happen very soon.

The idea of a long-distance relationship both excited and terrified her.

She had so many questions running through her mind.

How would they manage to see each other often enough?

Would their relationship be strong enough to withstand the distance?

These were all valid concerns, but Ella couldn't deny the strong feelings she had for Hugo.

It was something she had never experienced before, leaving her both exhilarated and scared.

But despite the uncertainty, Ella couldn't help but feel hopeful.

Maybe, just maybe, they could make it work.

As the day progressed, Jo hurriedly approached Ella, her face filled with remorse, apologising for ignoring her at the restaurant. With a sincere tone, she expressed her profound regret for her behaviour and reassured Ella that it would never happen again.

In response, Ella calmly acknowledged Jo's apology, observing that both of them seemed to be caught up in their own world at the time.

"You're right, Ella," Jo conceded, "we were completely oblivious to our surroundings."

The day had arrived, and bidding farewell to Hugo was tough.

Hugo and Ella exchanged contact details and said their goodbyes, hoping to catch up again soon.

Before parting ways, Hugo expressed his deep appreciation towards Ella for the understanding and support she had extended to him while coming to terms with the tragic incident in Annecy.

Ella, in turn, reassured him that she would always be there for him through thick and thin and that he could count on her for a listening ear or a shoulder to lean on whenever he needed it.

As Hugo returned to the office to say goodbye to Eric and Maria, he expressed his heartfelt gratitude for their warm hospitality and unwavering support during his time of need, both during his ordeal in the snowstorm and his journey toward recovery.

Ella's heart felt heavy with sadness as she watched Hugo disappear into the distance, leaving her alone with her thoughts.

She couldn't hide the feeling that she had let someone very special through her fingers and that she may never see him again.

Walking back to her chalet, she was lost in thought. The memories of him came rushing back to her like a tidal wave.

As she reflected on their past, she couldn't shake the thought of how different their lives might have been if he hadn't lived so far away. Memories flooded her mind - their deeply heartfelt conversations, the special moments they shared, the warmth of his touch, and the depth of their emotions.

The knowledge that they were now separated by miles tugged at her heart, leaving a lingering longing.

Despite the ache, she held onto the memories of the person who had left an indelible mark on her heart, yearning to meet him again in the future.

Days were now turning into weeks, and Ella curiously wanted to know about Jo's relationship with Ryan, as he, too, was travelling back to Canada within a couple of days.

As the morning sun shone over the snow-dusted peaks in a warm, golden glow, the girls took a stroll through Chamonix's picturesque town centre before starting their cleaning shifts at midday.

They wandered along the ancient cobblestone streets, taking in the beauty of the idyllic alpine scenery surrounding them, boasting quaint chalets adorned with vibrant flower boxes.

The girls took in every detail, from the intricate wood carvings on the buildings to the glistening snowy mountains towering overhead, creating a memory that would stay with them forever.

Ella wanted to find the perfect but friendly moment to ask about Jo's relationship with Ryan, so they stopped to savour the aroma of freshly brewed coffee wafting from their favourite café, where they sat by the window, sipping hot drinks and admiring the bustling yet tranquil atmosphere outside.

Over a hot cup of coffee, Ella began to feel a little nervous about bringing up the subject of Jo's relationship and didn't want to seem too inquisitive.

Ella began the conversation with a warm expression of happiness for Jo and genuine delight that she had found happiness with Ryan.

Ella's intentions were purely to offer Jo some friendly and caring advice.

Jo expressed her deep gratitude to Ella for her overwhelming kindness, emphasizing that Ryan was the one individual who had brought her immeasurable love and joy.

She reflected on the many similarities she shared with Ryan and acknowledged that her feelings for him deepened every time they met each other. Jo even hinted at the prospect of a future trip to Canada to meet Ryan's parents, leaving the question of what possibilities the future may hold for their relationship.

Once Ella became reassured with Jo's intention, she then realised that she and Jo were both wrestling with the challenges of long-distance relationships and understood that physical separation could impact their emotions, although the distance was even more significant in Jo's case, as it spanned thousands of miles.

After exchanging thoughtful words, Ella glanced at her watch and informed Jo that it was time to head back to work and begin tidying up the chalets!

Chapter 14

Now that Ryan and his friend Tyler had left for Canada, Jo spent the rest of the day reflecting on the good times spent with Ryan.

They had shared so many laughs and made unforgettable memories together.

Jo couldn't help but feel a twinge of sadness knowing that they had to say goodbye, but was comforted by the thought that they hoped to see each other again one day.

Looking out of the window, Jo watched the sky turn into a beautiful array of colours. The sun's warm glow on her face made her feel content and happy.

She closed her eyes and took a deep breath, feeling grateful for the memories she had made and excited about the possible future ahead.

As the days gradually slipped away and their inevitable departure from Chamonix was nearing an end, Ella and Jo were overcome with a bittersweet feeling.

The memories they had created in the picturesque town of this French Alpine town had left an indelible mark on them, and the thought of leaving it all behind was filling both girls with sadness but also excitement for the homeward journey ahead.

Nevertheless, Ella was determined to make the most of the remaining time in this idyllic destination.

She was adamant that they must take a trip up the mountain from Chamonix to Mont Blanc to experience the wonderful views first-hand before they leave.

The following day was their well-deserved day off, and they decided to embark on a cable car ride up the mountain, much to Jo's nervousness as she wasn't really very good with heights.

As Ella and Jo stood at the foot of the imposing mountain, a sudden wave of realisation engulfed Ella. She couldn't help but feel a sense of astonishment as she realised Jo had not mentioned her intense fear of heights when convincing Ella to join her on a skiing expedition up the daunting slopes.

Despite her reservations, Jo took a deep breath and prepared to step into the cable car, determined to conquer her fears.

As they ascended higher and higher, the panorama before them was nothing short of spectacular.

Further into the mountains, the scenery became even more breath-taking.

The snowy mountains that surrounded them seemed to stretch out for miles, and the towering peak of Mont Blanc loomed in the distance.

It was hard to believe that this mountain had been at its most destructive just a short time ago, wreaking havoc without regard for the consequences.

Standing here now, surrounded by such natural beauty, it was easy to forget about the past and appreciate the present moment.

Jo was gripping the armrests of the cable car with nerves, feeling unsteady with each sudden jerk.

She peered down through the glass bottom floor, which made her uneasy and caused her to feel nauseous due to the height and unexpected speed of the ride.

On the other hand, Ella was delighted to capture numerous photos of the picturesque view and didn't seem bothered by looking down at the ground as it moved beneath them.

As they neared the top of the mountain, the cable car gradually slowed down.

Jo's unease dissipated, and they both held hands and admired the beautiful views.

Upon arriving at the top station on the mountain, they couldn't help but feel a sense of awe and wonder.

Jo and Ella ascended the summit, the cool, gentle breeze enlivening their spirits. With each step, their anticipation grew, and a panoramic view unfolded before them, stretching endlessly in all directions, a vast expanse of beauty.

In the distance, they caught glimpses of Italy's picturesque coastline, its charm adding to the allure of the scene. Overwhelmed by the beauty that surrounded them, Jo turned to Ella, her face aglow with an uncontainable smile.

Their hearts raced with pure excitement, and the thrill of the adrenaline rush they had just encountered left them completely speechless.

Every detail was clear and vivid, from the glistening snow covering the mountainside to the unspoiled vistas beyond. It was one of the most unforgettable highlights of their journey, and they knew without a doubt that this was an experience that would stay with them for the rest of their lives.

As they stood side by side, taking in the beauty and peaceful scenery that enveloped them, it was time for them to make their way back, catching the downward cable car.

Walking back towards their apartment, Ella glanced down at her phone and saw a missed call.

Eagerly, she rang the number, amazed and delighted to know it was Hugo.

"Is everything okay?" she asked, her heart beating fast with excitement and anticipation.

Hugo happily shared that life had been treating him well since returning to Lyon. He described how he had been spending most of his time in private tutoring sessions for young students and attending numerous health and safety meetings, keeping him busy throughout the day.

Even though time seemed to pass quickly since his return, he felt a strong need to reach out and call Ella because he longed to hear her voice.

Hearing Hugo's words made her feel warm and happy inside, saying she had been missing him too, and knowing that he feels the same way is comforting.

As they chatted, she couldn't help but feel grateful for the intense connection between them despite the distance.

Ella shared that she and Jo planned to leave the resort soon.

According to the bookings, the number of guests would have decreased, and the resort would be closing until the next winter season.

Ella expressed excitement about seeing her mother again and sharing fantastic stories from her backpacking journey.

It was an unforgettable experience that taught her so much about herself and the world around her.

Hugo listened with interest to this independent, but most of all, very caring person.

As Ella shared her thoughts, he could feel her deep yearning for the comforting presence of her mother and her cherished dog, Sammy.

She expressed her desire to reconnect with her family and relish the everyday joys that had eluded her during her travels.

Despite encountering countless hurdles, Ella conveyed that she had emerged with newfound strength and resilience, prepared to confront whatever life might present.

As their conversation drew to a close, he promised to make plans for a visit once she returned to England.

Ella's heart skipped a beat, and she felt a rush of emotions that left her hands trembling. The mere thought of him coming to the Dales filled her with an irresistible sense of joy, one that she struggled to contain.

It all felt too good to be true, yet the prospect of seeing him again was enough to make her heart race with excitement.

Jo appeared excited for Ella, who looked so happy, and it was evident that love was just around the corner, or so she thought!

Jo was thrilled to hear from Ryan, too, eagerly anticipating the day they could finally be together.

Ryan mentioned inviting her to meet his parents in Banff, and she couldn't help but feel overjoyed at the possibility of being together once again.

Was it time for her to share this new person in her life with her parents, too?

Ella decided to ring her Mum and tell her about their impending departure and when she was expected to arrive back home.

Ella's mother was thrilled to hear her daughter's voice.

Upon her return, she eagerly informed Ella that she would have a hot meal and a comfortable bed waiting for her.

Ella expressed her gratitude and asked her mother to hug Sammy and tell him they would be walking together in the park soon.

Her mother responded affectionately and reassured Ella that Sammy would readily await her arrival.

The thought of reuniting with her loved ones filled Ella with happiness and contentment and even brought tears to her eyes.

Her mother also shared some exciting news that Ella's sister Lauren would be flying home from Australia for a four-week holiday shortly after Ella's return.

Ella was ecstatic at the news because she hadn't seen her sister in over two years and had much to catch up on.

Chapter 15

The day had arrived to bid farewell to Chamonix.

They had packed their bags and saved memories on their phones.

As they turned the key in the front door for the last time, they stood together on the chalet steps, feeling nostalgic.

They couldn't help but reminisce about the adventures they had experienced during their stay in this stunning place.

Even the snowstorm was something they would never forget because through this awful experience came hope, friendship and possibly love.

Every moment was memorable, from skiing down the snowy slopes to enjoying the magnificent views of the surrounding mountains.

They both agreed that this had been the most beautiful experience they had ever witnessed and who knows, perhaps one day they would return to the place they had called home for the past six months.

Eric and Maria conveyed their sincere best wishes and expressed much appreciation for having such outstanding and reliable girls working in their team. They also made sure to let them know that there would always be work available for them should they ever decide to return to the resort.

Eric then asked Ella about her relationship with Hugo, and although she was a bit hesitant to reveal too much, she did mention that he was planning to pay her a visit to England in the not-too-distant future.

Eric felt overjoyed and hopeful that their friendship would continue to grow.

When the taxi arrived at the office, Ella and Jo waved goodbye and expressed their desire to return someday.

Eric and Maria warmly replied, assuring them that they would always be welcomed.

As the taxi drove away on the slushy road, Ella and Jo reflected on the unforgettable trip, but they knew their journey wasn't over, as they still had 500 miles, possibly even more, to complete.

Despite this, they were grateful they had saved enough money to finish the journey without too much hardship and could afford a few luxuries on the way.

With time on their side, and as they arrived at the train station, Jo mentioned that instead of returning home to England immediately, perhaps they could catch a train to Nice, catching up with Tilly and Maddie in Antibes.

Ella was a bit hesitant because all she could think about was reuniting with her Mum and Sammy, but on second thoughts, it would only be another week at the most, or would it?

Jo remarked, "Let's surprise them and show up on their doorstep like Tilly did when she visited us in Chamonix.

We could even spend a few days at Mum and Dad's villa."

The thrill of the unexpected visit got the better of them, and they impulsively purchased two single tickets to Nice on the sleeper train.

They were now leaving the cold, frosty days of Chamonix and entering a much warmer climate, which they both welcomed.

After enduring a restless night on a crowded train surrounded by noisy passengers, the arduous journey lasted close to 10 hours.

Feeling exhausted, they eventually arrived at Nice-Ville station, and with a short bus ride to Antibes, they instantly recognised their surroundings – verdant palm trees, pristine sandy beaches, and azure skies peeking through fluffy white clouds.

Though the climate was slightly different from Chamonix, the scenery was equally captivating in its own unique way.

Jo contacted her parents to inform them that she and Ella would be lodging at the villa for a few nights, and her mother warmly invited them to stay for as long as they pleased.

Ella and Jo went to the local supermarket to buy supplies for a few days and planned to surprise Tilly and Maddie later that evening.

When they arrived at Maddie's apartment, they were shocked to see her looking upset and very distraught.

Maddie recounted the events of the previous day, describing how Tilly had been interrupted by an urgent phone call from England. Tilly had promised to keep in touch but expressed the need for some time alone to process the news she had received. Maddie, understanding Tilly's need for solitude, could only focus on Tilly's emotional state and the fact that she seemed reluctant to accept support from Maddie during this difficult time.

Ella, looking visibly agitated, inquired about Tilly's well-being. In response, Maddie conveyed that Tilly appeared deeply distressed and significantly troubled.

Despite feeling uncertain about Tilly's location and emotional state, Ella and Jo held onto hope and remained optimistic about finding her soon.

Meanwhile, they were grateful to have arrived in Antibes just in time to support Maddie through her struggles.

As they comforted her, they couldn't help but wonder where Tilly could be and what she could be going through.

Despite facing challenges such as Tilly's tendency to isolate herself and the difficulty in locating her, they remained steadfast in their determination to maintain a positive outlook, hoping to find Tilly finally.

Tilly, often lost in her own world, found a profound connection with Maddie. This strong bond caused a noticeable shift in Tilly's behaviour, a testament to the power of friendship.

Maddie's presence brought Tilly love, hope, and empathy, and both Ella and Jo had faith in Maddie's ability to continue providing this support. However, the urgency of the situation became apparent, as it was clear that additional assistance was needed to locate Tilly promptly.

As they discussed their action plan, they realised they had to consider every possible scenario to ensure Tilly's safety.

They considered that Tilly might be lost somewhere, unable to find her way back home, or worse, she might have been abducted. Who knows!

Both Ella and Jo had been through something similar like this with her before in Brussels at the beginning of their journey, and everything was beginning to look like it was happening all over again.

They decided to reach out to the local authorities and report her missing.

The girls knew that time was of the essence and every minute was vital in finding Tilly and providing her with the help she needed.

The past couple of days were tough as there had still been no news regarding Tilly's whereabouts, and the authorities have yet to contact them with any possible sightings, if any.

Ella and Jo thought it best to inform their parents of the situation, saying that it could delay their arrival back home.

They had been searching non-stop, talking to locals, and had also contacted not only the local Police but also the National Police, providing them with any information that could help in the search.

It had been exhausting, but finding Tilly was their top priority.

When talking with Maddie, Ella and Jo remarked on the striking positive change they had noticed in Tilly's demeanour whilst the friendship between Tilly and Maddie blossomed. Tilly appeared significantly happier and more cheerful, a transformation that was particularly evident during her recent visit to Chamonix. They attributed this shift in her disposition to the changes in her life. She appeared to have undergone a complete personality alteration from the Tilly they once knew and confided in Maddie that she had played a pivotal role in this remarkable change.

"Perhaps," Maddie said with such selflessness but admitted feeling sad and perplexed following Tilly's departure.

Despite the unexpected turn of events, Maddie decided to remain optimistic, hoping they would eventually find Tilly and offer her the help and support she needed.

It had been four days since Tilly had left, and they were becoming increasingly concerned.

The area had become a lot busier because it was now entering the holiday season, making the search for Tilly more complicated due to the vast number of people visiting the area. Nevertheless, they persisted with unwavering determination, scouring the region and beyond for any sign of her.

There were no reports of any unfortunate events in the area, which was welcoming news as they continued with their search.

The trio once again returned to the villa from their search without any luck.

Jo served some refreshing lemonade, which cooled them down in the warm late Spring sunshine as they pondered their next steps.

Suddenly, Maddie received a surprising text.

She exclaimed, "Oh my god, it's Tilly!"

Ella and Jo immediately inquired about what Tilly had said to Maddie.

With a sense of relief in her voice, Maddie explained that Tilly was safe. She revealed that she had received distressing news and was deeply upset, needing time to contemplate how she would tackle the situation. Jo immediately asked what the bad news was, but Maddie didn't know.

Tilly had promised to Facetime Maddie later that night to explain everything, as it was too long to put in a text message.

Knowing that Tilly was now safe and unharmed, the girls were now feeling slightly calmer and relieved but weren't going to pass judgment until they actually met up with her.

That evening, Maddie was all geared up for Facetime with Tilly, and after a couple of double gin and tonics, the laptop went into action.

The girls all stood around listening to Tilly and her news.

Tilly said surprisingly, 'Is that Ella and Jo I can see in the background?' Maddie replied, 'Yes, they had come all this way to see us both before returning home to the UK.'

Tilly fell silent as she began to cry.

Despite this, Jo couldn't help but ask her when she plans to return back with Maddie.

Tilly expressed her deep longing for Maddie and assured her that her leaving wasn't related to their relationship. She made a heartfelt promise to return soon, excited to be back with the person who brings her the utmost joy - Maddie.

A very distressed Maddie then asked the reason for her sudden departure.

Tilly explained that she had received an urgent message on her phone to ring her dad's next-door neighbour as soon as possible.

Having done so, the neighbour told her that there had been a fire at his cottage.

The neighbour went on to say that Tilly's brother had been driving past the cottage as occasionally he did when he saw smoke billowing out of the kitchen windows.

He stopped the car and raced up the uneven drive to the front door, opened it wide and could see his dad sitting in a chair with fire surrounding him.

He appeared slumped in the chair and unconscious.

Tilly was informed that her father had become very forgetful and extremely vague over the past six months or so, which may have contributed to the fire.

From what Tilly was told, her brother tried his hardest to save him and pull him away, but the fire got the better of them both, and the fire reports state that they were both pronounced dead at the scene due to severe burns and smoke inhalation.

"How did the fire start?" Jo asked."

I'm not sure, but it seems that a cigarette could have been the main cause of the fire.

Maddie was deeply shocked when she learned of the tragic news.

She couldn't comprehend why Tilly had chosen not to share this devastating information with her.

Tilly explained that she didn't want to burden Maddie with the grief of their deaths. She needed some time to come to terms with the loss on her own.

As they continued their conversation, Tilly shared some of her fondest memories of her brother and how much she loved him.

They all listened attentively, offering comfort and support to Tilly.

After the Facetime call ended, Tilly's mind was a whirlwind of emotions. She had spoken of her most profound feelings of grief to Maddie and the girls, and they had been incredibly supportive, offering compassionate advice and understanding that Tilly believed would assist her in dealing with her pain.

The knowledge that Ella and Jo were with Maddie provided Tilly with some comfort and she found herself yearning to go back home, within the familiar comforts of her surroundings.

As she confirmed her return, Tilly asked Maddie to put a bottle of Prosecco on ice, a small gesture of celebration in the face of her grief.

Maddie and the others were overjoyed to hear that Tilly was coming back, and they promised to support her through any future challenges she might face.

With a deep sense of gratitude for the love and support of her friends, Tilly felt reassured that she could face anything with them by her side.

Chapter 16

In the days since Tilly came back home, she had experienced a whirlwind of emotions. However, Jo and Ella's presence was a source of great comfort for both Tilly and Maddie, helping them navigate the challenges ahead. As they came together to talk about Tilly's next move, their primary goal was to provide unwavering support during this trying period.

One consideration was whether Tilly should return to England to take care of the funeral arrangements and paperwork, as she was now the only next of kin.

As they talked, it became clear that there was no easy answer and that Tilly would need to carefully consider her options before deciding.

After much consideration, Tilly ultimately decided to travel back to England to take care of the arrangements waiting for her.

When Tilly asked about Ella and Jo's return plans, Ella quietly informed Tilly that she and Jo planned to return once they knew her intentions.

Maddie also expressed interest in accompanying Tilly to England to ensure she didn't face any difficulties or setbacks alone.

Both myself and Jo thought it was a great idea, so we decided to plan the trip for the following Saturday.

As Saturday arrived, everyone gathered their belongings and went to the Nice-Ville train station. The atmosphere was filled with anticipation and growing excitement as Ella and Jo looked forward to the journey leading them back to their cherished English country homes.

Having reached Paris, they finally caught the Eurostar to complete the journey.

It was a long and arduous journey, and after all that travelling, the last thing they wanted to do was endure a 3-hour train journey back to Buckland Ridge, so they decided to spend a night in London before attempting the final leg of their trip, having both made sure to ring home to inform their respective families of their intentions.

Having both Maddie and Tilly with them during the journey back home added to the joyous atmosphere, and it also felt like a fitting end to Tilly's troubled journey.

Despite losing her beloved brother, they had faith that she would cherish his memory and move on from the bitter and very resentful memories of her estranged father.

It was a bittersweet moment, but knowing that Tilly had Maddie beside her was all that mattered.

Both families were excited to hear from their daughters and eagerly awaited their arrival.

Ella kindly asked her mother if Maddie and Tilly could stay for a few days so they could have time to arrange the funeral.

In addition, Jo also inquired about the possibility of staying the night. She wanted to make sure that Tilly had the necessary support to help her through the challenging days ahead, given the numerous arrangements that needed to be made.

As always, her mother was incredibly helpful in times like this and showed her true motherly spirit.

She didn't question it for a moment and was more than happy to offer them somewhere to stay.

Unfortunately, Lauren's visit from Australia had to be delayed by a week or two because of various flight issues.

Ella had to admit that amidst all the troubles with Tilly, she had utterly forgotten about Lauren's upcoming visit.

However, it excited her to think that she'd get to meet up with her sister after such a long time.

Finally, they returned home with their worn-out backpacks and boots showing signs of wear and tear from the rugged coastlines and mountainous pathways.

Their sun-tanned skin showed a golden glow on their cheeks.

However, they could proudly declare that they had experienced an exciting adventure and had much to tell.

As the girls approached the quiet and stillness of the late Spring afternoon in Buckland Ridge, Ella's Mum was patiently waiting at the door when she heard their footsteps trudging up the garden path.

Holding her arms out to Ella, she held her tightly, not letting her go, and said she was pleased she was home.

Ella's heart raced with anticipation as she turned the doorknob, knowing that Sammy was on the other side, eagerly awaiting her return.

His tail wagged with joy as he saw her, and she couldn't help but give Sammy the biggest hug ever.

She knelt and spoke to him gently, telling him how much she had missed him and promising that she would never leave him for such a long time again.

As she wrapped her arms around him, she felt a deep sense of comfort and contentment, knowing she was finally home.

Mum had prepared a hot meal for the girls, insisting they must be starving after their long journey and perhaps looking forward to a hot bath and a good night's sleep.

"You got that in three, Mum," Ella said laughingly.

Ella introduced the girls to Mum, and it wasn't long before all their adventures were spilling out one by one, showing excitement, drama, and, of course, newfound relationships, which they decided to discuss in more detail later.

After a restful night, the girls gathered downstairs for a delicious full English breakfast, something they hadn't enjoyed for a long time. The aroma of freshly brewed coffee and sizzling bacon filled the air, making everyone's mouths water in anticipation.

Tilly thanked Ella's Mum for a perfect breakfast, praising the perfectly cooked eggs and crispy bacon.

Savouring each bite, memories of her mother flooded her mind, and she couldn't help but begin to miss those precious times spent with her.

Tilly's voice was filled with deep emotion as she spoke, expressing how, in times like these, when faced with difficult situations, we tend to look back on our lives and become aware that we are truly alone in this world without our loved ones.

Ella listened attentively, offering a sympathetic ear and a comforting presence.

Brushing her hands down the front of her apron and with a very loving smile, Ella's Mum sat down and joined the girls for a cup of coffee, taking the opportunity to get to know them better.

It was the first time she had met all three of them, and she noticed that they had formed a strong bond of friendship that they would cherish for years to come.

As the morning sun streamed through the windows, casting a warm glow on the

late spring morning, all was right in the world for just a moment.

Jo gently said with a warm and caring smile, "That's what friends are for. I only wish I could have offered you more support with the unseen stresses you've been facing. But remember, Tilly, I'll always be here for you. I'm just a phone call away, any time of day or night." Tilly, in turn, reassured Jo, expressing gratitude for her immense support and encouraging her to think about herself. She deeply acknowledged Jo's selflessness, which made her feel even more grateful, and urged her to return home, emphasizing that her parents eagerly awaited her and, of course, her soulmate, Jellybean.

As the time came for Jo to depart, it was a bittersweet moment filled with mixed emotions. Despite the sadness of parting ways, Jo made a heartfelt promise to keep in touch forever. Each of them clung to the memories of their journey, a tapestry woven with both trials and triumphs, knowing that the deep bond they had forged during their shared experiences would stand the test of time.

Jo embraced Tilly tightly, their hug lingering for a moment longer than usual, and spoke to her in a soft, reassuring tone, assuring her of her unwavering and continual support. Tilly felt a profound gratitude for such a compassionate friend as she watched Jo Walk away, disappearing into the waiting taxi.

With the paperwork to sort out, the girls spent quite some time visiting various offices for the necessary form filling related to Tilly's father and brother's deaths.

During a challenging time, Tilly received invaluable support from Ella, who provided guidance and assistance to help Tilly navigate everything promptly and effectively.

Additionally, Maddie offered Tilly tremendous love and encouragement, which was uplifting during such a difficult period.

After both funerals had taken place, Tilly's life slowly returned to normal, yet something still seemed to be bothering her.

As Tilly brushed her long, auburn hair away from her face, revealing its natural colour from the bright pink it was when she first met her, she promptly asked to visit the cottage where her father and brother had lost their lives, hoping it would bring her closure and peace, believing this visit would help her focus on new opportunities and beginnings in her life.

Arriving at the scene of the fire, Ella and Maddie anxiously watched as Tilly courageously walked up the pathway alone to the destroyed, charred remains of the cottage.

A warning sign had been posted at the entrance of the cottage grounds, cautioning people about the risk of entering due to the possibility of a sudden collapse. The sign was visible to alert visitors to potential hazards and to promote safety precautions due to the severity of the fire.

Tilly clasped her hands together and said a prayer for her brother, saying that she hoped she would reunite with him someday.

Upon reflection, she expressed that the fear haunting her had dissipated, giving her a newfound sense of security.

Growing up, she had learned to hide her emotions and kept her feelings bottled up inside. She had been afraid that showing any vulnerability would only lead to more pain and heartache. However, she now realised that this fear had been holding her back and preventing her from fully experiencing life and love.

As Tilly embraced her newfound freedom, she couldn't shake off the feeling that she still had a lot of work to do.

She knew she needed to dig deeper and learn to be more open and honest with those around her. She also had to confront the painful memories of her past head-on, something that she had been avoiding for far too long.

Despite the daunting challenges ahead, Tilly felt a glimmer of hope.

With the unwavering support of her close friends and the knowledge that she was no longer alone, she felt more optimistic than she had in a long time.

As Ella bid farewell to Tilly and Maddie, she couldn't help but feel relief that all the hurt was finally over. Although she didn't know when she would see them again, she knew they could finally restart their lives and move on with the future. With renewed hope and determination, they would face whatever challenges lay ahead together.

Chapter 17

It was good to be back home with Mum, and Ella was getting very excited about the impending arrival of Lauren.

With her flight expected to land at London airport at around 6.30pm the following evening, the journey would have taken almost 24 hours with a stopover in Dubai.

Mum meticulously planned Lauren's arrival, and Ella had carefully kept her friendship with Hugo under wraps until she found the opportune moment to mention the subject.

Since returning to the UK, Ella and Hugo have stayed in touch less frequently than she would have preferred.

It was during a walk with Sammy that suddenly Ella's mobile rang and recognised the caller ID. It was Hugo.

Feeling extremely excited, she found a seat and sat down to hear his news.

Ella certainly had lots to tell him!

During the conversation, Ella shared the tragic news of the fire and the death of Tilly's father and brother.

Upon hearing this, Hugo expressed his shock and extended his heartfelt wishes to Tilly. He also emphasised the importance of standing together and supporting each other during difficult times. He quietly remarked, "It's reassuring to know Tilly has such wonderful friends."

He told Ella he had been busy teaching numerous pupils at the Ski School but also mentioned that the school had recently hired additional coaches to help with the workload. He apologised to Ella for not staying in touch regularly and felt guilty about the lack of communication.

As Hugo spoke, Ella found it strange that he didn't mention any forthcoming visit to the Dales, considering how much he discussed his plans in Chamonix.

He appeared vague when speaking and didn't seem like the same person he was in Chamonix. The uncertainty made her wonder if their relationship was still moving forward and if Hugo had any intentions whatsoever of visiting her. The thought of not knowing left her feeling restless and anxious. After the call ended, Ella couldn't shake off this uneasy feeling, so she decided to give it some time and see how things played out.

On her return from walking Sammy, Ella ventured into the dining room where her Mum was reading a magazine, awaiting the arrival of Lauren.

They both looked at the clock, hoping Lauren's flight had landed safely and on time in London and she would soon be home.

It seemed ages since they had all been together, and the anticipation was intense.

Not long afterward, they heard a taxi pulling up. Ella couldn't contain her excitement and immediately rushed out the door to greet her sister, with Mum following closely behind.

The gentle breeze brought the fragrant aroma of blooming flowers, filling the air with a sweet and welcoming scent as the two sisters finally reunited at the bottom of the garden. They hugged each other tightly, feeling the embrace of sisterly love and gratitude that filled their hearts with joy and calmness.

Mum and Ella embraced Lauren lovingly and did not want to let her go.

Mum whispered, "My girls are finally back home," and tears began to flow down her rosy cheeks.

After a warm welcome, they all returned to the house where Mum had prepared a late supper.

They were excited to hear about Lauren's adventures from the past couple of years but knew she must be tired from her journey. So, to ensure everyone was rested and refreshed for the next day, Mum suggested they all get a good night's sleep before catching up.

Funny how Mothers always know best!

As they settled into their beds, the house was filled with contented sighs. It felt so good to be together again, knowing this would be a special time.

The following day, despite feeling the effects of jet lag, Lauren's enthusiasm to hear about Ella's backpacking adventures was obvious. As they sat down together, Ella eagerly began sharing how her backpacking experiences had significantly influenced her life. She recounted how the challenges and rewards of backpacking had fulfilled their promise and bolstered her self-esteem and confidence, equipping her to confront any obstacles that crossed her path.

Most importantly, it ignited a renewed sense of purpose within her, empowering her to pursue her dreams with unwavering determination.

Of course, there were moments when Ella doubted her ability to persevere through the challenging times, but she said it gave her the courage to confront her fears.

Fortunately, being with two remarkable girls gave her the encouragement she needed to carry on.

Ella shared with Lauren the obstacles they encountered while supporting Tilly, detailing the emotional and practical challenges they needed to overcome. Despite the setbacks, Ella and Jo persevered, and Tilly ultimately discovered a sense of purpose and fulfilment, blossoming into genuine happiness and contentment.

Lauren was truly happy for Tilly, knowing she had finally found love and joy. She hoped that Tilly would continue to embrace this newfound happiness and never have to endure the painful and uncertain times from her past when she struggled to survive each day in total misery.

Ella then began telling how both she and Jo had to endure the snowstorm, which took them by surprise, but thanks to the generosity of those around them and their ability to handle unexpected situations, Ella believed everything was handled very well. It was a scary experience, but they remained calm and worked together to ensure everyone was safe.

The snow was deep, and it took lots of effort by so many people to help those caught up in the massive snow slide. Moments like this reminded her of the importance of being prepared for the unexpected.

After Ella had told Lauren about her travels, Lauren could see that her sister had emerged from the experience as a stronger and more resilient person.

Ella then started to tell her sister about her friendship with Hugo.

Lauren tentatively asked Ella what Hugo was like, including his appearance and fitness level, just like sisters do.

Ella answered all the questions as best she could, and Lauren could tell that her sister was becoming enamoured with Hugo.

The more Ella talked about Hugo; the more excited Lauren became for her sister. She could tell Hugo was a great addition to Ella's life.

However, their conversation was overheard by Mum, who entered the room at that moment.

"Lauren asked, 'Have you told Mum about your so-called friendship with Hugo?'

'Not yet,' Ella replied.

'Don't you think she deserves to know?' Lauren insisted."

In a sudden moment of courage, Ella opened her heart to her mother, who reacted with total surprise. Her mother was glad to see Ella finding someone who brought her so much happiness, which filled her with joy.

Ella went on to say that the relationship with Hugo was a special friendship without being too romantically involved, saying they were happy in each other's company, expressing her hope that they could both meet Hugo in person someday if he chose to visit.

Although Ella felt confident in their support for Hugo, she also acknowledged that they would have to wait and see where this friendship takes them.

Then, unexpectedly, Lauren shared some life-changing news with them, revealing that she had decided to make Australia her permanent home.

After much contemplation, which she admitted was an extremely hard decision to make, she realised that what with the current situation in the UK concerning the cost-of-living crisis, strike action everywhere, including the somewhat failing of the NHS, she felt it didn't offer the same opportunities and benefits of nursing as Australia did.

She explained that she had made many friends and had come to the conclusion that Australia was where she wanted to be.

Having resided in the glorious sunshine of Australia for nearly three years, she has come to refer to it with some affection as her home.

Lauren went on to tell them that she had already applied for a permanent visa to work and live in Australia, to be granted upon her return.

Although Mum appeared unhappy about the news, she knew in her heart that Lauren had made this decision long ago.

Mum quietly left the room, perhaps to make tea, but we knew she had gone outside to shed a tear.

After a brief moment of anticipation, Mum stepped back into the room, her arms outstretched towards Lauren as she said, "We hope you will be very happy, my darling." A warm embrace accompanied the words, and the three wrapped up in another group hug. It was a scene that they had become entirely accustomed to over the past few minutes.

Amidst all the emotion, there was a glimmer of excitement when Lauren announced that she would cover all expenses for Mum and Ella to visit her next year.

Ella greeted the news with joyous exclamations and exclaimed, "Wow, I need to start shopping for sun cream, a sun hat, and some new sunglasses!"

They both had a feeling that Lauren's recent trip to the UK was to share her move with them in person instead of over the phone or Facetime.

It turned out to be true; nevertheless, they were very happy for her.

The following day, Lauren shared her wish to visit the cemetery where their father had been laid to rest many years ago. The cemetery was in a beautiful remembrance garden overlooking the Fell Valley. The family went together and observed silence to honour his memory.

Lauren wanted to explain to him her decision to move permanently to Australia and hoped he would listen to her from somewhere above.

As they walked away, they interlocked their arms and felt at peace, knowing they had done the right thing.

Four weeks had passed so quickly before it was time for Lauren to depart and head back to Australia.

It was such a poignant moment for all of them.

They had all grown so close during her stay, and it was tough to say goodbye.

Mum was trying her best to hold back her tears, but it was evident that she was failing to do so.

Ella could feel a lump forming in her throat as she hugged Lauren one last time. However, they reminded her that no matter what, she would always have a home back in Buckland Ridge with them and that they were just a phone call away.

Chapter 18

Ella leisurely strolled along the narrow, twisting country lanes of Buckland Ridge, her faithful companion Sammy scampering beside her.

As they immersed themselves in the serene surroundings, Ella's heart filled with a kaleidoscope of emotions - from sheer wonder at the beauty of the landscape to an exhilarating sense of anticipation for the adventures ahead.

Despite the idyllic setting, Ella knew she had some critical decisions to make.

Her backpacking journey had ended, and it was time for her to focus on her future. She had to decide where to go next, what to do with her life, and how to make the most of the experiences she had gained from her travels.

It was daunting, but she was ready to face it head-on and embrace the challenges ahead.

Lost in thought and daydreaming, she couldn't help but notice how the locals were busy tending to their gardens and allotments. She could hear them chatting about the progress of their runner beans and ripened tomatoes, the weather, politics, and many other topics that elderly residents often gossip about.

It was a scene she had witnessed many times before, always making her smile. This was undoubtedly village life at its best.

With every step, Ella's mind was consumed with thoughts of the many young people from her village who had left in search of a better life. She couldn't help but ponder on the idea of whether or not she should join them, hoping to find better job opportunities elsewhere, with perhaps even more chances for success. The wind whistled through the trees as she walked, her mind racing with questions and uncertainty about what the future held for her.

Despite feeling doubtful about her plans, Ella was determined to discover the answer. Talking with her sister, Lauren motivated her to move forward, and although she admitted they shared some similarities, both sisters were so different in many ways.

One thing that made it difficult for Ella to consider leaving the village was the prospect of leaving her Mum alone. It was her greatest fear, and she felt incapable of deciding to move away. However, as she contemplated her options, she knew that staying in the village might hinder her chances of success and growth.

So, the question remained - should she leave, or should she stay?

It was a big decision that would require careful consideration and thought.

Ella couldn't stop thinking about Hugo's lack of communication. It had been troubling her for days, causing her considerable unease and making it hard to concentrate on anything else. She couldn't shake off the persistent feeling that something was amiss in their relationship.

She wondered if she had done something to upset him that had caused him to distance himself from her. Or perhaps he was going through a difficult time in his life, and that's why he had not been in contact recently.

The not knowing was driving Ella crazy, and she couldn't help but feel a knot in her stomach every time she thought about it.

Her mind raced with questions about whether their friendship was in jeopardy and whether she should try to contact him again. She had already sent him a few messages, but there had yet to be a response.

Should she call him? Or would that be too pushy?

She didn't want to come across as needy or desperate, but the uncertainty was eating away at her.

Despite trying to keep herself busy with other things, Ella constantly checked her phone for any sign of a message or call from Hugo. As the days went by, her anxiety grew, and she couldn't help but feel increasingly uncertain about the future of their friendship.

She missed him terribly and longed for the days when they used to talk and laugh together like they used to.

Thankfully, Sammy was always there to keep her company.

He enjoyed their daily walks together, and it was clear to anyone who saw them that they shared a special bond filled with love and affection.

Sammy's wagging tail and playful barks lifted Ella's spirits, if only for a moment., but you could see that he had undoubtedly missed her over the past months and was definitely making up for lost time.

The sun began to shine, casting a warm glow over the narrow lanes, and the leaves rustled gently in the breeze, Ella paused to appreciate the blossoming flowers and to greet other furry friends and their owners.

Making her way towards the local newsagents, she caught sight of Mrs Morris, who was busy arranging the evening newspapers.

She had been running the newsagents for almost thirty years and knew everyone in the village, well almost!

Upon seeing Ella, Mrs Morris paused and greeted her warmly, expressing surprise at not having seen her for such a long time.

Ella happily shared the details of her travels with her, who listened with great interest.

After finishing their conversation, Ella went to the counter and politely inquired with Mrs. Morris about buying a couple of lottery scratch cards.

Mrs. Morris responded positively, saying, "Of course, my dear, let's hope you're lucky!"

157

"Ella replied with some optimism, saying, 'Somebody has to win, and who knows, it could be me!' You have to be in it to win it," she said, laughing out loud.

As Ella left the shop, her mind wandered back to when she did win something.

It was a homemade jar of pickled onions in the local Christmas Fete draw when she was ten years old.

However, the mere thought of winning a significant amount of money and the endless possibilities that would come with it sparked her imagination and holding tightly onto the two cards. She hurried back home.

As she entered the front door, her mother was busy preparing a delicious dinner that made Ella's stomach rumble with hunger.

Dinner won't be long, she remarked, and it was evident by Mum's tone in her voice she was happy to have her youngest daughter back home.

Ella is facing a dilemma between pursuing her career goals and the possibility of causing emotional distress to her mother by moving away from Buckland Ridge. She is aware that it will be a tough situation for her mother to deal with, especially since her sister has already moved to Australia permanently. The thought of leaving her mother behind is making her decision-making process even more difficult.

Out of the blue and without any warning that evening, Hugo rang unexpectedly.

Ella hadn't heard anything from him for over a month, so she was more than happy to hear his voice.

Then suddenly, everything seemed different somehow, and Ella sensed there was something wrong.

"Are you ok"? She asked.

After a long pause, Hugo began speaking quietly and, with a hint of nervousness, said, "There's something you need to know," his voice trembling as he spoke.

Ella encouraged him to continue, asking, "Please tell me, what is it?"

Hugo expressed to Ella that the distance between them was causing him concern regarding trying to maintain a proper relationship.

As time passed, he came to the realisation that building a strong relationship required more than just relying on social media and phone calls.

He acknowledged that his busy schedules would only allow them to meet up at certain times of the year, and he wanted more than just brief, infrequent visits. Nevertheless, he valued Ella as a very close friend and cherished her deeply, not wanting to let go of their special bond.

He spoke passionately about their time together and how much he cherished being together, especially when the talking point revolved around Julienne, revealing that Ella had been a vital source of support for him, helping him deal with his grief and anxiety, praising her for being a good listener and for allowing him to open up about his most profound thoughts.

Ella's frustration bubbled to the surface as she questioned whether she was simply a confidant for him, a mere shoulder for him to lean on. In response, Hugo swiftly reassured her that his feelings for her remained steadfast and that the thought of her being just a shoulder to cry on had never crossed his mind. He emphasised how incredibly special she was to him in every respect.

However, he acknowledged the challenges of maintaining a strong connection when separated by distance.

Despite his reassurances, Ella could sense that Hugo was struggling to keep the conversation going.

The weight of emotional pain was evident in his voice as he spoke. His words came out in a rush, making it clear that the relationship was no longer sustainable.

All the plans Ella had made, showing him the beautiful Dales and meeting her mother, were shattered, and she couldn't continue the conversation any longer.

After saying a brief "Goodbye, Hugo," she abruptly ended the call and was suddenly overwhelmed with emotion.

Feeling stunned and teary-eyed, Ella quickly ran upstairs, laid down on her bed, and wept bitterly.

She couldn't understand how he could treat her so cruelly, especially after the wonderful time they had spent together in France, where their feelings for each other had seemed to be leading towards something more than just friendship.

It was only several weeks ago when Ella discussed with Jo the complexities of long-distance relationships and the effect they can have on both couples. A romantic liaison can finish as quickly as it started so it is important not to let your feelings run away with forever thoughts.

Little did Ella know that she would soon find herself in the same situation she had discussed with Jo, experiencing first-hand the reality of her own words as her romantic relationship took an unexpected turn.

Despite this, she held onto hope that Jo and Ryan's relationship would flourish with warmth and affection and that they would not succumb to the same challenges of prioritizing distance over love.

Ella had a difficult and emotional night. She found herself unable to sleep, tossing and turning in bed as she wrestled with her thoughts and emotions. Instead of drifting off into a deep sleep, she lay awake with her hands clasped behind her head, gazing up at the intricately patterned ceiling of her room. Her mind was filled with a poignant mixture of longing and hope, yearning for the day when she would find someone genuinely loving and caring, someone who would understand and appreciate her for who she truly was.

However, she made a conscious decision not to let it impact her life.

She wiped away any thoughts of Hugo from her mind and resolved to start a new chapter in her life.

The next day was a turning point for Ella as she confided in her mother that her friendship with Hugo had ended.

Her mother sympathised with her and advised her not to let this experience cloud her judgment in future decisions, reminding Ella that she had a bright future ahead of her.

Ella thanked her mother for her kind words but expressed that she sees herself as someone who helps people overcome crises in their lives, and once she has done that, her work is done.

Her mother encouraged her not to think that way, telling her that she was a kind-hearted and incredible person.

She assured Ella that one day, she would meet Mr. Right, and she would know instantly that he was the one.

Upon careful consideration, Ella came to the realisation that Hugo's decision to end their relationship was possibly the right thing to do.

Despite this, she still held on to the hope that they could still continue to remain good friends and who knows, perhaps one day they may meet again.

Suddenly, Ella remembered the two scratch cards in her jacket pocket, so she chased upstairs to see if she had won anything.

Still feeling somewhat depressed after hearing Hugo's news, Ella began to remove the scratch cards from her pocket and carefully scratched off the numbers.

She stood there, her body frozen in shock, her hands trembling with the weight of her substantial newfound fortune. The first scratch card revealed three identical symbols, instantly granting her a £1,000 win. But the incredible turn of events didn't stop there. The second scratch card also matched a total of five symbols, resulting in an unbelievable £1,000,000 prize. Two simple scratch cards, bought for a mere £5, had completely transformed her life with a mind-boggling £1,001,000 windfall.

"What happens next," she thought to herself.

Shaking in total disbelief, Ella read through the rules on the back of the cards and found a phone number to contact.

She waited patiently on hold for what felt like an eternity but finally received the confirmation she was hoping for – she was indeed a winner!

The arrival of this unexpected windfall would completely transform Ella's life. It couldn't have happened at a better time as she was starting to map out her future. With this money, she would have many choices available to her. The key for Ella now was to ensure that she used the money wisely and carefully considered the best path forward.

Ella was excited as she hurried home to share the news of her lottery win with her mother. As she walked through the front door, she could hear her mother softly humming a tune while she was busy ironing in the kitchen. "Mum, you won't believe what happened!" Ella exclaimed, urging her mother to sit down before she shared the incredible news.

"Whatever it is," she said.

Ella told her that she had some excellent news and began to tell her about the win.

"Are you sure you have won all this money?" her Mum said curiously, but nevertheless, she was over the moon with her sensational good luck.

Ella confidently assured her that the National Lottery had thoroughly verified her winnings. She proudly showed her mother the scratch cards, revealing that she had won a staggering £1 million and £1000 on two scratch cards.

They both sat together, laughing uncontrollably at the fantastic win and the possibilities it could bring them.

Last night, Ella received upsetting news from Hugo, but today, she has just received some fantastic news!

Life is about to change, Mum, and it's going to be amazing!

They discussed the possibilities and the potential for the future, both near and far.

"Let's call your sister, Ella, and share the excellent news with her," Mum shouted out loud.

Ella couldn't contain her excitement. Thanks to an unexpected stroke of luck, they now had the means to plan the trip of a lifetime to Australia sooner rather than later.

The thought of exploring the vibrant cities, soaking up the sun on the spectacular beaches, and experiencing the unique wildlife made her heart skip a beat.

Ella could see that her Mum was thrilled and was already packing her bags in anticipation of the trip of a lifetime.

With excitement overflowing, Ella exclaimed that she had become a millionaire. It's hard to believe that not too long ago, she was backpacking across Europe with a couple of friends, working to earn enough money for indulgences like delicious pizzas and exquisite cocktails.

How life can change in the blink of an eye Ella thought to herself.

They both decided to phone Lauren about the wonderful news.

Taking into account the time difference, they opted against calling her during the middle of the night, as Lauren may have been sleeping or even working, but Ella felt an immense excitement that she couldn't contain. With her heart racing, she immediately dialled Lauren's number and exclaimed, "It's ringing!" After a few rings, Lauren finally answered the phone, but her tone was irritated, and she asked, "Hello, who is it?"

Ella's voice trembled excitedly as she spoke, "It's me, Lauren. Ella."

Groggy from sleep, Lauren sensed the urgency in Ella's voice and asked if everything was alright. She could sense her sister's excitement and couldn't wait to hear what Ella had to say.

Ella couldn't contain her joy as she shared the incredible news— she had won a staggering £1 million on a lottery scratch card and an additional £1000 on a second card. The elation in her voice was contagious, and she expressed her plans to visit her sister as soon as possible to celebrate.

Amidst laughter and excitement, they spoke about how their lives would change after this unexpected windfall. Ella promised to FaceTime with Lauren later in the week and suggested she go back to sleep. Unable to contain her excitement, Lauren responded, "How can I get back to sleep after what you just told me, Ella?"

Later that day, when speaking to Lauren once again, Mum sounded excited at the thought of visiting her daughter in Australia much sooner than planned.

Lauren was thrilled to hear the news and replied, "That's excellent news, Mum! There's always a room here waiting for both of you."

As night fell, Ella realised she was unable to sleep as her mind was preoccupied with the best and most effective way of spending her money.

She acknowledged her mother's hard work in supporting her and Lauren and decided to spoil her with special treats so she wouldn't have to work anymore. Creating a comfortable life for her mother made her feel happy and content.

Ella knew her mother deserved the best and was determined to make it happen. With a smile, she drifted to sleep, dreaming of the happiness that would soon come to her family.

Chapter 19

Gazing through the kitchen window, Ella couldn't help but sense an air of luxury and indulgence around her.

Life was about to take a turn for the better, but thoughts of her past relationship with Hugo still lingered on. She had to forget him once and for all but was finding it very difficult indeed. She thought she had found love but has now been proved wrong.

Hoping for happier times, she was eager to pamper Sammy with special treats and perhaps even reward him with a new collar for good behaviour, giving out a slightly hysterical laugh.

Strolling down the tranquil pathway that meandered alongside the picturesque River Felling, Ella's phone began to ring, startling her out of her peaceful trance. Without hesitation, she answered the call, curious to find out who was trying to reach her.

The voice on the other end was bubbly and exuberant, instantly putting Ella at ease.

It was the Lottery team asking if she would like to go public about her recent winnings.

Ella's mind raced with possibilities as she contemplated the offer. Should she bask in her new wealth's glory and tell the world about her incredible luck? Or should she keep her good fortune to herself to avoid unwanted attention, harassment, or envy from those around her?

After much reflection, Ella decided to decline the offer of publicity. She cherished her privacy and didn't want to attract unwanted attention or jeopardise her relationships with those she cared about.

She wanted to remain the person she had always been, grounded, humble, and kind, but with a much larger bank account.

She planned to enjoy life to the fullest, but on her terms, without any unnecessary fuss or fanfare.

After ending the call, Ella received assurance that the funds would be deposited into her bank account by midnight.

With great delight and excitement, she was now planning how to spend her windfall.

Mum had been hesitant about quitting her part-time job at the school. The kids adored her, and she felt the same way about them, becoming a popular staff member.

Mum had to decide, and Ella wouldn't convince her either way.

Now that Ella's lottery win was safely tucked away in the bank, she was slowly adjusting to having loads of cash and had many ideas for her future.

However, she considered investing in property, possibly starting her own business, or even travelling. The world is her oyster, as they say!

She decided she wouldn't spend her money on frivolous things like expensive cars, jewellery, clothes and designer handbags as so many winners do.

However, she felt that it was important to have a car but didn't want anything flashy, just a dependable car that could get her where she needed to go.

Perhaps driving lessons should be a priority before anything else, as she giggled to herself.

Being thrilled to have the financial freedom to pursue her dreams and make them a reality, she knew that with careful planning and wise decisions, she could ensure a bright and prosperous future for herself.

Looking ahead, Ella felt excited and confident about what lay ahead and couldn't wait to see where her acquired wealth would take her.

Ella eagerly scoured the depths of the internet for business prospects within her specialised field of food technology. It wasn't long before she stumbled upon a property that instantly piqued her interest. Nestled alongside the enchanting River Felling and neighbouring the famous Felling Wishing Well, the property seemed to exude endless potential for a thriving business venture. Perhaps the possibility of a small-run restaurant, she thought to herself.

The allure of the well, which attracted many visitors eager to cast their hopes into its waters, instantly captivated her. "This is perfect," she mused with a renewed sense of excitement.

Ella had a vision of creating a warm and welcoming restaurant that specialised in locally sourced ingredients.

The restaurant would offer delectable homemade lunches and teas for visitors looking to venture out into the beautiful surrounding landscapes.

Her adoration for the stunning scenery of the Dales developed during her childhood when growing up in the region.

The picturesque Pennines, Fells, and Lake District offer abundant natural beauty, making it a popular choice for active and leisurely holidays.

The serene River Felling flows quietly, adding to the area's charm.

She longed for more people to experience the awe-inspiring landscapes and share in her love for the area.

She felt confident in pursuing her ambitions due to the experience gained whilst enduring her backpacking journey and, where she met so many different people from all walks of life.

Accompanied by her mother, Ella visited the property, and the positive ambiance of the place immediately struck a chord with both of them.

She began thinking of ways to design the property to attract customers who longed for a delectable homemade lunch or possibly an afternoon tea.

After much contemplation and deliberation, with valuable input from her mother, Ella finally reached a decision that would change her life forever.

As time passed, the idea of leaving the Dales that once crossed her mind slowly faded away. Instead, a new dream had started to take shape in her mind - the dream of owning her restaurant. This dream was no longer just a fleeting thought but a realistic possibility that she was determined to turn into a reality.

She quickly made an offer, and thankfully, it was accepted.

With this milestone achieved, she became excited about the future, although slightly apprehensive.

Regardless, Ella is determined to make the most of this new opportunity and embrace the challenges.

Thinking about the potential for success in bringing delicious and organic food to the community is exciting.

With her impressive credentials in food nutrition and her Mum's cooking ability, she feels ready and confident to take the exciting leap of opening her very own restaurant.

However, she realises that running a successful restaurant requires more than culinary skills, knowing she needs to learn about managing finances, marketing, and employing the right staff.

The location of the property is absolutely perfect! It is surrounded by stunning countryside and a serene river, while the Pennine Hills add to the beautiful landscape.

Additionally, the famous Cross Fell, which is England's highest point outside of the Lake District, is located nearby. Ella compared this location to Chamonix, albeit on a smaller scale, of course, although Cross Fell is still incredibly charming and mesmerizing.

In the coming months, Ella had to make difficult decisions as both the project manager and restaurant owner.

She was about to face numerous challenges but remained determined to do everything in her power to make her business a success.

The restaurant's renovation was progressing steadily when Ella unexpectedly received a phone call from Jo.

Ella was thrilled to hear from her, and after exchanging pleasantries, Ella eagerly shared her exciting news with Jo.

"Please sit down wherever you are and brace yourself," Ella said.
"

"What is it?" Jo asked.

Ella then revealed that she had won a large sum of money in the lottery.

Jo was speechless and, in a startled voice, said, "You're kidding me, right?"

However, Ella confirmed that it was true and that she was now a millionaire.

Sometimes, she had confessed to pinching herself to confirm that it was not a dream.

However, she reassured herself that it was indeed reality.

After taking a few minutes to update each other on all the events and goings-on in their lives since their last encounter, they made plans to resume their discussion the following day at the Stags Head pub. It was the same place where they had their first meeting a couple of years back and where they planned their memorable backpacking adventure together.

As she walked to the bus stop the following evening, preparing to take the short journey to The Stags Inn, she found herself lost in thought. Sitting on the bus, she looked out the window and quietly reflected on the past few months. A significant change in her financial situation left her uneasy about its impact on her family and friends.

She sincerely hopes that her lottery win will not change anything and that her friends will not become envious of her achievements.

At the same time, she is also aware that money can change people and relationships.

In the end, Ella firmly believes that genuine friendships are based on the foundations of trust, respect, and integrity.

Walking towards the entrance of the pub, her eyes caught sight of Jo, who was already inside, holding a couple of glasses.

Ella couldn't help but feel touched when she realised that Jo had remembered her favourite glass of wine, a refreshing Chardonnay.

"I believe this is your preferred drink, Ella!" Jo exclaimed with excitement.

Ella walked over and embraced her, as both talked for ages about how life had changed for them since their return from France.

When the topic of Hugo arose, Jo noticed a profound sadness in Ella's eyes. Jo shared her dismay about Ella's bond with Hugo but also provided reassurance, expressing relief that the friendship had concluded before causing additional heartache. With much sympathy, Jo told Ella she would eventually meet the right person to share her life with.

Oh well, Ella remarked, that's all in the past now.

There is much more exciting news to tell you.

In response, Jo suggested getting another drink before getting settled to hear what Ella had to say.

Shocked and totally amazed, Jo was flabbergasted when she heard about the lottery win and asked Ella how she planned to spend the money.

Ella remarked by saying that she didn't want to waste any of it, so she purchased a somewhat derelict building with the hope of turning it into a small restaurant alongside the River Felling.

Having discovered the perfect property that captured her imagination, she is unwaveringly committed to turning her dream into reality through dedication and perseverance.

Her background in Food Technology and Nutrition has instilled in her the belief and competence needed to bring her aspirations to fruition.

Jo was astonished by what she was hearing, but she had witnessed Ella's unwavering determination during the months they spent backpacking together. Knowing Ella's resilience, Jo knew in her heart that if anyone could succeed, it would be Ella.

Ella also mentioned that the builders were expected to complete the renovations in about four months, after which she could begin planning the restaurant's interior design.

After that, she intends to offer healthy lunches and delightful teas to the many tourists who come to see and explore the beautiful Fells, hikers considering the mountainous Pennines and even the locals who may want to indulge in a healthy prepared lunch or an afternoon cream tea.

Jo liked the concept and inquired about Ella's business background, offering to assist her in organizing the books.

Ella gratefully accepted Jo's offer and acknowledged that Jo's Business Studies degree would be exceptionally beneficial, confessing that Maths and Accounts were not Ella's favourite subjects in school.

Amidst laughter, Jo inquired about the restaurant's name.

Ella revealed that she had carefully considered several options before choosing "Tastebuds" as her preferred name.

Wiping a tear from her eye, Jo couldn't help but admire Ella's choice of name and wished her all the luck in the world in what was surely to be life-changing, not only for her but those around her too.

Ella then went on to share her excitement about Lauren's invitation for both her and Mum to visit Australia.

It brought immense joy, especially to Mum, who would love to travel and see where her daughter now lives with a plan to visit when the restaurant is launched and running successfully.

Jo's reaction to Ella's lottery win was a pleasant surprise for her because she was initially concerned about how Jo would take the news, but seeing her genuine excitement and happiness made her appreciate their friendship even more.

As they celebrated together, Ella couldn't help but feel a sense of relief that things had turned out so well.

Jo invited Ella to spend a few days with her and meet the family, introducing her two favourite dogs, Mollie and Monty, and, of course, Jellybean, her beloved horse.

"When you have some free time, maybe we could plan something," suggested Jo. Ella's face lit up with excitement as she exclaimed, "That would be amazing"!

She had heard so many good things about the farm and the animals.

It would be lovely to meet them in person.

Jo smiled and agreed, "Let's make a note of it in our diaries."

"Definitely," Ella replied with a grin.

Following a delightful catch-up, Jo and Ella agreed to arrange another meeting soon to further deliberate on the most efficient ways to manage the restaurant. Ella was undoubtedly thrilled to have Jo's assistance as it had weighed heavily on her mind for some time on how she would cope with the financial aspect of the business.

Jo had a keen eye for detail and would be able to help Ella create a budget plan that would keep the restaurant running smoothly.

After meeting up with Jo, Ella's mood had significantly taken a turn for the better. She now felt more positive and ready to tackle anything that came her way.

Jo's reassurance and encouragement gave her the confidence to embrace her future ventures wholeheartedly.

Ella was confident she could create an unforgettable menu for her customers.

She eagerly anticipated the challenge of preparing and cooking food that was simple, nutritious, and of the highest quality.

With her mother's help, Ella believed they could create a successful restaurant.

Although recognizing it would require hard work and dedication, she was ready to face the challenge head-on.

She knew that the road ahead would not be easy, but she felt well-prepared to overcome any obstacles that might come her way.

With all the help offered, Ella is optimistic that her business venture will go according to plan.

Additionally, she had just passed her driving test on the first attempt and is now the proud owner of a VW Beetle that resembles "Herbie" from the movie.

She is thrilled with her choice and has grown fond of her little car, naming it her 'little banana' because of its size and bright yellow paintwork.

Ella thought it would be a good idea to drive the small distance to meet up with Jo and her family for a few days, taking Sammy along with her to meet the Labradors in the hope they would all get along together.

After agreeing on a date, Ella cleared her busy schedule for a few days to take a much-needed break.

As Ella drove up the gravelled driveway, she was met by two energetic dogs, and Sammy couldn't wait to introduce himself as he quickly bounced out of the car with all three dogs wagging their tails in sheer excitement.

As she walked towards the stables, Jellybean, Jo's majestic horse, nudged her in a friendly manner, which struck her with a sense of awe in his presence.

Ella immediately felt at home with Jo's incredibly kind and welcoming family.

Jo's father appeared in very good health since his heart scare, and her mother attributed it to the fresh air of the countryside.

Jo's mother remarked that after they had decided to stay in the Dales permanently, they felt a sense of relief from the pressures of their previous life in the city.

Ella was thrilled when Jo's parents expressed their happiness with their new home.

After gaining substantial financial knowledge from their time spent in London, Jo's parents extended their unwavering support to Ella, too, with her new venture.

They promised to be there for her if she needed their help with bookkeeping and checking the accounts.

Ella couldn't help but feel overwhelmed by their kindness.

She spent the next few days cherishing her time with Jo's family, indulging in delicious meals, engaging in heart-warming conversations, and enjoying fun-filled activities with Mollie, Monty, Sammy, and Jellybean. The sheer joy on Sammy's face after meeting the two beautiful dogs was priceless, and he was invited to return anytime he wanted. The vast and lush green spaces surrounding the restaurant provided the perfect opportunity for Sammy to frolic around and have fun to his heart's content. The setting was nothing less than a picture-perfect landscape painting.

As Ella returned home, she felt incredibly refreshed and rejuvenated, thankful for the much-needed break and the unforgettable memories created with her friends.

Chapter 20

Ella couldn't be happier that everything seemed to be going well.

The restaurant's renovation is progressing smoothly and quickly, and she now feels that everything is falling into place.

She has even driven her Mum up to the Lakes to visit a cousin, and they spent a couple of days looking around and getting a few ideas for the restaurant.

With the restaurant now in its final stages of completion, Ella walked towards the entrance feeling a sense of pride at what she had achieved so far.

The restaurant features a log burner at the far end of the dining area for those chilly winter days, creating a cozy atmosphere perfect for enjoying meals with friends and family.

On sunnier days, guests can enjoy al fresco dining within a charming garden providing tables and seating areas. This space exudes a tranquil atmosphere and encourages relaxation. Umbrellas provide ample shade to shield against the sun's scorching rays, should the English summer allow.

The hanging baskets filled with colourful flowers add a touch of elegance to the already picturesque environment. Additionally, the restaurant has thoughtfully cultivated a small garden adjacent to the outdoor seating areas with various fresh herbs that fill the air with a delightful aroma. Ella's commitment to sourcing ingredients from local farmers ensures that everything is of the highest quality while supporting the local community.

All these beautiful features make the restaurant a favourite among locals and visitors alike.

The pre-opening of 'Tastebuds' had finally arrived, and Ella was pleasantly surprised by the large number of people who had gathered to take a peek inside. Guests were offered a variety of hors d'oeuvres and a selection of various wines while children played happily on the freshly cut lawns adjacent to the restaurant, enjoying squash and biscuits.

Ella overheard people commenting on the restaurant's beautiful location and healthy menu.

Despite not officially opening until the following Saturday, Ella had already received numerous bookings.

She couldn't believe how many people had found her restaurant the perfect spot for a peaceful and picturesque dining experience.

Ella's highly successful business endeavour attracted significant interest from the local media. However, when questioned about the funding behind her venture, she maintained secrecy.

Despite her preference to conceal her lottery win, speculations had already begun spreading throughout the village.

She realised it was only a matter of time before someone would uncover the truth.

Living in a close-knit and peaceful community means that news, especially significant or eye-catching, doesn't stay secret for long.

Ella had a grand vision that extended beyond simply starting a restaurant.

She intended to revive Buckland Ridge's diminishing charm and attraction while catering to all generations.

Her keen perception revealed that the village lacked essential amenities to meet the needs of older people and the remaining younger population.

She believed introducing something new that everyone would enjoy could help combat the ever-increasing issue.

She recognised that food is the spice of life and was committed to pleasing all tastes regardless of age, which is where the name 'Tastebuds' came to mind.

With its potential to serve as a vital hub for the local community, this restaurant could become a central gathering place for anyone wanting to socialise and savour great food and a place where people can feel connected and united.

Ella realised that promoting her restaurant in an idyllic area was not only helping the tourist industry but providing a much-needed boost to the local farming industry, too and she was extremely thankful for those wanting to promote their produce in her restaurant.

In preparation for the restaurant's grand opening, Ella was approached by numerous suppliers, all eager to offer their fresh produce. They expressed their desire to provide her establishment with top-quality vegetables, meat, fruit, and dairy products. Ella was thrilled by their interest, and she was keen to work together with local dairy and farm suppliers to feature their products prominently on her restaurant's menu.

Feeling a surge of confidence, Ella realised that although starting a business was an intimidating prospect, the overwhelmingly positive response from suppliers made her believe that she could overcome any challenge. She expressed her gratitude with a warm smile, genuinely appreciating the support and encouragement from the suppliers.

With this heartening response, Ella felt that her business had already begun its journey to success, and she eagerly anticipated turning her dream into reality.

Catching the sight of her Mum pondering in the kitchen of the newly renovated restaurant, she slowly walked over to her and asked if she had anything on her mind.

"Ella's mother gently responded, "I haven't made a firm decision, but I'm considering whether it would be better for me to leave my position at the school and join you, at least until the restaurant is fully operational."

Ella's eyes widened in surprise as her mother shared her thoughts.

She couldn't bear the idea of her mother giving up something she had been passionate about for so many years.

Urging her mother to think it through, Ella expressed her concerns.

Having a mix of determination and uncertainty, Ella's Mum promised to give it more thought, but deep down, she felt it might be the right decision.

Shortly afterward, Ella saw a missed call on her phone and could see it was from Jo.

Replying quickly, Ella asked Jo if everything was alright.

She quickly responded by saying that Ryan had called me last night and had invited me to visit him in Canada and meet his parents.

When Jo spoke about her plans to visit Canada, it stirred up a feeling of uneasiness within Ella.

Memories of Chamonix seemed to resurface for her, especially now that her relationship with Hugo had ended.

Despite this, she bravely expressed joy for Jo's impending visit. Nevertheless, Jo could sense how much the news of her trip to Canada could affect Ella. Painful memories of her time with Hugo in France make it hard to forget the joyful moments they had shared. Despite her determination, Ella knew it would take time to forget him.

She devoted herself totally to the restaurant, channelling her energy into its success. Over time, her recollections of Hugo gradually faded away, allowing her to shift her focus towards building a new chapter in her life.

Ella knew she had to continue making progress and had every faith that things would improve and move forward.

Since Jo's departure to Canada, Ella's restaurant has become more successful than ever imagined.

Ella's mother has been a great help with most of the prepping and cooking since deciding to give up her job at the school, while Ella has been busy with ordering and getting to know all the excellent suppliers who provide the best quality produce in the area.

A local farmer brings them the freshest free-range eggs, corn-fed chickens, and grass-fed beef. Ella couldn't believe her luck with the excellent food she now has on her menu.

Everything is homemade as far as possible, including Ella's mother's delicious quiches, lasagnes, chilli, herby chicken with asparagus, beef wellington, comforting fish pie, and there will be a special beef and vegetable hot pot, which will be going on the menu towards the end of November, enticing customers during the colder months.

So far, the customer feedback has been nothing short of amazing.

Ella has noticed that both locals and tourists are increasingly using the internet to locate her fantastic restaurant, nestled alongside the river.

She is delighted by the success and has worked hard to find a supplier in Cornwall who can provide her with the finest Cornish Clotted Cream. This cream complements the delicious homemade fruit scones and a variety of jams served with the afternoon cream teas.

At least two hundred assorted scones have been baked since the opening of the restaurant, and they are selling like hot cakes (no pun intended!)

Jams and Honey are locally sourced at one of the farms nearby and all ingredients to make a good restaurant run superbly is nothing short of remarkable.

It's been eight months since the restaurant opened its doors, and both Ella and her mother have been inundated with bookings.

They've even had to turn customers away because the restaurant has become so popular. If things continue like this, Ella plans to employ some part-time staff in the New Year.

Jo had recently come back from her amazing trip to Canada and couldn't wait to meet up with Ella to tell her all the news.

Jo was invited to the restaurant for a morning coffee before the lunchtime rush, and as they both sat down to chat, Jo's eyes sparkled with excitement as she revealed that Ryan had planned to visit her during the Christmas holidays.

Ella found herself caught up in her friend's overwhelming joy. She couldn't help but be captivated by the sparkle in Jo's eyes and the vibrant warmth that radiated from her face as she animatedly shared her deep affection for Ryan.

Ella started to sense that Jo and Ryan's relationship was undeniably unique, and she hoped it would be a source of enduring happiness for both of them.

Jo told Ella that Ryan lives in the town of Banff, a province of Alberta located within Banff National Park.

To be honest, Jo thought she was back in Chamonix with its beautiful chateau-style hotels, souvenir shops, and mountains displaying such beauty.

Some of the nearby parkland is home to wildlife, including elk and grizzly bears.

These majestic creatures may even venture to the surrounding houses and lodges to find food for themselves and their offspring, which can be a little scary at times.

The winter weather there is unbelievable, with snow that can reach up to seven feet deep in places, making it difficult to get around and purchase provisions.

In areas with heavy snowfall, especially where Ryan and his family live, the locals prepare extensively to ensure they can manage during winter.

They equip their large station wagons with wheel chains to make getting around even in the deepest snow easier.

Additionally, many of the population stock up their freezers with ample supplies before the onset of bad weather.

The snow can be so severe that they often stay in their homes for weeks, relying on their food stock to see them through.

Despite the challenges, the residents are well-adapted to their environment and come together to support each other when necessary.

Whilst Jo spent some time with Ryan at his parent's house by the lake, she couldn't wait to share the photos she had taken of her Canadian trip.

Ella's eyes were suddenly drawn to one particular photo as they went through the photos. It depicted a serene scene of a beautiful lake surrounded by lush greenery. In the foreground were two grizzly bears grazing peacefully on the grass. Ella was amazed and couldn't believe what she was seeing. "Is that bears?" she asked, her eyes still fixed on the picture.

Jo, sitting next to her, chuckled softly and confirmed that, indeed, it was.

Ella felt both fascinated and apprehensive at the same time.

On the one hand, she found the photo incredibly beautiful and awe-inspiring.

On the other hand, the thought of being so close to wild, potentially dangerous animals made her feel very uneasy.

After enjoying a brief coffee break, Ella suggested that Jo review the restaurant's financial records before heading back home.

After glancing through the books, Jo complimented Ella, saying, 'Looking good! You've been really busy, and it definitely shows. Keep up the great work, Ella. It looks like you're on track for success with your budget sales rising rapidly.' "

Both began talking about hosting a pre-Christmas afternoon tea that would include scrumptious sandwiches, homemade pastries, and mini trifles, together with a glass of champagne.

They thought that this event could be popular among both locals and visitors if promoted well, and it was decided between them that they would go ahead with this idea, placing a few posters up and down the village and beyond.

During their conversation, Ella suggested temporarily closing the restaurant in late December and reopening it in mid-February.

She believes the number of visitors during this period would be relatively low, and only committed walkers and hikers would be willing to brave the rough, wet terrain in the harsh weather.

The Dales are beautiful in the summer months but can be deadly in the wild winter months.

Ella also pointed out that this would be an ideal opportunity to visit Lauren in Australia. January is an especially favourable time to go, as it falls right in the middle of their summer Down Under.

During this time, temperatures can range between 26 and 30 degrees Celsius, creating a perfect environment for outdoor activities.

Additionally, a refreshing cool breeze adds to the pleasantness of the weather, making it a great time to explore and enjoy the beautiful Australian scenery.

Therefore, Ella and her Mum have decided on a trip to Australia at the end of December to visit Lauren, with a tentative return date in early February. Even though the details need to be finalised, Ella and her mother have thoroughly discussed the matter, and it seems to be the perfect time for a visit.

Chapter 21

Christmas was fast approaching, and the Christmas Party tea menu had been printed and placed on the board outside of the restaurant.

Posters were everywhere for all to see should they be interested in popping along for an afternoon Christmas Tea.

Bookings are being well received, with the first week of December fully booked.

With each passing day, Jo's excitement grows as the arrival of Ryan for the Christmas holidays draws near.

With definite plans made, she is eager to showcase the stunning beauty of the local area to him.

One of the trip's highlights will undoubtedly be visiting Felling Falls, which may not be as grand as Niagara Falls but is still a sight to behold in its own unique way.

Additionally, they're considering a trip to the many stunning lakes, and whilst the weather may not be perfect, Jo is confident that the scenery will live up to its amazing beauty, and she can't wait to share it with Ryan.

Moving on, the Christmas Tea Party was a great hit!

Obviously, they couldn't have pulled it off without the help of two local girls who kindly offered to wait and serve.

Their assistance was invaluable, and as a token of gratitude, Ella rewarded them generously.

Everyone had a fantastic time at the event, enjoying the delicious food, lovely decorations, and the vibrant, festive atmosphere that filled the air. The log burner added a cozy touch to the ambiance, lighting the room with warmth and relaxation. It made the fireplace even more inviting as guests gathered around, warming their hands and loving the crackling sound of the burning wood.

Overall, it was a perfect afternoon filled with laughter, joy, and warmth, leaving everyone with the Christmas spirit.

The sight of many happy faces was genuinely heart-warming.

Mrs Morris, the lady at the newsagents who initially sold the scratch cards that brought Ella her good fortune, asked with a knowing twinkle in her eye if she would be hosting the Christmas Tea party again next year.

Ella responded with a big smile and a resounding "Yes" based on the success of today's event.

After taking down the menus, stacking the tables and chairs, and thoroughly cleaning the restaurant, it was time to close the restaurant until mid-February.

Ella looked back and felt a sense of satisfaction, knowing that all the hard work and dedication she put into creating the restaurant was worthwhile.

Her profits were a testament to this.

When Jo told her the net income she had made since the opening of the restaurant, Ella couldn't believe her eyes. She was amazed to learn that she could recoup the purchase cost in just 12 months if business continued this way.

It was truly unbelievable!

Then, out of the blue, a letter arrived in the post informing her that the Food & Hygiene Department wanted to send an Inspector to visit the restaurant, possibly in early Spring, to ensure it met the required public-use standards.

Mr Tim Henderson will contact you via email to schedule a suitable date and time. Ella knew this visit was necessary as food hygiene is crucial for a successful restaurant, and she was obviously hoping for a favourable report.

Jo was excitedly anticipating Ryan's arrival for the Christmas holidays.

With only a week left until Christmas Day, everything fell into place for a great Christmas.

Ella couldn't help but think Jo was fortunate to have found someone she truly cared for, and somehow, she felt a twinge of envy towards Jo's relationship with Ryan.

However, she recognised that Jo had become more than just a friend to her and knew she had to let go of any envy inside her.

Ella and her Mum were excited as they walked into the travel agency to book their long-awaited trip to Melbourne. The idea of experiencing a new culture, exploring the city's landmarks, and creating unforgettable memories filled them with anticipation. However, Mum couldn't help but feel a bit apprehensive about the long journey ahead.

As they sat down with the travel agent, the itinerary displayed on the screen showed a stopover in the vibrant city of Singapore for a few days. This would be the perfect opportunity to rest, explore the city's sights, and indulge in some delicious local cuisine before continuing their journey to Melbourne.

Ella was determined to make the trip a once-in-a-lifetime experience. She kept reminding Mum to cherish every moment and enjoy the journey as much as the destination.

Finally, with their travel tickets reserved, they had set the date for New Year's Eve and planned to return at the beginning of February. Ella couldn't contain her excitement, knowing this would be their most thrilling adventure yet.

Christmas morning arrived, and Ella seized the opportunity to shower her mother with lavish gifts as a token of appreciation for her years of hard work and sacrifices while raising herself and Lauren during challenging financial circumstances when indulgent gifts were simply out of reach.

Her mother felt overwhelmed with gratitude and emotion as she reflected on all that her daughter had accomplished, especially since winning the lottery. This sudden stroke of luck completely transformed their lives, bringing a sense of security and comfort they had never known.

Amid this newfound financial stability, Ella understood that money alone could not guarantee happiness and well-being. She appreciated the significance of prioritizing contentment and good health above all else.

It became clear to her that genuine happiness couldn't be purchased with money and that one's well-being holds more value than any amount of wealth.

As Sammy snuggled into his new fluffy bed, Ella couldn't help but feel sad about him being placed in kennels for the time they were going to be away in Australia.

Upon hearing this, Jo quickly messaged Ella to offer Sammy a stay at her Mum & Dad's farm.

Ella was relieved and grateful for the kind offer, knowing that Sammy would love it and be well taken care of.

Jo assured her that they would spoil Sammy just the same as Mollie and Monty.

With compassion in her voice, Jo reminded Ella that friends are there to help each other.

With Sammy in good hands, Ella could now enjoy her trip without any worries.

Jo informed Ella that Ryan will be staying with them until mid-January.

They have several sightseeing trips planned, but they hope the weather doesn't worsen as snow is expected shortly in the Pennines. Unfortunately, some of the lakes have frozen over, so they may not be able to showcase the usual beauty of the Dales.

However, Felling Waterfalls are always stunning no matter when you visit.

It will be lovely just having time together and walking the dogs, especially having Sammy in tow too, taking in the cool fresh air, and hopefully planning further visits together.

"Jo, that sounds absolutely lovely," Ella expressed with a warm smile. "I sincerely hope that all your plans and dreams come true."

With Sammy now safely settled at Jo's farm and enjoying the company of Mollie and Monty, it appears they have become great friends and are happily playing together in the vast fields beyond.

After much planning, the day had finally arrived, and Ella and her Mum were now travelling down under in readiness to meet Lauren.

So far, so good, the plane landed in Singapore on time (which is quite unusual giving the disruptions of flights recently) and what a beautiful country it is, too.

Tall skyscrapers fill the city's headline, together with the many restaurants which line the famous street serving their traditional and speciality street food.

Feeling somewhat hungry, it was time to venture into the town where all types of cuisine were being catered for.

Mum didn't think the Hainanese Chicken Rice, covered in various sauces and gravies, looked very appetizing, mentioning that possibly it wasn't something they would serve at 'Tastebuds.'

Therefore, it was decided to go for a simple rice dish with crab instead.

After a good night's sleep in a magnificent 5-star hotel, both Mum and daughter ventured out into the city, where they walked the famous street of Orchard Road selling exquisite jewellery, clothes and leather goods.

You name it, they sold it!

Chinatown was another place on their list to visit and it was definitely an area not to be missed.

They just had enough time to visit a couple of the famous temples and an art gallery, but Ella could see that her Mum was getting weary, so they decided to take a break and take a taxi ride to the famous Raffles Hotel for tea.

They both sat down to an English High Tea displaying a classic three-tier stand of finger sandwiches, home-made scones and a selection of patisseries.

A tea pot was provided with proper loose-leaf tea, something you don't see quite so much nowadays.

This was certainly an experience they would never forget.

As they stepped onto the Airbus bound for Melbourne, they knew the final stretch of their journey was about to begin. Ella had planned this trip for some time, hoping to give her mother the experience of a lifetime. Judging by the look on her face, she was beaming with excitement, and you could tell she couldn't wait to be with Lauren once again.

Despite the late hour of their arrival, Lauren was waiting for them as they walked through the arrivals gate, waving frantically and jumping up and down like a jack in the box as they appeared.

After much kissing and hugging, they arrived at Lauren's apartment, when her mother suggested that they unwind with a soothing cup of tea and take a moment to relax. They had planned to catch up on the latest news the following day, as Lauren had accumulated a well-deserved three weeks of annual leave, which had included working late shifts and overtime. She looked forward to using this time off to spend quality time with her mother and sister.

The following day, they all enjoyed a delicious breakfast on the sunny patio, although they were adjusting to the 9-hour time difference with the UK. As they ate breakfast, they reminisced about old times.

The atmosphere was incredibly calm and peaceful, with the faint whisper of the breeze and the delightful melody of birdsong blending to create a sense of utter tranquillity. In the distance, the gentle lapping of waves against the shoreline added to the feeling of serenity. It was the ideal beginning to what will hopefully be a holiday of a lifetime.

Ella was thrilled to discover Lauren's apartment within a gated complex, which had its own swimming pool and sauna, as well as a BBQ area for residents to gather and enjoy outdoor activities with one another.

Later that day, they decided to stroll around the neighbourhood to explore the local shops and restaurants.

They stumbled upon a quaint bookstore where they spent an hour browsing through the shelves, and Ella found a book she had wanted to read for months. They also tried a new sushi restaurant and enjoyed the delicious food.

After a long day, they spent the evening relaxing in the apartment and watching movies.

Mum asked in a joking tone, "Do they still have 'Neighbours' on TV over here?" They all laughed so hard that their sides hurt.

Lauren expressed her gratitude for Mum's presence, "What would we do without you, Mum?"

Lauren was excited to show Mum and Ella all the exciting places, stunning surfing beaches, and some of Australia's national parks.

Ella was in awe of the city's fantastic architecture and shopping areas.

Despite knowing that capturing its beauty in such a short time would be impossible, they were determined to make the most of it.

Lauren's friend Sally, who accompanied her to Australia, was spending time in Sydney with her friends, having an extended holiday, giving Lauren all the time needed to spend with her family.

As Ella gazed at Australia's stunning landscape, she couldn't help but think it was a country ideally suited to those wanting a better life in the warm sunshine, with possibly more opportunities than could be offered back in the UK.

In the past, before she had decided to buy and run her restaurant, she might have given serious thought to starting a new life in this beautiful land down under. However, the idea of leaving her mother all alone had always been a significant deterrent. Despite this, Ella felt confident that opening Tastebuds had been the right decision for her, and she was grateful for its success.

At the same time, she remained keenly aware that life held unpredictable surprises and that anything could happen at any moment.

Mum seemed satisfied, rejuvenated, and relaxed, and Ella knew she had made the right choice by bringing her to see Lauren.

Lauren took them to places she knew would interest them, and with only two weeks left before they had to head back home, Lauren wanted Ella to experience the city's vibrant nightlife, with Mum taking a backseat and allowing the sisters to enjoy themselves on their own.

Lauren chose an underground nightclub that offered a unique experience, and Ella wouldn't have missed it for the world.

They enjoyed each other's company, sipping cocktails, dancing, and just being sisters.

During their chat, Lauren suggested throwing a beach BBQ party before they returned to the UK, which excited Ella as she would get the opportunity to meet some of Lauren's colleagues from the hospital.

The party was scheduled for the following week, giving Ella and her mum enough time to rest before returning home.

Pebble Island Beach was the perfect setting for the evening BBQ, and Lauren worked hard to make it successful.

Friends were arriving on the beach for the party, and Ella looked stunning in her gorgeous dress, which showed off her incredible figure and sun-tanned body, with her hair tied back in a French plait, completing the look.

Mum was excited to meet some of Lauren's friends who were quietly sitting nearby.

They began discussing the differences between life in England and life in Australia.

Mum said that the English weather is a well-known and unpredictable phenomenon worldwide. Still, England and its beautiful countryside and landscapes can also be the most beautiful place on earth.

Meanwhile, Australia's hot summer climate and bushfires can be very frightening. There are pros and cons to both countries.

Mum remarked, "Home is where the heart is, and my heart is in England."

The atmosphere became even more magical as the sun set on Pebble Island Beach. The sound of waves crashing on the shore and the music playing in the background created perfect harmony.

Lauren had cooked her famous BBQ ribs, which everyone couldn't wait to try, and Ella had prepared her signature potato salad, which was always a hit.

As the night went on, more and more people arrived, and the party became livelier.

Lauren introduced Ella to her work colleagues, who just loved Ella's English accent and friendly personality, with the evening ending with a surprise fireworks display put on by one of the partygoers.

"What an amazing evening," remarked Ella's mother as they all walked back to Lauren's apartment, feeling tired but satisfied by the delicious food and several bottles of wine.

Chapter 22

It was difficult to bid Lauren farewell, especially for Mum. However, it was time to leave and return home to England's cold and damp winter weather. Mum was reluctant to leave Lauren, but Ella could sense that she was eager to return to her little haven, Buckland Ridge, which she will, and always call home.

Their brief stopover in Dubai, which lasted only 36 hours, gave them little opportunity to explore the country's beauty and culture. Nevertheless, they were fortunate to stay in a luxurious five-star hotel once again with tremendous views of the city's iconic skyline.

So many expensive cars like Maserati's and Lamborghinis, cruising on the wide streets was astounding. Even with her lottery winnings, Ella knew such extravagance was beyond her means.

The famous Burj Khalifa, the world's tallest tower, stood tall above everything else, and Ella took advantage of the opportunity to snap many photos to share with those back home.

Returning home amid cold, wet and windy weather was expected after leaving behind the heat of Australia.

However, lighting the log burner, snuggling up with Sammy, knowing he enjoyed his stay with Jo and her family, brought a sense of continued contentment.

Today's plan was to visit the restaurant quickly to make sure everything was ship shape and Bristol fashion, as they say, in readiness of opening once again after two months holiday shut down, but importantly, having a catch up with Jo.

As Ella glanced at her phone, there was a message saying that Jo had something important to tell her and would meet her at the restaurant shortly.

As Ella sat at the table, waiting in anticipation, her fingers idly tapping on the smooth surface, she went over in her mind the details of

Jo's message and couldn't help but wonder what this important news could be.

Her mind whirled with curiosity and apprehension as she awaited Jo's arrival.

Was she going through a tough time? Or perhaps the opposite and something exciting had happened in her life?

The uncertainty made Ella feel anxious, but at the same time, trying to stay positive and hopeful.

Finally, Jo walked in, and both girls embraced warmly.

Jo seemed a little nervous but also eager to talk.

Suddenly, Jo took a deep breath and looked Ella straight in the eyes.

"There is something I have to tell you," she said, sounding serious.

Ella felt her heart rate increase, anticipating what was to come.

However, as Jo spoke, Ella discovered that her worries were unfounded.

Jo had exciting news to share – she was engaged!

They embraced and laughed with relief and joy.

"Is Ryan the lucky guy," Ella asked.

"Of course," Jo replied, sounding a bit smug.

Who else!

Ella couldn't help but notice the glow of happiness on Jo's face.

Jo's eyes sparkled with excitement as she said her parents were happy about the engagement.

Jo moved closer to Ella, proudly showing off her stunning diamond solitaire ring. The precious stone shone brilliantly, enhancing her fingers' elegance and perfectly manicured nails.

"What's the big plan then?" Ella inquired.

During their heart-to-heart conversation, Jo couldn't contain her excitement as she shared her plans to move to Canada with Ryan to start a new chapter of her life. She spoke about looking forward to exploring Canada's diverse landscapes, immersing herself in its rich culture, and taking advantage of the country's many opportunities.

Ella listened attentively to Jo's concerns about moving to a new country, offering her sincere friendship and support.

Despite understanding Jo's fears, Ella felt inspired by her courage to pursue her dreams.

As they chatted, the two girls agreed that life was full of endless possibilities and that it was essential to follow one's heart to live a fulfilling and meaningful life. They talked about their experiences together and how they had always supported each other through thick and thin.

Ella reassured Jo that she would always be there for her, no matter what challenges she faced in her new life.

Jo felt grateful for Ella's support, and they both agreed that their friendship was a valuable asset they cherished.

Jo was feeling a mixture of excitement and worry as she thought about her beloved horse, Jellybean.

Who would take care of Jellybean?

He can be quite a handful if not nurtured correctly, and Jo knew that he would be too much for her Mum and Dad to handle on a daily basis.

Jo's love for Jellybean was immense, and she wanted to ensure he would be in good hands without her.

Quick thinking Jo suddenly remembered that a local girl had been taking care of him when she was away backpacking.

She had become a trusted friend and carer for Jellybean, cleaning his stable, grooming, feeding him, and taking him for canters across the moors.

Jellybean has always been Jo's faithful companion, and Jo knew that if he were content and happy with someone, he would instinctively take a liking to them.

Jo's Mum also said that his new carer had received the Jellybean nudge, indicating that he trusted her to provide him with the best care and attention.

Jo was adamant that she would return home to be with him if anything unfortunate happened. He had always been there for her when she needed him and always there for her when she felt lonely or down.

Although sad about leaving Jellybean behind, Ella realised that Jo was about to make the most important decision of her life, but care arrangements for Jellybean had to be part of that, too.

Suddenly, Ella called out, "who is going to sort out my accounts?
"

No worries, Ella!

Mum said she would take over your books at no cost.

She would be only too pleased to help because it would give her something more to do than feed chickens, round up the six sheep, and make endless cups of tea for Dad.

Upon careful observation, Ella couldn't help but notice that Jo was standing at a significant crossroads in her life, faced with crucial decisions that would change her future.

Driven by a strong sense of responsibility and concern for her friend, Ella felt compelled to ensure that Jo was equipped with all the necessary guidance to make well-informed and sound choices, and if she needed a friend, Ella would be there.

With her parents' unwavering support, Jo is looking forward to starting a new chapter in her life with Ryan by her side.

What's even more exciting is that Ryan recently qualified as a lawyer and secured a stable job just outside his hometown of Banff.

Jo is optimistic about their future, and his career prospects look bright.

But that's not all - Jo has always had a passion for business and is determined to turn her dream of becoming a Business Consultant into a reality.

Following a successful job interview conducted over Zoom, she eagerly anticipates the opportunity to land a role within a prominent organization located close to Ryan's office in Banff ultimately enabling her to achieve her career aspirations also.

Chapter 23

It has been three weeks since Jo left for Canada, and Ella has been acutely aware of the changes in her life and those of her closest friends.

Tilly, for instance, has found love and contentment with her partner Maddie in the southern region of France and Jo is now living in Canada permanently with her fiancé Ryan.

During her most recent visit, it was immediately apparent that Lauren had settled into her new life in Australia quite comfortably. She has immersed herself in the local culture, forming solid and meaningful connections with the people around her.

Her vibrant and joyful demeanour reflects her deep sense of contentment in her new home, Down Under. It's clear that Lauren has fully embraced her new surroundings, and the love and happiness she radiates are a testament to her thriving in Australia with no intention of returning.

Back at Buckland Ridge, Ella is staying put and going nowhere, for now anyway, with 'Tastebuds' preparing for yet another busy time.

Fresh menus have recently been printed and prominently displayed inside and outside the restaurant.

Mum, as always, is bustling around the kitchen, preparing and cooking various delectable dishes, such as savoury quiches, hearty bowls of chilli, and tasty lasagne dishes, all locally sourced, of course!

Meanwhile, Ella is making wholesome loaves of bread for the midday lunches and a variety of scones for the afternoon teas.

A very busy lunchtime, but everything was ticking over as it should when the phone started ringing.

Ella's hurried footsteps echoed through the restaurant as she approached the front desk to answer the phone.

The caller asked if he could speak to Ella Manning.

Without missing a beat, Ella responded, giving her name.

The caller introduced himself as Tim Henderson and informed her that he had been sent by his office, which had requested him to carry out a Health and Hygiene Inspection at Tastebuds.

Without showing any signs of surprise, Ella responded in a composed tone, conveying that she had been eagerly awaiting a visit from the department in question.

The Inspector proposed Friday for the visit, to which Ella agreed, asking for an exact time as Fridays are usually the busiest.

He began to explain that he needed to observe the restaurant in full operation to assess the cleanliness and efficiency of the restaurant's operations and that he couldn't give Ella an exact time of his arrival.

Ella felt a sense of unease as she hung up the phone and nervously sat down, unsure of what to expect.

While her restaurant had a reputation for serving high-quality food, she couldn't help but worry if the Inspector would agree.

Her business could be at risk, and she needed to do everything in her power to ensure it met the Inspector's standards.

Ella was determined to ensure that every aspect of the restaurant looked absolutely flawless, from the interior to the exterior. To achieve this, she contacted a couple of villagers and asked them, with great kindness, if they would mow the lawns, tend to the herb garden, and place potted olive tree plants by each entrance.

She also wanted the delightful fragrance of lavender to welcome customers as they stepped inside.

Thankfully, the weather was behaving itself, and despite Easter being just around the corner, the temperature was slightly higher than usual for this time of year.

Lambs were starting to appear in the nearby fields, the grass was getting greener every day, and the birds were chirping with the sounds of spring.

The transparent River Felling was flowing over the rocky terrain, with just a few leaves floating downstream in a very organised manner.

Everything looked beautiful.

The day arrived for the arrival of the Food Inspector, and at almost one o'clock, Ella heard a car pull up alongside the restaurant.

A smart, tall man appeared, carrying a clipboard and a mobile phone.

Ella approached him and introduced herself.

Hello! My name is Tim Henderson, the Food and Hygiene Inspector, and I am here to evaluate and inspect your restaurant for cleanliness and safety.

The location of your establishment is absolutely stunning, he told her, and the sight of the River Felling flowing beside your restaurant is simply captivating.

You certainly chose a beautiful location for this exquisite restaurant.

She told him that with the right amount of effort, she could turn it into something truly magical.

Ella went on to say that her goal was not just to renovate the derelict building but to significantly enhance the area's charm and make it a destination that people from near and far would be drawn to.

With unwavering determination and a passion for her dream, she opened 'Tastebuds,' turning her vision into a reality.

Well, he said, "you have certainly done that".

Having made several notes regarding the location, he asked if he could take a short tour of the outside area.

"Of course, let me know if you need anything," she said with a slightly nervous tone in her voice.

Ella informed him that she would be inside with the customers who were departing slowly before the afternoon tea session commenced at four o'clock. She always preferred to say goodbye to them and express gratitude for their patronage.

He reassured Ella that there was no need to rush and asked her to take her time while he took some notes.

He mentioned that the inspection would take little time if everything went as planned.

Soon after, the inspector walked inside the restaurant and spoke with Ella, and she could tell he was impressed by what he saw.

He complimented her on the herb garden, mentioning that it was a lovely addition to the restaurant, which looked exceptional and very well maintained.

Everything looked fresh and up to the mark.

Ella replied light-heartedly, saying, "We aim to please!"

The inspector smiled warmly at her and stood beside her again with a twinkle in his eye.

During his inspection, he showed a keen interest in the kitchen area, taking detailed notes and snapping several pictures with his phone.

Ella remained quiet and allowed him to continue his assessment.

As he explored the restaurant further, the inspector observed that the customers appeared very content and happy, and at one point, he even approached one lady and asked her if she had enjoyed her lunch.

In response, she praised the restaurant with glowing words by saying, "this establishment is the best for miles. The food is exceptional, and the staff are incredibly accommodating and attentive".

The lady said she would return and bring a few of her friends from the local Women's Institute Flower Group along on her next visit, mentioning that everyone should know about this fantastic and homely restaurant.

After thoroughly inspecting all of the meticulously maintained and organised spaces, he informed Ella that the assessment was complete.

The Inspector was thrilled to present Ella with the Certificate of Excellence, the highest rating a business can receive. This confirmed it was a distinguished and highly recommended establishment. Ella was so excited that she almost stumbled to the floor, overwhelmed with joy and appreciation. Winning such a prestigious award was beyond her wildest dreams, especially considering she had only been in business for less than 18 months. This was an incredible honour that she would cherish forever and a testament to her hard work and dedication, not forgetting her mother's dedication and input too.

After Ella expressed gratitude for his time, he mentioned that he might consider returning to this beautiful location to enjoy a meal for himself.

Without hesitation, Ella replied hastily, "Please feel free to visit anytime. You would be most welcome."

"Would your reservation be for one or two?" asked Ella inquisitively. "Just for one."

"Perhaps we could have a drink together if you're not too busy," he said, replying with a friendly smile.

The unexpected invitation took Ella aback, and she didn't know how to respond.

She cautiously replied, "That would be nice," mindful of her past mistakes with Hugo and not wanting to appear too forward.

As Tim Henderson bid farewell to Ella, he took a moment to express his genuine admiration for her restaurant's potential for success.

He highlighted how impressed he was with the many customers who travelled miles to experience fresh and home-cooked food. Tim mentioned how the restaurant's focus on healthy dining was a major draw for customers seeking a wholesome and delicious dining experience. His parting compliment left Ella confident and motivated to continue delivering exceptional service to her loyal customer base.

He also praised the great location, which he believed would contribute to its popularity and success.

After getting into his car, he mentioned that he would call soon to book a table. Ella was left with a plethora of questions, pondering if there was an ulterior motive behind his request to have lunch at her restaurant so soon after his last visit.

Was he interested in the bustling activity of the restaurant, or was there more to his intentions?

After a hectic Friday that proved to be successful, Ella and her mother were grateful for some much-needed downtime to unwind.

They finished their afternoon teas, embracing a sense of calm and contentment, cherishing the memories of their productive day.

Chapter 24

As Ella walked through the beautifully kept restaurant gardens, she was immediately struck by the natural beauty surrounding her. The green foliage with blossoming buds suggested new growth, and the colourful vegetables growing in the fertile soil under the warm sun were visually stunning, while the fragrant herbs added another layer of sensory pleasure. The gentle flow of the nearby river completed the peaceful and serene atmosphere, making it a truly spectacular experience that left her feeling rejuvenated.

The sense of happiness that this particular place brought to her was absolutely irrefutable, and she simply couldn't imagine herself living anywhere else but here.

As Easter draws near, Ella realises she must prepare the restaurant for the upcoming busy season. However, her mind appears to be preoccupied with other matters.

Ella found herself consumed by thoughts of the visit of the Food Inspector, Tim Henderson, wondering if he would call her and make a reservation at the restaurant.

Despite her attempts to focus on the daily running of the restaurant, she couldn't help but secretly hope for another chance to meet with him once again.

Confused and uncertain, she questioned the reasons behind her constant thoughts, asking herself, "Why was she thinking this way?"

Ella could not resist acknowledging his undeniable handsomeness and charm.

Regardless of her attempts to focus on other things, thoughts of him lingered in her mind, making it difficult to concentrate on anything else.

However, she needed to proceed cautiously, trying to avoid getting her hopes up too high and risk being disappointed like she had been before with Hugo and not wanting to make the same mistake again!

Today was going to be a good day, she thought to herself.

Having rearranged tables outside in the glorious sunshine, with many of the locals enjoying a lunch of fish pie, with new potatoes and a fresh green salad from the restaurant garden, nothing was going to spoil this wonderful day, or so she thought.

Ella glanced at her phone and noticed a message from Jo's mother.

Her eyes quickly filled with tears as she read the text.

It was a very sad text to read, but at that moment, Ella's mother rushed over and asked in a gentle tone what was wrong.

Ella explained that Jellybean, Jo's beloved horse, had broken his leg while exercising with the stable hand that morning.

Because of Jellybean's age and the severity of his injury, undergoing surgery and recovery would be lengthy and might not yield positive results.

The vet had determined that the kindest decision was to euthanise Jellybean. This news left Ella completely heartbroken, especially knowing that her friend Jo was miles away and unable to be present during this difficult moment.

Despite the heavy weight of grief that enveloped her, Ella took a deep breath, clutching her car keys tightly. With a determined voice, she turned to her mother and informed her of her intention to visit Jo's parents. "I want to be there for them," she said during this incredibly difficult time.

Her mother, understanding the gravity of the situation, reassured her. "Don't worry, Ella. I'll take care of everything at the restaurant. Go and be there for Jo's parents. They'll need someone to lean on."

Upon entering Jo's home, Ella immediately sensed the heavy and sombre atmosphere.

Jo's parents, their faces marked with visible anguish, approached her with tears in their eyes. It was genuinely heart-wrenching to witness the profound sorrow that gripped them as they shared the devastating news that Jellybean had been peacefully laid to rest.

Jo's father's voice, quivering with emotion, lovingly recounted the vivid memories of Jellybean's long and vibrant life. He expressed disbelief at the tragic turn of events, unable to comprehend how a simple fall could have led to such a devastating outcome. His words were filled with deep sorrow, a testament to the irreplaceable void left by Jellybean's departure.

Ella wondered how Jo would handle the news so far away but was told that Jo had received the devastating news, and as you can imagine, she was distraught and in a state of shock.

They comforted her with the assurance that he was now pain-free, advising her to stay put and cherish the fond memories she shared with Jellybean.

The day had such a delightful beginning however, it had ended so very tragically.

As Ella bid farewell to Jo's parents, they expressed their heartfelt gratitude for her kindness, support and thoughtfulness over Jellybean's death.

That evening, despite the seven-hour time difference, Ella Facetimed Jo in Banff.

However, the conversation took an emotional turn when they discussed the sad death of Jellybean.

Fortunately, Ryan was there to comfort and support Jo, who sincerely appreciated his help during this difficult time.

She also thanked Ella for comforting her parents who too were very upset by the sad events.

"Thank you, Ella, for being an amazing friend!" she said.

Jo had difficulty discussing Jellybean, so she changed the conversation to Ryan's friend Tyler, who had recently relocated to Montana, a beautiful part of the North American mountain states region renowned for its stunning landscapes, including the Great Falls, Glacier National Park, and Yellowstone National Park.

Ella spoke with excitement as she told Ella about Tyler's relocation, emphasizing that this move began an exhilarating new chapter in his life. Unfortunately, upon Tyler's return from his backpacking expedition with Ryan, his engagement with his fiancée ended. One can't help but wonder if the time spent apart during the expedition played a role in the change of their feelings upon his return. Who knows!

Thankfully, Tyler has now moved on and found employment at a City Hospital just outside Billings and relishes life to the fullest. He keeps in touch with Ryan and assures him that he has never been happier in his personal life and enjoys his role as a junior doctor.

He told them that after spending time in Chamonix, he gained clarity in his life.

Taking a break from his girlfriend had its benefits, as it made him realise that absence doesn't always make the heart grow fonder - a first-hand lesson Tyler learned.

After their emotional Facetime call, the girls promised to contact each other again very soon.

As the call ended, Ella couldn't help but feel a sense of hope that Jo would eventually find some comfort after Jellybean's tragic end. Grief impacts us differently, but Ella believed that with time, Jo would gradually find it easier to cope with the loss of someone so dear.

With the Easter period well and truly out of the way for another year, the restaurant is once again thriving.

More and more customers are visiting to savour the delicious menu.

In the meantime, Ella had noticed a change in her Mum's behaviour after she confessed to feeling tired, but she continued to work diligently to ensure the restaurant's success.

Ella suggested that her mother take it easy while working in the kitchen and reassured her that plenty of people were available to help.

Although her mother brushed off her concerns and said she would ask for help if needed, Ella emphasised the importance of her mother's well-being, sharing a warm embrace.

Even so, Ella kept a close eye on her mother to ensure she didn't overexert herself.

Chapter 25

It was a lovely summer day in Buckland Ridge, where the village eagerly awaited the annual Flower Show.

This event was a significant highlight of the year, and locals warmly welcomed visitors from far and wide.

However, the influx of cars and coaches into the small community posed a significant challenge. Nevertheless, the weather was perfect, and the playing fields were adorned with tents, creating an idyllic backdrop for the Annual Flower Show and its many attractions.

When Ella was asked to bring her delicious cakes and scones to exhibit in the Refreshments Tent, she enthusiastically accepted without hesitation.

She saw this as an opportunity to generate additional income alongside her restaurant business.

As Ella was preparing to carefully pack the freshly baked cakes and pastries for the flower show, she suddenly looked behind and noticed a familiar car parked just alongside the entrance of the restaurant garden.

Despite the familiarity of the car, she couldn't quite place where she had seen it before. Shrugging off the thought, Ella began arranging the cakes in her car's spacious boot, ensuring each delicate creation was secure for the journey to the Flower Show.

The stunning array of flowers, fresh herbs, and even vegetables was going to make the Flower Show the best year ever.

Even the local press attended to showcase the event.

As a local reporter strolled to the refreshments tent, Ella offered him a slice of her homemade lemon drizzle cake on a paper plate, proudly stating that she had baked all the cakes herself.

As Ella was about to explore the show, the reporter tapped her on the shoulder and complimented her on the delightful cake.

He promised to return for another slice after he had taken photographs of the prize-giving event.

Ella jokingly replied, "If there's any left."

As Ella wandered leisurely through the beautiful and vibrant Flower Show grounds, she saw Tim Henderson making his way toward the entrance of the expansive marquee.

A thought sparked in her mind: Did the car Ella noticed earlier parked outside the restaurant belong to Tim Henderson?

This notion piqued her curiosity, prompting her to consider the possibility as she continued her stroll amidst the delightful scenery of the Flower Show.

Ella warmly greeted him as he approached, and they engaged in light-hearted conversation for some time.

During their chat, he mentioned his struggle to find parking for his car, expressing his hope that she wouldn't be inconvenienced by his decision to park alongside the restaurant entrance. She responded with a cheerful assurance, "Not at all."

Tim inquired about the restaurant's performance during the busy Easter period, to which Ella replied enthusiastically that it did very well, exceptional in fact.

Out of the blue, she asked him why he hadn't called to book a table as he had promised.

He explained that his busy work schedule had made it impossible to arrange anything, but now that he was here, he would like to reserve a table for himself next week.

"Just for one," Ella asked inquisitively.

"Yes, that's correct, unless you would like to join me," speaking rather flirtatiously.

Ella started blushing, slightly embarrassed, turning her head to the side.

During this hectic time of year, and with the restaurant bustling with customers, Ella made a mental note to check the bookings, making sure there would be a table available for him.

Leaving the Flower Show, he provided her with his mobile number, for which Ella was grateful and promised to contact him soon.

He explained that he was excited to return as a customer instead of the Food Inspector.

Once again, Ella blushed profusely as she thanked him for popping along to the

Flower Show and also showing interest in her restaurant.

"Perhaps we will see each other next week," he shouted.

"Maybe", Ella said.

Taking a slight detour back to the restaurant, Ella impatiently unlocked the door and walked over to the counter where the reservations were made.

After checking, she could see an available table for the following Wednesday at 1 o'clock.

She was still determining whether to call him immediately or wait a little longer.

Eventually, she decided to call the number he had given her, hoping the day and time were convenient to him.

He responded positively, expressing his interest in having an aperitif before lunch and invited her to join him.

Feeling bashful and slightly overwhelmed by his comments, she expressed her gratitude and took a moment to consider her response. After a brief pause, she suggested that a pre-lunch drink would be very enjoyable.

With everything sorted with Tim, Ella made her way back home.

As Ella walked through the front door, she noticed her mother sitting in her favourite old chair, which was now showing signs of wear and tear.

She kindly suggested getting a new chair with the addition of new, fresh and comfortable cushions.

Her mother was relentless in her decision to keep the cherished chair, a piece that had been a fixture in the family home for many years. Ella felt that the chair possibly held sentimental memories, perhaps dating back to when her father was still alive. As the evening progressed, Ella noticed that her mother appeared visibly fatigued and gently advised her to get an early night's rest.

The next morning, Ella prepared breakfast and offered her mother some muesli with fresh fruit and yoghurt.

Her mother's voice sounded weak when she replied that she would be down for breakfast shortly.

Finally, when her mother eventually walked down to the kitchen, Ella noticed a distressed look on her face and asked if anything was wrong.

After a slight pause, her mother then revealed that she had noticed a lump on her right breast during her shower the previous morning and felt that she needed to get it checked out.

Ella adamantly agreed and suggested that they make an appointment with the doctor right away.

However, Ella couldn't stop thinking about her mother and began feeling very afraid. Could it be the awful 'C' word?

They would only know after visiting the doctor and undergoing tests.

The following day, in the late afternoon, Mum received her appointment, and they drove to the surgery with apprehension and fear, unsure of what to expect. After a thorough examination, Mum was referred to the hospital for further scans and tests.

The waiting was the most challenging part, as they were both unsure of the outcome.

Despite her worries, Ella ensured that everything at the restaurant ran smoothly, which gave Mum the chance to rest if she felt exhausted.

The following day, Tim arrived at the restaurant as planned, looking smart in a blue blazer, white shirt, and jeans.

Ella escorted Tim to a cozy corner table by the window overlooking the picturesque garden. They settled into their seats, and Ella gracefully poured a glass of aromatic red wine for Tim and a refreshing elderflower mocktail for herself. As they sipped their drinks, Ella gently broached the topic of her mother's recent health scare, her voice tinged with concern and vulnerability. Tim leaned in attentively, offering words of empathy and reassurance. He expressed his willingness to lend support and an empathetic ear during this uncertain time, emphasizing that she could rely on him whenever needed.

Ella recalled having said the exact words to Hugo in the past.

Tim departed from the restaurant after a delightful lunch and expressed his gratitude to Ella for the exceptional hospitality provided by her and the staff.

"You must visit again soon," she suggested.

"Definitely," he replied, mentioning that he hoped her mother's health would improve soon.

After a couple of weeks, Mum received some news that wasn't what she had hoped for.

The results showed that she had a malignant tumour on her right breast, and it was unfortunately advanced.

The prognosis was not good, and nothing could be done to change the situation.

Despite this, Mum remained positive and tried to live her life to the fullest as much as she could.

However, after several weeks of chemotherapy, Mum's condition appeared to worsen, and the treatment didn't seem to be working as well as the doctors had hoped.

Ella received additional help at the restaurant so she could spend more time with her Mum as much as possible.

After hearing from Ella that Mum's health had deteriorated, Lauren made the tough decision to fly back to the UK to be by her side. The hospital in Melbourne granted her compassionate leave, allowing her to take as much time off as necessary to be with her mother during this difficult time.

As soon as Lauren arrived, Mum held out her arms and sat up in bed to caress her daughter despite being exceptionally weak.

Having Lauren back home was like having an angel sent from heaven.

Ella was deeply grateful for Lauren's exceptional nursing skills. Lauren cared for Mum remarkably professionally and compassionately, and Ella couldn't imagine how she would have managed without her.

As sisters, they were always very close, but now, with the deterioration of Mum's health both Ella and Lauren have become inseparable, having to make important decisions together.

Occasionally, Lauren would pop over to the restaurant and give a hand, waiting on the tables, whilst Ella was back home comforting and making many cups of tea for her Mum, who had lost a considerable amount of weight, but Ella did her best to entice her with some of the fancy cakes from the restaurant, which she appeared to relish.

Chapter 26

After a few weeks of complete worry, Mum declined steadily and now constantly remains in bed, with a specialised nurse calling twice daily to relieve her pain.

Both girls were preparing themselves for the worst outcome.

Even Sammy knew something wasn't quite right, as he tried to sniff underneath her bedroom door, but Ella tried her best not to encourage him to enter due to all the drugs and sterilised areas in her room.

"Good dog, Sammy," Ella would say.

Ella cuddled him tightly and took him back downstairs.

At eight-thirty that evening, the Nurse came downstairs and told us that Mum had fallen into a deep sleep and to prepare ourselves.

Lauren and Ella cried uncontrollably and decided they just wanted to be at her bedside.

They sat and held her hand for what seemed hours and hours, but it could only have been about 30 minutes when her hands began to feel cold.

Ella shouted for the nurse who was in the next room preparing medication, who quickly rushed to her bedside and checked her pulse.

Quietly and softly, she told them that she had peacefully passed away.

She was now sleeping and free of pain.

Ella and Lauren sat silently before saying their final goodbyes to the most loving mother anyone could have wished for.

With tears streaming down their faces, they embraced each other tightly. The weight of their loss was heavy, but they found solace in the knowledge that their dearest mother had left behind a lasting legacy of love that would continue to inspire and guide them for years to come. Despite the pain of their grief, they were grateful for the memories that would forever remain in their hearts.

It had been extremely hard running the restaurant during this very traumatic time following the sudden death of Ella's mother, but she expressed gratitude towards her committed staff, who had worked tirelessly to ensure everything ran smoothly.

Lauren pledged to support Ella until she was confident enough to manage the restaurant alone, regardless of the many obstacles she faces, and will only travel back to Australia when she knows her sister is ready to carry on.

Upon hearing about the death of Ella's Mum, Jo offered to help in any possible way and insisted on returning home to be with her friend.

At first, Ella refused her kind offer, feeling overwhelmed by the gesture. However, Jo's kindness deeply touched her when she said that she had booked a flight to London Airport scheduled for tomorrow.

After the emotional phone call, Ella hung up, eagerly anticipating her friend's arrival.

Despite the distance that separated them, Jo had made the effort to travel to be with her. Ella's heart swelled with gratitude and joy.

The following day both Ella and Lauren awaited Jo's arrival.

As they heard the taxi draw up outside, all three girls were overwhelmed by emotions, especially when introducing Jo to Lauren for the first time.

Ella, Jo, and Lauren gathered in the evening to reflect on the unfortunate events of the past year, which included the loss of Jellybean and, of course, the recent loss of their dear mother.

Curious about Lauren's experience in Australia, Jo asked her how she liked it. Lauren responded positively, mentioning the awe-inspiring scenery, excellent surfing opportunities, and beautiful climate, saying she couldn't ask for more.

Her voice changed suddenly when she spoke, saying there are times when homesickness takes hold, and she longs to be back in the UK, especially now, since the death of her mother.

She expressed concern for Ella, who is now living alone without any close family nearby.

Ella reassured her sister she was doing alright and was content and happy running her business.

She hopes to keep it going since she is now reaping the rewards of her hard work and dedication.

Amid the overwhelming sadness and tears, there were beautiful moments filled with heartfelt laughter as Ella fondly recalled the good times spent with Jo. The memories of their backpacking journey through Europe stood out, as it was a defining experience that solidified and strengthened their relationship.

"Do you have a boyfriend yet, Ella?" asked Jo. "No, I don't have time for that," replied Ella nervously.

"Well, you should make time," advised Jo. "Life is too short, and you're young, confident, and truly gorgeous. Someone is out there waiting for you."

Changing the subject, Ella said, "Another gin and tonic, anyone?"

Ella and Lauren were touched by the many people who attended their mother's funeral at St. Peter's Church to pay their respects to a wonderful and kind person.

She was an essential figure in the community, especially at the school where she had dedicated over 25 years of service. Her kind and generous nature had won many hearts, and she was always ready to lend a helping hand to those in need.

The sisters were proud of their mother's impact on others, and though the day was filled with tears, they also celebrated the life of a hardworking and loving mother who will always be remembered and never forgotten.

The restaurant was closed that day for the funeral, so they could host a buffet lunch for friends and family in the surroundings loved by their Mum.

As they prepared to serve their guests, the two sisters felt their mother's watchful presence hovering over them.

They knew that she would expect nothing but the best - from the sizzling hot food to the matching crockery. "That's Mum," they whispered to each other, taking comfort in her unwavering standards and guidance.

A small, joyful laugh assured them their mother was not far away.

Ella and Lauren received a friendly tap on their shoulders, reminding them that Jo would be departing to Canada the following day.

They expressed their gratitude towards Jo for helping them arrange the buffet and being there for them when they needed her.

Jo felt sad as she prepared to depart, but she reassured Ella that she would always be there for her. "You're so fortunate to have Jo as a friend," remarked Lauren, acknowledging Jo's unwavering support for Ella.

It has been precisely two weeks since Lauren left for Australia, and Ella now feels a sense of longing for her dear sister and with that comes a feeling of somewhat loneliness and isolation.

The restaurant is now her top priority, but as she steps into the kitchen where the culinary magic happens, she experiences a profound sadness as her mother is no longer present.

However, Tastebuds continues to thrive, and Ella works tirelessly to maintain the same level of success and quality that her mother instilled in her.

Tim Henderson had tried to contact her several times and offered assistance if needed.

Although there appeared to be no romantic connection between them, Ella felt grateful for his kindness and decided to call him to invite him to her home for a drink to express her gratitude.

He happily accepted, and they planned to meet the following Saturday evening.

As Saturday drew closer, Ella was now beginning to feel a little more like herself, but she had to make sure the relationship was strictly platonic and nothing else.

As arranged, at precisely 7 pm on Saturday, Ella answered the doorbell to find a pleasant surprise: a beautiful bouquet and a beaming smile from Tim.

He hoped the flowers would brighten her day, and she eagerly accepted them before arranging them in a vase.

As the night progressed, they found themselves completely engrossed in conversation, each sip of wine accompanied by a story or insight into their lives. They discussed the twists and turns that led them to where they were now, sharing their triumphs and challenges whilst enjoying each other's company.

As Tim prepared to leave, he thanked Ella and kissed her gently.

"We should do this again sometime," he said.

Ella's response was a noncommittal "perhaps," her mind a whirlwind of uncertainty and intrigue.

Chapter 27

Ella had been profoundly contemplating her relationship with Tim.

Their evening together was a significant event that she couldn't shake from her mind. Although they were just friends, she wondered if their relationship could be more than that.

However, Ella was mindful of avoiding repeating the same mistake she had made with Hugo.

She was cautious about adding any complications to her relationship with Tim, especially considering the other important things she had going on in her life. Running the restaurant was a big responsibility, and she was also dealing with the grief of losing her Mum.

Eventually, she disclosed her emotions to Tim by asking him to meet her at the restaurant.

After their heartfelt conversation, Ella felt a wave of relief and joy, knowing that they could continue to be close friends and nothing more at this stage.

After successfully resolving that issue with Tim, Ella finally found a moment to contemplate her future.

As she sat in the restaurant's quiet area, a question lingered: Was it feasible for her to continue managing and running the restaurant on her own?

Gathering her belongings, Ella prepared to head back home when the familiar ringtone of her phone rang out loudly.

Surprised to see Tilly's name on the caller ID, Ella swiftly answered with an eager "Hello Tilly, how are you?"

However, Tilly's response was laced with caution. Her voice carried a sombre tone as she relayed the news that Jo had informed her about the recent loss—the death of her beloved mother.

Overwhelmed with emotion, Ella's eyes welled up with tears again, her voice quivering as she vulnerably spoke to Tilly about the profound impact her mother's absence had brought into her life.

Tilly spoke very caringly to Ella, saying that although both she and Maddie had only met her mother once, they were very much taken by the kindness shown to them on their visit to Buckland Ridge.

Ella was grateful for Tilly's genuine concern and empathy as she continued to struggle with her grief. Tilly offered her support and assistance, assuring Ella that she was there for her whenever she needed to talk or simply have someone to listen.

Recognizing the critical importance of prioritizing self-care during such a challenging period, Tilly thoughtfully proposed that Ella take a short holiday to visit her and Maddie in France. She believed that spending time with close friends in a comforting and supportive environment would be immensely helpful for her.

Ella was comforted by Tilly's kind words and appreciated her offer, hoping to take her up on it soon.

Still wrestling with indecision, Ella finds herself pondering the uncertainty of her future, a task that has suddenly grown overwhelming.

She needs guidance, hoping to make the right decision either way.

For Ella, this realisation is a bitter pill to swallow. The restaurant, a symbol of her aspirations and a testament to her love for her mother was meant to be a means to success.

Working alongside her Mum was a delightful experience for Ella, and their combined efforts resulted in a noticeable feeling of satisfaction.

As they ran the establishment, both wore proud smiles on their faces, and the contentment they shared was immeasurable.

Life is so very different now without her, Ella thought to herself.

The thought of selling her restaurant and potentially her home had become unbearable for Ella, and she required time to evaluate all the best options before committing to a decision she might regret.

Enthusiastically, Ella decided to take up Tilly's offer and fly over to Antibes, giving her some time to clear her head of many decisions.

Tilly was thrilled to hear the news and, during a Facetime chat, offered to meet Ella at the airport, saying she could stay for as long as she wanted.

Arrangements were made and Ella was feeling excited about her trip.

"See you next Saturday," Ella said, sounding more cheerful.

Feeling confident in her capable staff, Ella was reassured that she could entrust the restaurant's operation to them with complete confidence in their abilities, but she also needed to thank the staff for their constant support and kindness during challenging times.

Still, she had to ensure that her top priority was for her staff to warmly greet loyal customers and ensure timely delivery of fresh produce while she was away.

After ensuring Jo's parents would look after Sammy, Ella felt relieved and was finally ready to leave for Antibes.

She eagerly boarded the plane with excitement and anticipation, knowing that she was leaving behind the stresses of daily life and stepping into a more relaxed and carefree atmosphere.

Upon her arrival at Nice Airport, Ella was greeted by a wave of intense heat emanating from the tarmac.

Despite feeling slightly overcome, she couldn't help but feel a twinge of excitement at the prospect of experiencing a different climate and being with her friends once again.

As she carefully stepped off the plane, the temperature soared to a scorching 30 degrees Celsius, starkly contrasting with the cooler 17 degrees Celsius she had left behind in the United Kingdom.

Yet, as the sun's warmth encircled her, Ella couldn't help but feel a sense of contentment.

She imagined what it would be like to live in this idyllic setting, surrounded by palm trees and the sparkling Mediterranean Sea.

The endless possibilities ahead made her ponder if her life would lead to the picturesque South of France or possibly Australia, something which has constantly been on her mind.

As soon as Tilly spotted Ella walking through airport arrivals, she rushed to hug and kiss her while Maddie kindly took her suitcase and affectionately touched her shoulder. The three of them chatted non-stop during the drive home.

Once Ella had unpacked, they opened champagne to celebrate her lottery win.

"Congratulations, Ella!

We're both very happy for you," they said.

Tilly then asked Ella if she had any plans.

Ella began telling them that after investing a large portion of her winnings in the restaurant and with its remarkable success, she now feels that something is missing without her Mum.

She confided to Tilly and Maddie, revealing her ongoing struggle with the decision to sell 'Tastebuds.'

Ella recognised that selling the restaurant could be attractive to potential buyers due to its ongoing success, but she felt sad at the thought of letting go of something that had held such significant value in her life.

She understood the importance of carefully considering her choices before making drastic decisions, and both Tilly and Maddie agreed with her.

Although the restaurant had been Ella's idea from the beginning, her mother was a strong motivator for its success.

Ella acknowledges that the restaurant will always have a special place in her heart because of the cherished memories it has created, and yes, Ella needed to make the right decision.

During a conversation with Tilly and Maddie, Ella opened up about her feelings and the loss of her mother.

Tilly and Maddie did their best to offer comfort and support, reminding Ella of the beautiful memories she'll always have.

Ella was deeply touched by their kindness and expressed her gratitude, saying, "Thank you both so much.

Ella's heartfelt words resonated with emotion as she expressed that each passing day was becoming more manageable. She gratefully acknowledged the support of her wonderful friends, including our Canadian friend Jo, and with a gentle giggle, she added, "Having amazing friends like yourselves helps me stay strong."

During their conversation, Tilly began showing genuine concern for Jo's well-being and expressed her hope that Jo and Ryan would enjoy their life in Canada.

In response, Ella said Jo appeared happy and contented with her new life.

Ella went on to mention that Jo had recently flown to London to be with her and her sister Lauren following the death of their mother.

Jo had been an immense source of comfort and support during the funeral, providing much-needed assistance to the family.

Whilst sipping a refreshing chilled glass of champagne, she admired the stunning bougainvillea draped across the white-washed walls.

Reflecting on her past experiences, including the failed relationship with Hugo, winning the lottery, the purchase of 'Tastebuds,' and the loss of her mother, Ella pondered her next steps in life whilst enjoying the warm Mediterranean evening sunshine and feeling very relaxed which was something she hadn't felt in a long time.

She turned around and saw Maddie finishing a painting while Tilly prepared a cold meat platter and salad for dinner.

Although cooking wasn't Tilly's forte, she did her best to improve her culinary skills, and to be honest, she wasn't bad.

After dinner, the girls strolled along the promenade's white-paved pathway and stopped for a refreshing gin and tonic at the Sunshine bar, a favourite of both Tilly and Maddie's.

Tilly savoured the cool, refreshing sip of her perfectly mixed gin and tonic. She had just finished creating a delightful dinner for Maddie and Ella, and now, at last, she could settle down and indulge in a thoroughly earned moment of peace and relaxation.

With only a few days remaining before returning to the UK, Ella was determined to make the most of her time with Tilly and Maddie.

Without hesitation, Ella revealed that she had a small gift for them.

Ella had been thinking about what to give her dear friends for a while, knowing that although they were content and happy together, their casual earnings sometimes made finances somewhat tight.

Ella gathered her closest friends around her on the patio and shared her desire to transfer 10,000 euros to Tilly's bank account, with the understanding that it would be shared with Maddie.

She expressed gratitude for their unwavering support and friendship during difficult times.

Ella encouraged her friends to use the funds to do something special for themselves, whether travelling to new places or indulging in small luxuries that could enhance their daily lives.

Tilly and Maddie found themselves taken aback by Ella's sudden monetary gift and momentarily were lost for words.

The silence hung heavily in the air until Tilly finally found her voice and softly said, "You didn't need to do that," her eyes locked on Ella's face.

Calmly, Ella replied, "There's something priceless about seeing such happiness and having such wonderful friends, and no amount of money could ever replace that feeling."

The sincerity in her words was palpable, and Tilly and Maddie felt Ella's warmth and kindness surrounding them.

They embraced Ella, showing their gratitude and thanking her for her generosity.

The following day, Tilly and Maddie arranged a delightful beachside dinner on Ella's final night as a small token of appreciation for her kindness and generosity.

They came equipped with their trusty portable BBQ and eagerly began to cook some Savoury beef burgers and juicy sausages. The refreshing sound of the gentle waves and the sight of happy couples strolling hand in hand under the starry night sky made the atmosphere genuinely enchanting.

The girls spent their evening relishing delectable food and chilled wine as they basked in the serene ambiance of the sunset.

Suddenly, a loud noise interrupted their peaceful moment and caused Ella to jump in alarm.

Initially, she thought the sound was similar to the rushing snow slide, just like she had experienced in Chamonix, but the circumstances obviously proved otherwise.

Tilly observed Ella's unease and inquired about her well-being.

Ella hesitantly revealed that she has struggled with anxiety ever since the terrifying avalanche incident. Sudden loud noises often trigger intense fear and apprehension within her. However, despite this ongoing challenge, she remained determined to overcome her anxiety.

As Ella glanced up at the dark, starry sky, she suddenly noticed a series of fireworks lighting the night in a dazzling symphony of vibrant colours and radiant light. The captivating performance left her feeling completely entranced and peaceful.

In that enchanting moment, she discovered herself enveloped in an overwhelming sense of serenity and calmness, the anxiety stemming from that dreadful incident in Chamonix slowly dissipating from her thoughts.

The following day, Ella had packed her bags and was ready to leave the charming resort of Antibes.

Tilly, however, wished she could stay longer. Ella reminded her that she still had a restaurant to manage, but Tilly assured her that she was always welcome to stay whenever she wanted.

Saying goodbye to her dear friends was very emotional, and as she boarded her flight to Manchester, where a coach was waiting to take her back to Buckland Ridge, she realised how much she was going to miss them.

Upon returning home, Ella hurriedly headed towards her restaurant, feeling anxious. However, there was no need as she was relieved to see that the restaurant was clean, lively, and filled with customers enjoying their afternoon tea.

In a rush, Ella headed to the kitchen and noticed the staff working diligently to clean down the work surfaces before leaving for the day.

The head chef whom Ella had appointed before leaving for France had done an excellent job, with many clients reporting positive feedback.

Ella was impressed with their dedication and attention to detail and took a moment to commend them on a job well done.

As Ella watched her team working hard, she couldn't help but wonder if her mother, who had played a significant role in building the restaurant's success, would approve of her selling it.

She felt grateful for their efforts and became confident in the staff's capabilities.

This made her consider revising her previous thoughts about the restaurant's future.

Chapter 28

Ella decided to pick up some accounts from the restaurant before heading back home after her flight and was surprised to see Tim walking towards her. "Hello," she called out. "How are you?"

"Good," he said elatedly.

Tim acknowledged that he just wanted to ensure she was okay, as he called the restaurant last week but learned she was taking a restful break.

Ella couldn't believe it; she thought Tim had read her mind!

She had been thinking about him on her flight home, thinking how nice it would be to catch up.

He suggested meeting at the Stags Head for a drink the following evening.

"Sure, that sounds good," she replied.

However, Ella mentioned that she couldn't stay chatting because she needed to pick up Sammy from a friend's house and was eager to do so because she had missed him and knew he would be excited to see her.

Ella frantically waved goodbye to Tim and called out, "See you tomorrow!"

Walking up the winding path to Jo's parent's house, Ella noticed Sammy playing in the sprawling garden with Mollie and Monty.

She called his name, and he came bounding towards her, wagging his tail in sheer delight.

Filled with joy at seeing her beloved dog, Ella hugged him tightly as he jumped up and down in an ecstatic frenzy.

Just then, Jo's mother approached Ella and asked if she had a pleasant time in France.

"Yes, it was pure bliss. In fact, it was absolute heaven."

As they walked over to the patio, a pot of tea and biscuits awaited them.

They began discussing Jo and Ryan's life in Canada during a welcoming cup of tea.

Both Jo and Ryan had found secure jobs and were earning good money.

They were hoping to rent or buy a place of their own soon.

Nevertheless, Jo's Mother told Ella she was beginning to miss her daughter.

However, it seems that Jo's parents appear to be harbouring remorse, believing they didn't devote enough time and attention to Jo during her childhood due to work and social obligations.

As a result, they may be grappling with anxiety about the potential repercussions of their past actions.

Ella understood the pain of missing someone, as she deeply missed her mother, and it would take time for the healing process to end.

Ella suggested they could take a trip to Canada to visit their daughter, but the response she got was different from what she expected.

"We can't do that because we have to think about the animals," Jo's mother said hastily.

Ella felt disappointed and frustrated, knowing there were always excuses for not taking time to be with their daughter.

However, she didn't want to interfere, as Ella only cared about Jo's happiness, which was essential to her.

After picking up Sammy, Ella rushed home to take a hot bath and find something to eat, either from a can or packet, before heading straight to bed.

It had been a long day, and tomorrow looked no different.

Upon returning to work the next day, Ella could see that the restaurant was in good hands and running smoothly.

Happily, greeting new and old customers gave her a sense of purpose.

Having checked the restaurant's books, Ella realised it had been doing exceptionally well since her short break away.

At that moment, she reflected on many things, including the future of the restaurant.

She decided that she could discuss this with Tim later that evening and ask his opinion on what he would do in her position.

Ella decided to look her best that evening, not to impress but to feel good about herself.

The Stag's Head was bustling with tourists and locals, but she soon caught sight of Tim, who was waiting at the bar when she arrived.

As he approached her, he asked what she would like to drink.

"A glass of Chardonnay please?"

"Of course, no problem," he replied with a smile.

Ella brought up the topic of the restaurant and whether she should sell the restaurant or keep it running.

She said she hadn't felt the same about the restaurant since the death of her mother.

Ella finds herself at a crossroads, feeling uncertain about her ability to navigate life without her mother's guidance. Seeking advice, she confides in Tim, who provides her with valuable insights. Tim advises her to take her time and carefully weigh her options before making decisions. He reassures her that she is capable and independent, highlighting how she has managed to run a first-class restaurant at such a young age. Tim's words of reassurance instilled a sense of confidence in Ella, making her feel more secure about her future.

Additionally, Tim offers his ongoing support, assuring Ella that he will be there for her whenever she needs it.

Ella was grateful for Tim's wise words making her feel more at ease with the situation.

She decided to give herself more time to think before making any final decisions.

During their lengthy discussion, Ella and Tim planned to keep in touch, and Tim promised to be available whenever she needed him.

As Ella waved goodbye to Tim, suddenly, she felt a sense of loneliness.

Most of her friends have either moved away or emigrated, leaving Tim as the only person she can call a friend in the village.

Although the older villagers are kind, Ella craves a connection with someone her own age.

After a tiring day, Ella was exhausted but nevertheless decided to ring Lauren.

Considering the time difference, Ella planned Facetime at 10 pm UK time since it was morning in Melbourne and Lauren would be making breakfast and getting ready for work.

Since their mother's death, the two sisters have grown closer than ever. They stay in touch by calling or facetiming whenever possible, providing much-needed comfort and support to one another.

During their recent conversation, Lauren suggested to Ella that she should consider booking another trip to Melbourne when it was convenient for her, knowing that she could afford it and stay as long as she wanted.

Lauren expressed how much she missed Ella, and her feelings were reciprocated. After saying their goodbyes on Facetime, Ella closed her laptop and got ready for bed.

She knew she would fall asleep quickly, but not before taking Sammy outdoors for his nightly wee break.

As the gentle morning light filtered through her bedroom curtains, she slowly awakened from her peaceful slumber. With a soft stretch, she lifted her arms above her head and whispered to herself, "Another busy day lies ahead."

She thought about having a good breakfast to start the day.

Sammy sat by her feet, making the moment even better.

As she gazed out at the picturesque landscape of the Yorkshire Dales, with their magnificent rolling hills and meandering valleys, she couldn't help but marvel at the beauty surrounding her.

The peaceful serenity of the countryside filled her with a sense of contentment and admiration.

She wondered why anyone would want to leave such a stunning and idyllic part of England.

It was what she had always known, and she couldn't live her life anywhere else. After careful consideration, a firm decision was made - she was here to stay.

The very idea of leaving was not just unthinkable, and it was sheer madness!

Chapter 29

During the Christmas season, Ella seemed constantly occupied with all the festivities at the restaurant.

However, now that the holiday rush is over, the restaurant is pretty quiet.

It's a stark contrast to the constant buzz of the Christmas season, and Ella now decided to finally take some much-needed downtime.

Sitting in her living room on a chilly January evening, she snuggles up on the sofa with Sammy, who is nestled comfortably at her side. The fire crackled, casting a warm and inviting glow throughout the room and creating a peaceful and cozy atmosphere.

As she gazed into the flickering flames, Ella pondered the new year's possibilities and felt a sense of anticipation and curiosity building within her.

Eventually, she finally made up her mind and decided to book airline tickets for a visit to Australia to see Lauren as soon as possible.

She felt a sense of excitement at the prospect of finally being able to see her after a long time.

However, as the reality of the situation sunk in, she couldn't help but feel a twinge of restlessness at the thought of travelling to the other side of the world on her own.

With a mix of anticipation, nervousness, and determination, Ella stood firm in her decision to embark on the upcoming trip to Australia.

As the departure date drew near, she carefully gathered all the necessary documents, ensuring that each detail was in perfect order and up to date, from her passport to travel insurance, instilling a sense of reassurance as she prepared for the adventure ahead.

In addition, Ella took great care in ensuring that Sammy would be well taken care of during her absence.

With Sammy's well-being in mind, she arranged for him to stay once again. Jo's parents knew that he would be in safe and loving hands while she was away.

With all the necessary arrangements made, Ella set off for Jo's parents' house, taking Sammy along for his upcoming four-week stay, relieving any worries about his safety.

Once again, Sammy was welcomed with warm smiles and open arms, his tail wagging with uncontrollable joy. Ella sensed the genuine warmth and affection, knowing that Sammy was in loving and capable hands. The immediate bond between Sammy and Jo's family quickly filled the room with love and joy, creating a heart-warming atmosphere for everyone involved.

Returning back home, Ella was excited as she reached for the phone and dialled Tim's number. She couldn't wait to share the news of her upcoming visit to see Lauren. "I've made up my mind to see Lauren," she declared excitedly. "I'm scheduled to fly out next week, and we're already planning an array of activities and sights to explore. We might even sample some new cuisines, and who knows, I might come back with some menu ideas for my restaurant, as long as they offer healthy options," she added with a laugh.

Tim's voice brimmed enthusiastically as he replied, "What an amazing plan! This trip will undoubtedly be an extraordinary adventure for you.

Travelling alone will inspire you to embrace new experiences with confidence."

When Tim offered to keep an eye on the restaurant and update her on any local gossip, Ella's eyes lit up with gratitude and appreciation.

It was like a deep and meaningful friendship was forming, or could it be much more?

Arriving in the bustling city of Melbourne, Lauren eagerly awaited her sister's arrival at the airport. As soon as her sister entered the arrivals area, Lauren's eyes lit up, and she instantly spotted her. The sisters embraced each other tightly before leaving and walked towards where Lauren's sleek, silver VW Golf was parked.

"Is this a new car?" Ella remarked, her eyes gleaming with curiosity.

"Yes, I bought it just for you," Lauren said with a playful glint in her eyes, lovingly teasing her sister.

They drove off into the distance, chatting non-stop all the way to Lauren's apartment.

Under the scorching sun, Lauren meticulously organised activities and places to visit. Despite the relentless heat, they cherished each other's company and found joy in the coolness of the evening air, enjoying refreshing swims in the pool.

During her stay, Ella relished spending quality time with Lauren, rekindling old memories, and sharing beautiful stories. They giggled endlessly until their stomachs ached. But amidst the joyous moments, there were also times of sorrow when they spoke of their much-loved mother. However, as usual, their tears soon turned into laughter, giving them the courage to continue their lives.

Ella couldn't help but reflect on it being the best holiday she had ever experienced, and she felt a pang of sadness, knowing that her time in Melbourne was drawing to a close.

Sadly, the time had come for Ella to bid farewell to Lauren once again, leaving behind nothing but cherished memories of their time together.

As they held each other close, tears streamed down their faces. They both knew how hard it was to be apart, but they promised to stay in touch and try to visit each other at least once a year.

With a heavy heart, Ella wiped away her tears, turned around and walked towards the boarding gate.

As she glanced behind her, Ella saw Lauren standing alone, her hand raised in a wistful farewell, tears glistening in her eyes. A wave of emotion hit Ella, and she felt a lump in her throat. Despite the distance that would soon separate them, Ella held onto the certainty that their bond as sisters would endure, no matter where their paths may lead.

After taking a month-long holiday, Ella wanted to stay up to date on everything that had happened in her absence.

So, she decided to call Tim and ask for an update.

Tim replied quickly with a text message, telling her that everything was going well and assuring her that there was no need to worry.

Ella was grateful for his reassurance, and she suggested meeting up with him for a coffee to catch up.

To her delight, Tim eagerly agreed and expressed his desire to see her again and said he would pop over to see her later.

Today, being Ella's birthday, she woke up with the same determination as any other day, ensuring her restaurant was perfectly prepared for a bustling service ahead. Despite it being her special day, she was more concerned about the running of the busy day ahead than celebrating herself. She knew it would be a hectic service, but perhaps she might enjoy a drink or two later in the evening to celebrate.

Quite suddenly and without any warning whatsoever, she felt someone tapping on her shoulder, and to her surprise, Hugo was standing right behind her.

She was so startled that she couldn't believe her eyes.

She was completely at a loss as to why he was at her restaurant.

Ella was in a state of distress as she grappled with the unsettling questions that were racing through her mind.

How could he possibly know where she lived?

How did he have any idea about the location of my restaurant?

Hugo confessed that he had taken the initiative to look up her name on the internet. To his surprise, he found the restaurant Tastebuds and its location. He seemed rather smug as he remarked how simple it had been.

It was the only information he needed to track her down.

Hugo then confessed that he had been unable to get her out of his head since their breakup and was constantly thinking about her.

She noticed he seemed slightly arrogant and reckless and wasn't the Hugo she once knew.

Following a few minutes of casual conversation, Ella found herself experiencing a mixture of emotions - surprise at seeing him and confusion regarding his intentions of trying to rekindle their relationship.

She hoped that during his visit, she would be able to gain greater insight into what he truly wanted and expected.

Ella had already made her mind up, believing there was no chance of reconciliation with the person who had shattered her trust and broken her heart in many ways and was therefore determined to remove him from her life forever.

Nevertheless, she asked about Eric and Maria.

"Oh, they're alright, but I haven't seen them for a year or so.

I've been quite busy," was his reply.

As Hugo's voice broke into an abrupt tone, Ella's senses pricked up, and she couldn't help but notice an inexplicable change in his demeanour.

His response was curt, sharp, and unfriendly, a complete deviation from the warm and friendly person she had known in the past.

The sudden change in Hugo's attitude left Ella uneasy and unsure of what could have prompted such an abrupt change.

As Ella and Hugo were engrossed in conversation, Tim suddenly appeared from around the corner, carrying a beautiful bouquet of flowers.

Although it was an unexpected surprise, Tim couldn't contain his excitement and exclaimed, "Happy Birthday, Ella!" before gently kissing her on the cheek.

Ella was delighted with the flowers and thanked Tim for his kind gesture.

However, Hugo's expression changed as he saw Tim's gift, and a hint of jealousy was visible.

Ella then introduced Tim to Hugo, explaining that Tim had been a great friend who had supported her through a tough period, particularly after her mother passed away.

The tension between them was visible as Ella found the courage to express to Hugo that she was ready to move forward with her life and the idea of reigniting their relationship was far from Ella's thoughts.

With unequivocal determination, she communicated to him that she was steadily moving forward with her life and intended for it to remain that way.

She had experienced many changes in her life, including coming to terms with her lottery win, owning her restaurant, and losing her mum.

She wasn't willing to give up her personal growth for anyone or anything.

As Tim stood standing in the doorway of the restaurant, somewhat bemused, he could sense the tension, so he suggested calling Ella later that day and began walking away.

The realisation finally sank in for Hugo that there was no point in pursuing the relationship further.

As he rose from his chair, Ella noticed his unsteady figure and perplexed expression.

She watched, her curiosity piqued, as he casually picked up his holdall from the gravel pathway and started walking down the driveway, disappearing into the distance.

The mystery of his sudden visit hung in the air, leaving Ella with more questions than answers.

A mix of relief washed over her, and as he walked away, he turned around and gave her a cynical smile, got into his parked car, and drove away into the distance. Ella's mind was ablaze with questions.

She couldn't help but be consumed by his true intentions for coming all that way to visit her.

Was it solely to make amends and offer an apology, or was there a hidden agenda behind his visit?

She wondered if he had somehow learned about her recent lottery win and was now hoping to benefit from her newfound wealth.

These thoughts lingered on her mind and perhaps she might never really know the real reason for his visit.

Lost in her thoughts, Ella walked back into the restaurant, determined to move forward and close that chapter of her life.

Seeing Hugo had only reinforced her decision, and she knew it was time to focus on running her restaurant and concentrate on her future ahead.

Ella took a deep breath and told herself to snap out of it.

After all, she had a business to run, a dream to fulfil.

Chapter 30

In spite of the fact that Hugo's unexpected visit had the potential to ruin her special day, she was determined to make the most of it.

She hurriedly made her way to the restaurant kitchen, where kitchen staff were waiting for her.

They had all got together and had taken the time to create a small birthday cake, complete with a single candle that flickered in the soft light of the kitchen.

The sight of the cake brought an immediate smile to her face, and she felt a deep sense of gratitude towards them.

The cake was adorned with a few carefully placed sprinkles, and the frosting was a perfect shade of pink, her favourite colour.

The gesture was small, but it made a huge impact on her day.

Overwhelmed with emotions, she thanked them for their kindness and poured them all a glass of bubbly, a bottle she had been hiding in a cupboard for special occasions.

As they raised their glasses to toast, she felt grateful for the small but meaningful celebration with the people who mattered a lot to her.

That evening, Ella decided to phone Tim and ask him over for a birthday drink and thank him once again for the lovely flowers.

He accepted graciously.

As Ella paced the length of the lounge, she couldn't help glancing down at her watch, anxiously waiting for his arrival, and her excitement had only increased as minutes ticked by.

Hugo's visit earlier in the day had left her slightly distressed, with his sudden appearance leaving her shaken and extremely upset by his visit.

But despite this emotional upheaval, she was determined to move on and enjoy her evening with Tim, a man she is beginning to become increasingly fond of.

As she paced back and forth, she couldn't help but feel a sense of calm wash over her.

Tim had always been a kind and gentle presence in her life, and she knew that in his company, she would be safe.

Was Tim now becoming more than a friend?

As Ella gazed out onto the grassland of the moors, she reflected on the profound transformations that had taken place in her life in recent years.

The once timid and uncertain young woman who had never travelled further than Cornwall, England, had blossomed into a self-assured and independent individual, capable of carving out her path in the world.

Her mind took her back to the days when she encountered numerous obstacles in her young life, especially backpacking through various parts of Europe, where she met people from different walks of life, each with their own unique stories to tell.

When Ella suddenly acquired substantial wealth, it brought unique challenges. She had to manage her finances carefully; make important investment decisions and handle the attention it brought from others.

On top of that, Ella was also dealing with the loss of her mother, which made the situation even more difficult.

However, despite these challenges, Ella found solace in the lifelong friendships she made throughout her journey. These friendships were the most valuable thing Ella gained from her journey, and they brought her joy and comfort that nothing else could.

Jo and Tilly were very important to Ella, and she knew that regardless of any challenges she might face in life, she could always count on the support of her closest friends.

Lauren was also someone she could rely on, and that was something Ella valued more than anything else.

Despite encountering numerous setbacks and challenges, she refused to succumb to defeat and remained steadfast in her unwavering pursuit of her aspirations. However, deep in her heart, she yearned for someone to share her future endeavours with.

Ella knew she had made the right decision ending her relationship with Hugo, and now there was a place in her heart for that special someone who could bring her love and happiness.

With a beating heart, she couldn't shake off the thought that Tim might be the one she had been searching for.

Would he feel the same way?

Suddenly, car headlights beamed through the kitchen window, and the sound of a car crunching up the gravel pathway signalled Tim's arrival, shaking Ella from her thoughts.

As she opened the door, Ella welcomed Tim into her cottage. Sammy, the dog, jumped up to greet him, too.

Ella poured Tim a glass of celebration bubbles, and they both sat together for a birthday drink.

Ella apologised to Tim for Hugo's behaviour earlier that day.

She then proceeded to tell Tim about how she and Hugo met and the relationship they formed while they were in France.

Tim responded calmly, assuring her that she didn't need to apologise and that her well-being was all that mattered to him.

However, he did mention that Hugo's behaviour did not leave a good impression.

Giving Ella a warm look, she responded in a tender way as they spent the evening together.

Tim informed Ella that he is an only child and that his parents reside in the market town of Cheswick Bridge, on the Scottish border.

After completing a couple of years at university, Tim realised he was passionate about ensuring the safety and quality of food products. His interest in meeting new people and attention to detail led him to pursue a career as a Food Inspector.

Due to the scarcity of job opportunities in his hometown, Tim was advised to relocate to other areas for personal growth. His passion for the food industry led him to move to the Dales, where he was offered a job and where he found a modern one-bedroom flat just outside Buckland Ridge.

The location is ideal for commuting to work, and he is excited to be living in yet another beautiful place.

As they spoke, Tim expressed his amazement at Ella's success in running a restaurant, having only a limited understanding of how it works.

He admired her enthusiasm and hard work and pointed out that her efforts had certainly paid off.

However, after talking to Tim, Ella was reminded of why she had started the business in the first place. It renewed her pride and purpose in the life she had built in Buckland Ridge.

Within the comfort of her home, cherished memories with her loved ones and the strong sense of community she had found in the village had meant everything to her.

Not being sure of her future and the path to take, she now knows that Buckland Ridge and its surrounding area are where she belongs and where she will forever stay.

As the evening ended, they walked towards the front door, and as Tim stepped outside into the cool night air, he turned around and passionately kissed Ella.

As they embraced, Ella's response was filled with tenderness, as if every part of her body longed to hold on to that moment forever. They held each other tight, their bodies intertwined, creating a sense of comfort and safety that only two people finding love could understand.

Finally, they let go, and as they separated, Ella's eyes sparkled with joy, hinting at the possibility of something special happening between them.

Her heart was filled with so much happiness that it could burst at any moment.

Standing in the doorway of her cottage, she gazed into the night sky and felt hopeful for her future and its possibilities. The soft breeze carried the sweet scent of blooming flowers, and the stars twinkled above like diamonds.

Ella wished she could hold onto this moment forever as it filled her heart with peace and serenity.

After bidding each other goodnight with a lingering embrace, Ella made her way to her bedroom.

The warm light of the bedside lamp casts a soft glow over the room, creating a comforting ambiance.

She wasn't sure if she could easily drift off to sleep after such a delightful evening and possibly one of her best birthdays ever.

She could still feel the gentle touch of his hand and the sound of his laughter echoing in her mind, a soothing memory from the night.

Feeling the angry exhaustion of the day meeting up with Hugo slowly ebbing away, Ella undid the delicate clasp of her necklace and placed it on the dresser.

Resting her head on the soft pillow, she yawned a contented sigh, her body sinking into the familiar comfort of her bed. The rhythmic ticking of the old grandfather clock in the hallway filled the room with tranquillity as Ella closed her eyes.

It wasn't too long before she fell into a deep and undisturbed sleep, carried away by the peaceful embrace of the night, her heart filled with contentment.

The next morning, Ella wandered up to the bustling restaurant; the warmth and aroma of freshly cooked food being prepared added to her joyful mood.

As she scanned the room, her eyes fell upon Tim, who was unexpectedly waiting in the doorway of the restaurant.

Suddenly, everything around her faded into the background, and she lost herself in his gaze.

The thought of being with him made her heart race, and she couldn't help but think back to her Mum's wise words, 'You will always know when Mr Right comes along.'

She silently thanked her Mum for the advice that had guided her in the right direction.

She knew there was still a long way to go, but for now, she was content to enjoy the moment and savour the possibility of what might be.

As Ella nervously approached Tim, her heart pounded loudly, making her voice tremble ever so slightly as she called out to him, "What brings you here?"

With a gentle smile, Tim replied, "You."

Tim seemed to sense her thoughts and extended his hand to her, slowly making his way towards her, his eyes locked onto hers.

Ella couldn't take her eyes off him and suddenly felt the urge to be close to him and hold him once again.

Without any hesitation, they fell into each other's arms and shared a long and passionate kiss.

They pressed their bodies against each other, leaving no doubt about their feelings for one another. They lost themselves in each other's embrace, and for a moment, time stood still. They relished the moment alone, knowing it was just the beginning of something new and exciting.

Chapter 31

Everything seemed to be going well for Ella these days!

The restaurant is going from strength to strength, and she is feeling happy and fulfilled.

Ella was thrilled to share the exciting news about her relationship with Tim during her FaceTime with Lauren that evening.

Of course, Lauren was happy for her sister, but she also couldn't help but worry slightly about the possibility of Ella getting hurt again.

Thankfully, Ella was quick to put her sister's mind at ease, telling Lauren, and she was now very confident that Tim was the one for her.

Ella eagerly suggested that Lauren meet Tim on her next visit to the UK, explaining that she had told him so much about her big sister.

Lauren's face lit up with a big smile, and she couldn't help but giggle at Ella's teasing remark. "I hope you have only said good things about me," Lauren playfully replied.

As Ella started to talk about Tim, Lauren noticed a dreamy expression on her face, indicating her deep fondness for him.

Ella was now living the life she had always dreamed of.

Every little thing that was significant to her was now becoming a reality, and she felt fulfilled.

Nothing and no one in the world could ever take away the happiness and contentment she felt at that moment.

Lauren could sense the depth of pure contentment as her sister spoke and could only wish that this newfound joy would finally bring her the genuine happiness she rightfully deserved.

As Ella prepared to say goodbye to Lauren, she couldn't shake the deep sadness that always accompanied their goodbyes. However, as time passed, Ella found that the pain of parting was becoming more bearable.

Just then, in a sudden jolt back to reality, Ella remembered that she had invited Tim for dinner the following evening.

Her heart began to pound with excitement at the thought of spending more time with him, and she felt a rush of anticipation as she envisioned the evening ahead. She was determined to make it a memorable occasion, and her mind began to race with ideas for what she could prepare for dinner, how she could set the table, and how she could make the atmosphere warm and welcoming.

She couldn't wait to see him again and was eager to make the most of the time they would spend together.

Having informed the restaurant staff about taking a day off, Ella set out to prepare a delicious chicken dish with a unique twist: marinated with a blend of spices and garlic and slow-roasted to perfection.

She carefully selected the ingredients, spices, and herbs and spent several hours preparing the meal perfectly.

As she began creating what she envisioned as the perfect meal, her hands trembled with anticipation, and her heart raced nervously, hoping that everything would be perfect for their romantic evening together.

Ella, with a hint of anticipation, glanced at her watch.

It was time to shower and change her clothes because she wanted everything to be perfect.

She just wanted to look her best.

Ella's heart skipped a beat as she saw Tim's car pulling up outside. Little did she know, this was the beginning of a night she would never forget.

As they exchanged greetings, they made their way to the candle-lit dining table. The flickering light casts a charming spell, enhancing the romantic atmosphere of the evening.

Ella had taken great care to lay the table with the crockery she had inherited from her Mum, each piece gleaming in the soft light.

Tim's face lit up with excitement as he saw the beautifully presented food prepared especially for him.

She hoped he would enjoy eating it as much as she had enjoyed creating it.

She needn't have worried because she could see the satisfaction on his face, and it made her feel relieved and content.

As Tim continued to enjoy his meal, he praised her for her skills and attention to detail, making her blush with happiness.

Ella thanked him with a grateful smile, pleased that her efforts had been appreciated.

Throughout the meal, Ella couldn't help but feel a deep sense of contentment.

Could this be the start of something beautiful?

As the night ended, saying goodbye proved difficult for Ella and Tim.

However, they both knew they would have many opportunities to spend time together in the future if everything worked well for them.

As Tim walked down the pathway towards his car, he suddenly turned around and briskly walked back to where Ella was standing in the doorway.

Their gaze locked, and time stood still as they shared a passionate and meaningful kiss, expressing their deep affection for each other.

Ella felt a sense of enchantment wash over her.

She knew, with absolute certainty, that Tim was the one she had been waiting for all along.

In the weeks that followed, Ella and Tim had become inseparable. Their bond had deepened, and they had made the exciting decision to take their relationship to the next level. They both knew in their hearts that it was time to start a new chapter by moving in together, a decision that filled them with anticipation and joy.

They agreed that living in Ella's more spacious accommodation was better than living in Tim's cramped flat.

Tim's parents, whom Ella had now met on several occasions now, fully embraced her as a member of their family, treating her with a warmth and affection that made her feel right at home.

It was evident that they loved their son dearly and were grateful that he had found someone as loving and caring as Ella.

A symphony of natural wonders unfolded as Buckland Ridge basked in the warmth of Summer once again. The gentle breeze carried with it a sweet medley of floral fragrances, intertwining with the crisp, pure scent of the flowing river. Ella and Tim leisurely strolled along the meandering riverbank, with Sammy eagerly exploring the delightful surroundings with his playful sniffs and boundless curiosity. The gurgling melodies of the water caressing the pebbled riverbed provided a soothing backdrop, harmonizing with the joyful chorus of chirping birds and the tranquil rustle of leaves stirred by the gentle breeze. Amidst this serene setting, they immersed themselves in each other's company and peaceful embrace of the river's tranquillity.

However, their peaceful moment was about to be abruptly shattered when Ella returned home and found a letter that had been delivered by hand through her letterbox.

This letter was about to devastate her world.

As she lowered herself onto the chair and took the sealed brown envelope in her hands, she carefully tore open the envelope with trembling fingers and extracted the letter inside.

Her eyes raced over the words, trying to understand their meaning as her heart thudded rapidly.

She struggled to maintain her composure as she absorbed the news before her, her mind reeling with the implications of what she had just read.

As she read the letter, her face turned pale, and her body trembled with fear and sadness.

Sensing something was wrong, Tim approached her and asked, "is everything alright"?

Ella showed him the letter, and he read it nervously, wondering what the next steps would be.

The letter outlined the joint efforts of the Local Authority and National Highways to develop new infrastructure near Ella's cherished restaurant. The proposed bridge construction along the River Felling promises to improve pedestrian and local community access significantly.

However, this project's completion necessitates removing Tastebuds, as its current location hinders the planned developments.

Ella's eyes widened in disbelief as she looked at Tim, her heart racing in panic. "Can they really do this?" she asked him, struggling to keep her voice steady.

After a brief hesitation, Tim spoke in a low and serious tone. "Yes, they have the authority to do this."

Overwhelmed with fear and uncertainty, she could feel her emotions spiralling out of control.

Tears streamed down her face, her body shaking with sobs as she tried to make sense of the situation. It was all too much, too overwhelming, and she didn't know how to cope.

Tim offered comfort and support, patiently listening as she expressed her fears and anxieties.

Amidst the turmoil and confusion that engulfed her, Ella was fortunate to have Tim by her side. His reassuring presence and constant support gave her the strength to regain her composure and confront the daunting obstacles ahead.

The battle against the local authority and the numerous departments involved in the project was arduous and exhausting, and Ella knew she couldn't have fought it alone.

Despite her valiant efforts, the plans to construct a bridge adjacent to her restaurant were approved very quickly.

Ella's hard work and cherished memories were now fading into obscurity, overshadowed by the new bridge that threatened to erase everything she had worked so hard to build.

The decision to construct a bridge caused a lot of commotion among the villagers because Tastebuds had become more than just a dining place. It had been a community landmark where people gathered to share meals, make memories, and enjoy each other's company.

Ella felt despair at the thought of her restaurant having to be demolished and gone forever.

The restaurant had been the centre of her life for quite some time, and she knew her life would never be the same again.

Without it, she would be left with nothing - no job, purpose, or direction.

She couldn't help but feel numb at the prospect of losing her restaurant and the memories it held for her.

The once peaceful village was now filled with angry and resentful residents, who held up banners and protested against the planned demolition.

Despite their efforts, nothing was going to stop the mechanical diggers and men in hard hats from changing any decisions made, whether the villagers liked it or not.

Eventually, Ella lost the battle, and the authorities went ahead with their plans, resulting in the demolition of her restaurant.

However, Ella received a significant amount of compensation for the loss of her business. It was a bitter pill to swallow, but the compensation helped her to move on from the ordeal.

As the day of the demolition drew near, the atmosphere in the village became increasingly tense.

Large machinery and digging equipment now dotted the landscape, an ominous reminder of the impending destruction.

Standing amidst the wreckage of the almost demolished restaurant, Ella watched as heavy machinery continued its work, crushing the remaining debris into dust and rubble.

Her heart felt heavy with a sense of loss and nostalgia as she remembered all the good times at the restaurant.

Ella stood still, gazing out at the wide expanse of desolate land that stretched before her.

Standing in silence, Ella could hear her mother's comforting voice echoing in her mind. "Be brave, Ella," her mother had said. "You have the determination to start again. I know you can do it".

Those empowering words filled her with renewed determination and strength, a strength she needed to face the world that seemed to conspire against her. She would not give up, if not for her, but for the love and memory of her mother.

After some reflection, she realised that building a bridge over the River Fell would not only enhance the safety of hikers and walkers but would also offer a splendid view of the nearby countryside. As she pondered on it further, she came to terms with the decisions made by the planners, although it meant surrendering her own beloved restaurant.

With substantial money in her bank account, Ella knew there wasn't any rush to make any hasty decisions.

However, a small glimmer of hope flickered within her, reminding her that every ending comes with a new beginning.

Ella's world had been upside down since losing her restaurant. The pain of that loss still lingers, and it's a wound that refuses to heal.

Tim suggested they take a break from their routine and go away for a short time to help Ella forget the painful events of the past few months.

"That's a fantastic idea, Tim!" she exclaimed, a broad smile lighting up her face.

Ella suggested they visit Tilly and Maddie in the South of France and rent an apartment for a few weeks, relaxing and soaking up the warmth of the Mediterranean. Tim was excited about Ella's suggestion.

Before the evening sun disappeared, they decided to take Sammy for a walk alongside the riverbank and start to plan their forthcoming trip.

As they walked, they couldn't help but gaze up at where the restaurant once stood.

Building work had commenced, and according to reports, it was going well, but it had left Ella with countless memories that would remain with her for the rest of her life.

She began to think how life had dealt her a series of harsh blows.

The sequence of events begins with the painful loss of her beloved mother, followed by the difficult choice to part ways with Hugo.

Most recently, she has had to cope with the devastating closure of the business, a venture she had poured her heart and soul into, only to see it come to an end.

Amid all this chaos and upheaval, there was one constant shining light in Ella's life: Tim.

He was the unwavering pillar that brought stability and hope to her life, the sole person she could trust to infuse substance and meaning into her world.

She clung to him with a determination that knew no bounds, never willing to let go.

Chapter 32

After confirming all the details for their upcoming trip to meet up with Tilly and Maddie, Ella excitedly phoned Tilly to share the wonderful news of their impending visit.

Tilly was thrilled to hear from Ella and very excited about meeting Tim.

She assured Ella that she would have chilled wine ready for them upon their arrival.

Jo's mother kindly offered to let them stay at their villa, leaving Ella grateful for her kind offer.

As Ella and Tim meticulously readied themselves for their upcoming departure, and with the comforting knowledge that Jo's parents would take care of Sammy, they felt excited about the journey ahead.

Excitement brimmed within them, although Tim couldn't help but feel nervous about meeting Tilly & Maddie for the first time. However, Ella reassured him quickly, emphasizing that the couple were not just delightful friends but also shared a deep love for each other and had a unique connection that made them incredibly easy to connect with.

With a confident smile, Ella declared, "I know they are going to adore you, Tim." Her words carried a reassuring warmth that eased Tim's apprehensions.

After a pleasant flight, Ella and Tim decided to hire a car for the rest of their stay.

As they arrived, they saw Tilly was busy in the garden tending to the colourful plants and flowers which surrounded her.

Maddie, a talented painter, was putting the finishing touches on a stunning painting of the nearby mountainside with so much pride and joy.

It was a beautiful mix of colours, bringing the landscape to life.

As Ella and Tim walked through the smelling fragrance of lavender bushes, Tilly warmly greeted and welcomed them into their home.

As Ella pulled Tilly into an embrace, she could feel the warmth of her friend's tears on her cheek. "It's okay," she whispered, "they're happy tears."

Looking into Tilly's misty eyes, Ella could sense the depth of her emotions.

"It's lovely to see you," she murmured, feeling grateful for the tender moment they shared.

As Tilly gazed upon Ella and Tim, she couldn't help but feel moved by their depth of love.

The way they looked at each other, the gentle touches they exchanged, and the warmth in their voices all spoke volumes about their bond.

Tilly's heart skipped a beat as she took it all in, grateful to have witnessed such tenderness. "It is truly a pleasure to meet you, Tim," she said, smiling warmly. "Please take good care of her. She means the world to us." Tim's voice was full of conviction as he replied, "I will undoubtedly do that."

Quietly, Tilly told Ella, 'You have a keeper there. Hold on to him.'

Ella's voice trembled as she spoke, revealing to Tilly the profound impact Tim has had on her life so far.

Ella began recounting the heart-breaking story of the restaurant's demolition. Tilly and Maddie listened intently, their compassionate expressions offering comfort and hope to Ella.

Tilly's heart was heavy as she felt the weight of Ella's words, her empathy growing as she sensed the pain that still surrounded her.

Despite the significant personal tragedies Ella had recently faced, Tilly remained steadfast in her belief that every event in life, no matter how distressing, unfolded for a specific purpose.

Tilly's comforting words reassured Ella, emphasizing that even in the face of adversity, there was a silver lining, a purpose to be found, which required patience and time.

Ella's words lingered in the serene stillness of the evening air her voice filled with such sincerity.

"What would I do without you, Tilly?" she pondered, her eyes reflecting a deep sense of gratitude.

Looking back, Ella had seen the tragic events that had affected Tilly during her youth, leaving her emotionally hurt and shattered.

However, Ella realised that life could offer a way out, so long as there are people around who can provide support and assistance when someone is going through a difficult period.

Ella found the villa an indispensable sanctuary, providing her with a peaceful retreat and a home away from home whenever needed. With its four spacious bedrooms, the villa starkly contrasted Tilly and Maddie's quaint one-bedroom apartment. Despite these differences, both spaces exuded their unique charm.

After unpacking and having a light snack, Ella and Tim decided to call it an early night, but not before taking a stroll to Tilly & Maddie's to bid them goodnight.

The next morning, they all relished in each other's company, savouring a hearty brunch altogether before exploring the exquisite surroundings.

The beautiful azure blue waters and the picturesque landscapes of the snow -capped Alps behind left them both spellbound and rejuvenated, reminding them of the beauty that still exists in the world.

It's fascinating how time seems to pass by so swiftly when you are having a good time.

Such a common phrase, yet so true.

On the evening before their departure back to England, Tim wanted to do something special for Ella to thank her for the fantastic time they had spent together in France.

While Tim was out on his morning run, he stumbled upon a hidden gem—the charming Bistro Valentino. The cozy and inviting atmosphere instantly captivated him. He could already picture it as the perfect setting for a romantic dinner with Ella.

Filled with excitement and a touch of nervousness, he promptly secured a reservation. He couldn't wait to see her reaction to the charming brasserie and the romantic evening he had planned.

In the coolness of the evening, and with such excitement, they walked side by side towards the hire car, their fingers intertwined, radiating an unmistakable air of affection and intimacy.

Ella wore a flattering black dress that artfully showcased her elegant silhouette. The shimmering diamond pendant around her neck, a cherished heirloom from her mother, lent her an undeniable sense of grace and confidence.

She felt radiant.

Tim's well-fitted blue denim jeans and pristine white linen shirt, tailored to perfection, accentuated his bronzed complexion, infusing his appearance with a rugged and captivating look.

Tilly and Maddie couldn't contain their excitement as they observed Tim and Ella's undeniable chemistry. With a shared giggle, they watched as the couple drove off into the horizon, a picture of timeless allure and romance.

Walking towards the restaurant, Ella and Tim felt overwhelming joy and anticipation.

Ella couldn't help but feel a sense of excitement as she imagined the perfect evening with the perfect man.

Even as they sat down at their table, Ella wanted the evening to go on forever and never end.

The meal was delectable, the wine was a perfect complement, and the ambiance was simply enchanting. The conversation flowed effortlessly, punctuated by laughter and animated storytelling. In each other's presence, it felt as if the passage of time had become inconsequential.

As they finished their meal and said their gratitude to the staff, Ella felt a twinge of sadness. She didn't want the night to end, but she knew that it would.

They were now both closer than ever before.

They say Paris is a romantic city –

Ella had to admit that Antibes is a close second!

The following day It was time to part company with Tilly and Maddie and head back to the UK.

Ella expressed her heartfelt thanks to Tilly and Maddie for their kindness. Making their stay in France a truly memorable experience.

Tilly and Maddie assured them that they would always be welcome anytime, day or night or whenever they felt the need for friends.

For Tim, the days that followed their return were a battle with a sense of melancholy.

The stark contrast between the serene, relaxing holiday and the chaotic routine of daily life left him feeling a pang of sadness.

He found it hard to shake off the lingering tranquillity and let go of the cherished memories of their time away. As he sat at his desk, his mind wandered, eventually settling on memories of the unforgettable moments he had shared with Ella. The vivid images of her infectious smile, her melodious laughter, and the profound way she made him feel filled his mind with a comforting warmth.

Each day, his emotions seemed to intensify, becoming more overwhelming.

Amidst these reflections, a weighty question loomed over him: the prospect of taking the next step and proposing to her.

He grappled with the decision, questioning whether the timing was right or if he should bide his time and allow their relationship to evolve more before embarking on such a monumental undertaking.

Meanwhile, Ella found herself reflecting on the days following their return.

Ella found the holiday to be a deeply rejuvenating experience. It allowed her to set aside any worries about her future plans and fully embrace each precious moment she shared with Tim.

However, as the comfort of the holiday began to fade, she knew it was time to confront the challenges ahead and channel her energy into navigating the uncertain path that awaited her.

Taking a moment to appreciate the peacefulness of the surroundings, she allowed herself to get lost in her thoughts.

Ella stood frozen; her eyes fixed on the spot where Tastebuds once stood.

The whirring sound of mechanical machinery and the sight of workers in fluorescent jackets filled the air, replacing the once-beautiful landscape with rubble and piles of earth.

Her mind was flooded with memories of happy times spent at the restaurant, making her feel incredibly nostalgic. It had been her little gem, a place where she had poured her heart and soul into making it a success.

For her, it had been a special place, one where she had created cherished memories with family and friends.

She began to wonder if she could ever rebuild what she had lost and if it was at all possible to start over again, not knowing where her journey would take her, what challenges and opportunities would come her way, and whether she had the strength and courage to face them.

With each passing moment, there was a glimmer of hope that with her experience and the love of everyone around her, it could be possible to achieve her dream once again.

Feeling very restless, she found herself yearning to make significant changes in her life.

While Tim was inspecting new restaurants in Greater Manchester, Ella decided it was time to follow her heart.

Feeling overwhelmed with her thoughts, and nothing much to occupy her mind, Ella decided to take a drive to clear her head.

During her travels, she stumbled upon a magnificent three-story building known to the locals as The Old Brewery, which, despite its dilapidated state, stood out as an impressive and distinctive landmark that had been an integral part of the surrounding area for over 80 years.

The property was now available for purchase and was located on the outskirts of Buckland Ridge, on the other side of the River Felling.

The building offered superb panoramic views of the surrounding moorlands, valleys, and hills, greatly enhancing its already considerable charm.

Ella couldn't help but imagine the potential of converting this old building into a 'posh 'restaurant, even though it would require a lot of hard work.

Despite the building's current condition, Ella firmly believed that her energy and enthusiasm could revive it. So, she expressed her interest in buying the old red brick building, determined to turn her dream into a reality.

Although she felt slightly nervous about the size and potential of the new venture, she knew, with a lot of help, she could create something truly exceptional.

Ella now found herself at a crossroads.

The building was in the right location; everything in her head told her it was a good decision.

However, she knew she couldn't do it alone – she needed someone she could trust completely, who shared her vision and would be willing to work alongside her as a partner.

Before, she had her Mum beside her all the way, and together, they made 'Tastebuds' work.

Ella needed that same support, but as she thought about who she could ask, one name kept popping up in her mind – Tim.

He had been there for her through good and bad times and had always been honest and loyal.

She knew he had the skills and experience she lacked, and she hoped he would be interested in joining forces with her.

With anticipation and nervousness, she finally approached him and explained her plan.

She laid out her vision for the business, the goals she hoped to achieve, and the challenges she anticipated. She then asked him if he would be willing to partner with her, knowing he was the only person she would consider asking.

Ella's heart beat faster as she waited for his response.

She desperately hoped he would say yes, and they could embark on this new adventure together.

During a conversation, Tim agreed by saying, "Absolutely."

He expressed his belief that forming a partnership would be instrumental in ensuring the success of their new venture.

Tim also suggested the idea of asking the staff who had proven their loyalty and trustworthiness to work alongside Ella once again.

Ella, upon hearing this proposal, responded with excitement, saying, "It's like a dream come true!"

After a period of anticipation, Ella received confirmation from the vendors that the sale of The Old Brewery had been finalised, making it joint ownership with herself and Tim.

Chapter 33

After months of hard work and dedication, the restaurant was finally complete. The three-story building was impressive, with elegant chandeliers in the entrance room and plush sofas surrounding the reception area.

The compensation money was a help in furnishing the new restaurant with something beautiful yet still maintaining a friendly and relaxing atmosphere.

Customers could sit comfortably, sipping on an aperitif and browsing the specialty menus while waiting for their table.

The downstairs dining room had enough seating for 25 tables, while the upstairs space could accommodate an additional 20 tables.

Tim devised the brilliant idea to design the top floor as a banqueting suite for special occasions, such as weddings, conferences and the like - something Ella wouldn't have considered.

Ella was thrilled with how everything was developing.

Two heads are better than one, and that was very clear from the start.

They both had put a lot of effort into creating a warm and welcoming atmosphere, and it showed. The decor was tasteful and sophisticated, with a touch of whimsy that made it feel unique.

The walls were adorned with beautiful artwork, and the lighting was just superb.

As they stood in the doorway of their new venture, Tim and Ella couldn't help but feel proud of what they had accomplished.

Ella was grateful for Tim's much-needed input and encouragement throughout the process, knowing she couldn't have done it without him.

Now that the restaurant was complete, the next challenge was choosing a name.

After much discussion with Tim, Ella finally named the restaurant 'Attwoods,' which held a special significance because it was her late mother's maiden name.

Looking closely at Ella, Tim could see a hint of emotion in her eyes as she began to share the story behind it.

Ella spoke about her mother, who had always been the epitome of strength and resilience, and how she had been her inspiration throughout her life.

She went on to explain how the memory of her mother kept her going, even in the toughest of times.

With tears in her eyes, Tim could see that she must have been an incredible woman and noticed the sadness that had been weighing her down slowly fading away.

Instead, a spark of hope and anticipation began to fill her. The mere mention of the name had a positive impact on her, filling her with a renewed sense of purpose and drive.

The name had a magical quality to it, instilling in both a deep sense of enthusiasm and determination to make their new venture a success.

With huge excitement, 'Attwoods' was finally opened, bringing the community together once again and creating a sense of enjoyment and anticipation.

People were eagerly waiting to taste the delicious food served at this new restaurant.

The surge in bookings that the restaurant experienced was exceptional and was a testament to the hard work not only of Ella and Tim but also the pure dedication of the team working behind the scenes.

Everyone, from the talented chef to the friendly waiting staff, had played a significant role in getting 'Attwoods' up and running as quickly as possible.

Their unwavering commitment to delivering exceptional food and service caught the attention of many, which is evident from the high number of bookings they had received.

Ella was delighted to have taken on her previous staff, who were equally thrilled to be back and working together again, creating an exceptionally happy atmosphere within the workplace.

The team members' positive attitudes and enthusiasm for their jobs were evident in the quality of their work and the way they interacted with one another.

The overall atmosphere was incredibly positive and energised, characterised by a strong sense of teamwork and a shared commitment to achieving success. These qualities were a direct reflection of Ella and Tim's exceptional leadership.

Ella had recently employed two new front-of-house staff members. Their primary responsibilities included guiding guests to their seats, providing comprehensive explanations of the updated menus, and accommodating guests with specific food allergies.

This was the idea of Tim, who, with his previous experience in the food industry, had always been proactive in finding new ways to enhance the customer experience.

The entire team worked seamlessly together, and now the restaurant is poised to provide an even more exceptional dining experience for all its patrons.

After a year filled with hard work and dedication, 'Attwoods' has finally transformed from a derelict building into the establishment it is today.

As Ella gazed up at the building and beyond, she was filled with a sense of gratitude. "I believe you would be proud of me, Mum," she whispered. "You were my rock, my inspiration, pushing me forward for a second shot at success.

I love you, Mum."

Due to a hectic few weeks, Ella completely forgot that her 30th birthday was coming up shortly.

However, Tim hadn't forgotten.

He had been thinking of ways to celebrate her birthday in style and wanted to surprise her.

Despite facing numerous challenges along the way, Tim had persevered and was now on the verge of successfully completing all the arrangements for the highly anticipated upcoming event. He had made countless phone calls, overcame numerous hurdles and spent endless hours ensuring that everything would be perfect. After much consideration,

Tim had finally selected the banqueting suite at their restaurant as the ideal location for the event.

He had personally instructed one of the staff members to decorate the room with an abundance of colourful balloons and flowers, which would create a warm and inviting atmosphere for the guests. The tables had been meticulously set up, with elegant tablecloths, fine China and polished silverware, all designed to create a sense of luxury and sophistication.

As for the catering, Tim had left nothing to chance and had instructed the cooking staff to prepare a sumptuous hot buffet filled with mouth-watering delicacies for this very special occasion.

Tim's anxiety grew as the birthday celebrations drew nearer, for he had a lot riding on the evening's success. He had tried everything he could to persuade Ella to stay away from the restaurant but was finding it very difficult indeed.

He knew Ella was feeling down on her birthday, and the disappointment was evident.

She had been eagerly waiting to receive cards and gifts from her loved ones but hadn't received many.

To make matters worse, Lauren had yet to call or send a Facetime message on her special day, leaving Ella feeling sad and let down.

After a while, Ella realised she couldn't wait for others to make her day special.

She decided to take matters into her own hands and drove into town to indulge in some retail therapy.

She carefully selected a couple of dresses, each one a potential showstopper, hoping they would catch Tim's eye and inspire him to take her somewhere

special for her birthday celebration that evening.

Little did she know what was about to unfold that evening: a series of events that would change her birthday celebration plans.

Upon returning from town, Ella took Sammy for a stroll along the serene riverbank, planning to indulge him in a lively game of fetch with his much-loved thrower and ball.

Meanwhile, Tim, eager to coordinate the evening's arrangements at the restaurant, was keen to know how long Ella would be.

Tim was fortunate that Ella's absence was brief. After a short while, she returned with a satisfied smile, carrying numerous shopping bags filled with her latest purchases.

Tim had yet to mention celebrating her special birthday to Ella.

Feeling a tinge of melancholy, Ella reached for a bottle of her beloved Chardonnay and opted to indulge in a leisurely and soothing bath. Just as she was about to immerse herself in the warm water, Tim's voice called out, gently reminding her not to take too much time. He excitedly informed her that he had made a reservation at The Garden Thai restaurant for a special and romantic dinner for them to celebrate her birthday, sparking a wave of excitement in Ella.

Ella's face lit up with joy, knowing he hadn't forgotten her birthday after all.

Ella mentioned to Tim that she had been shopping in town and had bought a couple of dresses, asking if they would suit the occasion.

Tim smiled and reassured her that she would look stunning no matter what she wore.

It was almost seven o'clock, and as Tim glanced nervously at his watch, he reminded Ella it was almost time to leave.

Luckily, one of the staff at Attwoods had texted him to inform him that everyone had arrived and was just waiting for Ella to make an entrance.

Tim had hired a young girl from the village to dog-sit Sammy, as it could be a late night.

Feeling a little unsure why Tim had done this, Ella wanted to know more.

He explained that the girl was looking for extra pocket money to finance a backpacking trip she hoped to arrange with her friends.

It brought back many memories for Ella, and she wanted to stay and talk to the girl because she had so many stories to share about her backpacking experiences. But Tim gently pulled her away, saying they could speak later.

While they were engrossed in conversation in the car, Ella observed that Tim was not heading towards the town as she had anticipated, but instead, he was driving in the direction of Attwoods.

Being curious, she asked him which direction he was taking into town.

Tim replied, saying that he thought he had forgotten to turn off one of the lights in the restaurant kitchen.

As they exited the car, Ella noticed a row of parked cars outside the restaurant. It was unusual to see vehicles parked there at night, especially considering that the restaurant should have been closed by now.

Nonetheless, she followed him towards the entrance, wondering what could be going on inside.

She couldn't help but ask whose cars they were. Tim smiled, knowing that Ella would find out soon enough.

As he opened the front door, all the lights were suddenly turned on, and a loud cheer and applause filled the air.

Ella was stunned as she looked around the room, taking in the beautiful decorations and the smiling faces of her friends and family.

She suddenly spotted Tilly and Maddie through her teary and blurred vision. Overwhelmed with emotion, she hurried over to them and hugged them tightly.

Tilly made it clear that Ella's 30th birthday celebration was an event that couldn't be overlooked.

Ella's eyes scanned the room until they settled on Jo and Ryan, whom she recognised immediately.

She couldn't believe they had flown from Canada to be there for her. Overwhelmed, she once again burst into tears, her body shaking as she tried to regain her composure. Tim, ever her rock, held her tenderly, offering his unwavering support and a couple of tissues.

After a few moments, Ella managed to speak, her voice choked with emotion. "You all came all this way for me?" she asked incredulously.

Jo nodded; her eyes warm with affection. "Of course. We've been through so much together; this was the perfect opportunity to be together again."

Ella wiped away her tears, still shocked at the lengths her friends had gone to be there for her. It was then that Jo revealed a surprise that left Ella speechless: her parents had been staying with them in Canada for the past month, helping with the preparations for a wedding.

"A wedding?" Ella repeated, stunned.

Jo had a mischievous expression on her face. She said with a grin, "We are getting married this fall, or as they say in England, Autumn."

Ella couldn't help but laugh at Jo's use of Canadian terminology and felt a sense of joy and affection in the conversation. She congratulated the couple and asked if she could be invited to the wedding.

Jo smiled, saying she was already on the guest list.

This was the first time Tim had met both Jo and Ryan, and it was apparent they hit it off immediately.

Jo couldn't help but remark on how nice Tim was and hoped that they both had a future together.

As friends and family mingled with each other, the atmosphere was electric.

Tilly and Maddie were catching up with Jo and Ryan, chatting and laughing about all that had happened during their time apart.

Ella was so proud to have Tim with her, and during a quiet moment, they looked into each other's eyes and kissed passionately.

Ella thanked Tim for the beautiful surprise he had planned, which she would never forget. Tim then whispered that the surprises were not over yet.

Tim and Ella strolled towards the dimly lit bar, surrounded by the crowd's lively chatter. Tim suddenly reached out to Ella and handed her a glass of chilled champagne.

As Ella turned to express her gratitude, she caught sight of Lauren vigorously waving her hands in the distance, rushing towards her. Ella's heart leaped with joy as she realised her sister had joined the celebration.

'You can't get rid of me that easy Lauren said out loud.

Ella sprinted towards Lauren, extending her arms eagerly to welcome her but unable to regain her composure.

At that moment, and once again overwhelmed with emotions, they held each other tightly, reluctant to part as if they feared losing that precious moment.

Once again, tissues were on hand for yet more tears of joy.

Lauren and Ella linked arms as they strolled toward the bar, sharing a sisterly bond. Seeing them, Tim extended his arms to greet Lauren affectionately. "It's wonderful to finally meet you," he said. "Ella hasn't stopped talking about you." Lauren blushed at his kind words and reciprocated his embrace, holding him warmly. "It's a pleasure to meet you too, Tim," she replied. "Likewise, Ella has been singing your praises nonstop."

The three stood amid a lively party, surrounded by chatter and laughter.

They talked for quite some time, exchanging pleasantries and stories.

Lauren hoped Tim would take care of her sister and not make promises he couldn't keep.

Despite her worries, Lauren couldn't deny their affection. The way they looked at each other, the way their hands gently touched, spoke volumes of the love and happiness they shared.

276

As Ella and Tim stood chatting to the party guests, their cheeks slowly reddened, perhaps from the party's warmth or probably from the deep love and fondness they felt for each other. It was a beautiful sight to behold. The joyful sound of laughter and clinking glasses filled the air, creating an atmosphere of pure happiness and celebration. Everyone was gathered to celebrate Ella's birthday, a night she or everyone else would never forget.

Suddenly, Tim stood up and raised his hands, signalling for everyone's attention. The room fell silent, with only a few guests shuffling back to their seats. Then, Tim turned to Ella, his heart full of love and devotion.

As he drew closer to Ella, his heart pounding with nervous excitement, he knelt on one knee, his eyes locked with hers as he reached into his pocket and pulled out a small velvet box. With a trembling hand, he opened the box to reveal a stunning diamond ring that caught the light and shimmered like a million stars in the dimly lit room. His voice shaking with emotion, he asked for her hand in marriage, hoping with all his heart that she would say yes.

As Ella moved closer to him, her cheeks blushing and her heart beating with anticipation, she proudly said, "Yes, Tim, I will marry you."

The room erupted in cheers and applause as the two embraced and sealed their love with a kiss.

Chapter 34

As she gazed proudly at the exquisite diamond ring adorning her left hand, she couldn't help but feel an overwhelming sense of joy and contentment. The radiant sparkle of the ring reminded her of the deep love and tenderness that her soon-to-be husband had consistently shown her throughout their time together. She felt immense gratitude and excitement at the thought of spending the rest of her life with him.

Earlier that day, Ella had found herself believing nobody truly cared about her birthday. Moments later, she was entirely surprised when Tim arranged a delightful gathering at Attwoods, surprising her with the presence of her closest friends and cherished family members. The atmosphere was filled with love and warmth, and she couldn't express enough gratitude to Tim for turning what initially seemed like an ordinary day into the most extraordinary and unforgettable birthday celebration.

Ella has encountered challenges in recent years that have left her with vivid and poignant memories. She has navigated a roller coaster of emotions, experiencing many highs and lows. Despite these tumultuous experiences, she embarked on a remarkable transformation that ultimately brought her a deep sense of fulfilment, contentment, and unbridled happiness, with the unwavering support of Tim and her forever friends playing a crucial role.

One of the most significant events in Ella's life was the wedding of her close friends Jo and Ryan. They got married and settled in the scenic town of Banff, Alberta, which is nestled in the heart of the Canadian Rockies.

Whilst Ella and Tim were invited to the wedding, they were assigned important roles during the ceremony.

Ella was her one and only flower lady, while Tim was asked if he would be an usher.

Their trip to Canada was quite remarkable as they got to see many beautiful sights. They found the country to be amazing, just as Jo had described it. Ella understood why Jo had chosen to start a new life in this exceptional country.

Seeing the joy and contentment on the faces of Jo and Ryan, Ella felt a deep sense of happiness for them. The couple seemed to be living the life many only dream of, and witnessing their joy meant the world to her. It was heart-warming for Ella to be told that Jo's parents visit regularly.

She knew how much it meant to Jo to have them in her life, especially considering their absence during her childhood.

Jo now had the love and support of her parents, which filled Ella's heart with immense joy.

Upon their return from Canada, Ella found comfort in the rhythm of her daily life.

She often daydreamed about all the places she had visited. She was lucky to have seen some parts of Europe and, further afield, Australia's beautiful scenery, wild outback, and diverse wildlife.

Canada's majestic mountains and clear lakes also made a lasting impression on her. But her time with Jo, Tilly, and Maddie in Antibes, France, will always hold a special place in her heart.

Yet, in those rare moments of silence, Ella was struck by the unique allure of her hometown, Buckland Ridge. Its offerings, so familiar yet so special, deepened her appreciation for life's simple pleasures.

What more could she ask for?

Tim now spends all his time at Attwoods, overseeing and managing the restaurant's day-to-day operations.

His expertise in food safety and hygiene has been instrumental in ensuring that the restaurant meets the highest standards of quality and service.

Ella, on the other hand, focuses on the creative side of things, constantly coming up with innovative menu ideas that keep customers coming back for more.

Her attention to detail and dedication to using only the freshest, locally sourced ingredients, puts Attwoods among some of the best restaurants in the area by far.

Their unwavering commitment to quality and innovation has recently been acknowledged with a prestigious food award, a recognition highly coveted in the culinary world.

This certificate hangs on the reception wall for all to view.

Ella and Tim, together with the Attwoods team, are incredibly proud of what they have accomplished. They have worked tirelessly to bring their vision to life, and the recognition they have received is a testament to their hard work and dedication.

They look forward to continuing to provide customers with an unforgettable dining experience.

One of the most memorable moments during the past 12 months was when Ella and Tim joyfully tied the knot after a brief engagement.

A gorgeous and sentimental wedding ceremony celebrating their marriage was held at Attwood's, set against the beautiful backdrop of the Dales.

The entire atmosphere was enchanting, with the natural beauty of the surroundings enhancing the already magical occasion.

Surrounded by their nearest and dearest, the couple exchanged meaningful vows, creating a cherished and unforgettable experience.

After the wedding breakfast, the newlywed couple set off on their honeymoon to the beautiful Provence region in the South of France, possibly one of their favourite places to spend a romantic time together.

As they arrived in Provence, the air was filled with the sweet scent of lavender and wildflowers that grew in abundance across the fields, creating a picturesque and serene atmosphere.

The couple spent their days exploring the winding roads and narrow streets of the charming towns and villages, each with unique architecture, history, and culture. They visited the bustling markets filled with fresh produce and artisanal crafts and sampled the local cuisine, savouring every bite of the delicious Provençal dishes.

As they walked hand in hand through the fragrant fields of lavender and sunflowers, the couple felt a sense of pure joy and contentment, knowing together they were sharing this magical experience. It was the perfect destination for the couple to spend their honeymoon and create unforgettable memories.

After a profoundly romantic and unforgettable honeymoon in the captivating region of Provence, Ella and Tim were filled with hope and decided to purchase a lavish apartment in a picturesque village just 20 kilometres south of the vibrant city of Marseille. They saw this investment as a wise decision and envisioned themselves enjoying extended periods in Provence, basking in the sunlight and savouring the delightful Mediterranean weather. This vision of a peaceful and relaxing life together filled them with hope and excitement.

After much contemplation, Tim and Ella carefully decided to step back from the day-to-day operations of their restaurant. They approached their staff with sensitivity and assured them that with their exceptional team, Attwoods would maintain its high standards even without their constant involvement.

Ella expressed her confidence in the team's ability to professionally and warmly welcome customers. The head chef, while initially surprised and saddened by the news, quickly assured Tim and

Ella that he and the rest of the staff would work tirelessly to uphold the restaurant's esteemed reputation.

One more reason for stepping back is that very soon, the gentle pitter-patter of little feet will be heard.

It's true - Ella and Tim are expecting their first child, and the whole community, as well as friends from near and far, are thrilled about it.

Lauren is over the moon at the prospect of becoming an Auntie and has already begun planning a trip that perfectly coincides with the little one's arrival.

Ella has been experiencing a tumultuous range of emotions lately. She has been realising that this moment in her life is when she would have needed her mother's guidance and support the most. Despite this, she finds solace in Tim's mother, who is a true blessing in disguise.

Initially hesitant, Ella has come to treasure her mother-in-law's constant presence. She sees her not only as a mother-in-law but as an unwavering friend who has supported her during her pregnancy.

From accompanying her to the doctor's appointments to helping her prepare for the baby's arrival, she has gone above and beyond to ensure that Ella is comfortable and well taken care of.

The day little Ethan entered the world, miracles were unfolding. Despite the initial fear and apprehension caused by some complications during birth, Ella and Tim experienced an indescribable surge of joy and relief when they finally cradled their precious baby boy in their arms. The rollercoaster of emotions they had navigated throughout Ella's pregnancy, from the initial joy to the intense anxiety, culminated in an overwhelming sense of peace and wonder.

For Ella and Tim, Ethan's safe arrival was not just the best thing that had ever happened to them but also a deeply cherished blessing that filled their hearts with immense gratitude.

The arrival of a new baby is always a joyous occasion, and for Lauren, the birth of her nephew Ethan was no exception.

She is overjoyed to have a little bundle of joy to dote on and watch grow and can't wait to meet him as soon as possible.

The family is looking forward to a long-awaited reunion to celebrate Ethan's arrival and to revel in the special bond of welcoming a new member into the family.

Tim's parents have taken to their roles as first-time grandparents with enthusiasm, showering Ethan with love and affection.

The joy of recently becoming a mother has been overshadowed by a significant loss for Ella.

Her beloved dog, Sammy, recently passed away, leaving her feeling completely devastated.

Though Sammy lived a good life and reached the age of 14, it did not help Ella overcome her grief.

Sammy was a constant source of comfort and support for Ella, and his absence has created a massive void in her life. Through countless difficult times, they shared a journey filled with joyous moments and weathered many storms together, forming an unbreakable bond.

When Ella's mother passed away, Sammy provided the most comfort, enabling Ella to move forward despite the immense pain. Rest assured, Sammy's memory will always be cherished and will forever hold a special place in Ella's heart.

RIP, my dearest Sammy. xxx

Chapter 35

After much contemplation, Tim and Ella finally decided to move from the house where Ella had spent her entire childhood. The memories were significant, good and not so good, but Ella believed that it was time to let go and start afresh.

She eagerly looked forward to building new memories with Tim and their son, Ethan, somewhere new but not too far away from Buckland Ridge.

Tim was fully aware of the emotional strain Ella had been under over the past couple of years, with the loss of her mother, the demolition of Tastebuds, and, most recently, the loss of her dear pet dog, Sammy.

Tim was determined to support Ella in every way possible and make this transition as smooth as possible. Tim appeared to be in a state of concern, perhaps bordering on anxiety, about the potential repercussions that the memories associated with the loss of Ella's loved ones and the traumatic time of losing her beloved restaurant could have on her emotional state.

It had deeply impacted her, and Tim felt it was his responsibility to take appropriate measures to ensure her well-being.

Therefore, he believed it necessary to move away to a place where they could start and create a brighter future with Ethan, feeling confident the move would be best for his family.

The couple eventually found their dream home, a beautiful Victorian architecture house in the serene and picturesque hamlet of Stoney Brook, just outside Buckland Ridge. The house boasts spacious and comfortable rooms, providing ample space for them to spread out and unwind. Inside is tastefully designed with a perfect blend of old-world charm and contemporary style, adding to its overall appeal and character.

They feel fortunate to have found a home in such a lovely and welcoming community, and they look forward to creating many wonderful memories in their new home.

They believe that Stoney Brook is the perfect place to raise their family and feel grateful to call it their home.

They wonder what the future holds and are excited to think about the possibilities ahead.

Who knows, perhaps, one day, Ethan will have a younger brother or sister with whom he can share his adventures.

In addition to the beautiful surroundings, the family is lucky enough to have Tim's parents living just ten minutes down the road. This proximity means that they can easily rely on them for help with babysitting duties, which will undoubtedly come in handy for Ella and Tim as they adjust to their new life with Ethan.

Six months have passed since they settled into their new home, and they have decided to throw a party in the spacious grounds, which happens to coincide with Ethan's second birthday.

Unfortunately, Lauren cannot attend the party due to her work commitments and limited holiday allowance.

However, she can still be present virtually through Facetime.

Lauren was informed that Ethan, a spirited and lively little boy, is doing well despite a few minor scrapes on his knees.

He's been his usual energetic self, running around, stumbling, and falling occasionally, just like any other toddler.

It's a familiar scene of a young boy in his element, full of curiosity and eagerness to explore and learn. Ella and Tim, always present and attentive, are his steadfast companions, ensuring he's safe and cared for.

On the other hand, the timing was perfect for Jo and Ryan, who will be flying back home from Canada to visit Jo's parents. They are excited to join Ella and Tim's house party and cannot wait to share some exciting news with them.

Ella received a message notifying her that Tilly and Maddie wouldn't be able to attend her party. They were in Milan attending an Art Exhibition showcasing a couple of Maddie's landscapes. However, they wished Ella and Tim the best for a great party and couldn't wait to get in touch when they returned from Italy.

The long-awaited day of the party had finally arrived, and Jo and Ryan were the first ones to arrive, carrying a case of Champagne, a striking bouquet, and a beautifully wrapped gift for Ethan. The sprawling garden was adorned with marquees, and the atmosphere was buoyant with music and chatter.

There was sheer delight on the faces of Jo and Ryan as they wanted to share some of their news with Ella and Tim.

Ella was extremely curious and couldn't help but ask what the news was.

With a playful smile, Jo teased Ella and asked her if she could guess.

She then rubbed her tummy up and down, and Ella laughed, saying, "Do you have wind?"

However, Ella soon realised Jo was pregnant, and they hugged each other excitedly.

Tim shook Ryan's hand and congratulated them on their happy news.

"Sleepless nights ahead," Tim said light-heartedly.

"Oh, that's Jo's job," Ryan remarked jovially.

Ella expressed her concern and exclaimed, "Oh my! You shouldn't be drinking Champagne in your condition, Jo!"

Jo responded graciously, explaining that the Champagne was a gift from her and Ryan to celebrate Ella's new home.

Jo also promised to opt for soft, non-alcoholic drinks instead.

Ella felt relieved and brushed her hands across her brow, satisfied that Jo had made the right decision for a young pregnant lady.

The atmosphere was electric as they all walked into the house, where Ethan played with his grandparents in the playroom.

The party was in full swing; champagne corks started popping, and the sound of laughter filled the air.

Suddenly, a tap on the window caught Ella's attention.

Looking outside, she saw a man walking up the pathway carrying a large plastic box.

Ella was surprised but curious as she walked towards him.

The man explained that he had a package for a little boy named Ethan

Ella returned to the house to fetch Ethan, saying somebody wants to meet you.

Ethan and Ella stepped outside, holding hands tightly

As the man approached them, he smiled, knelt, and opened the box, revealing a nine-week-old black and tan cocker spaniel.

Ella's heart swelled with happiness at the sight of the tiny puppy.

She had missed having a dog since the loss of Sammy, and the thought of having a new furry companion filled her with immense joy.

As the man handed the puppy over to Ethan, his face was beaming with delight. He gently stroked the puppy's soft fur, and Ella could see the love and affection in his eyes.

Although she was a little apprehensive about introducing a new puppy to the family so soon after the loss of Sammy, Ella knew it was the right thing to do.

The puppy would have plenty of space to run around and exercise in the large garden, and it would be an excellent opportunity for Ethan to learn about animals at a young age.

As they all went back inside, Ella could feel the warmth in her heart, knowing their family had just grown by one more adorable member.

Ethan's eyes widened with excitement as he gazed at the adorable puppy in his arms. "Can we keep him, Mummy?" he asked, looking up at Ella with pleading eyes. Ella smiled warmly at him. "Of course, it's a birthday gift from your grandparents just for you," she replied, her voice filled with affection.

Without wasting a moment, Ethan rushed down the hallway to the room where his grandparents were sitting, the puppy wagging its tail excitedly in his grasp. As soon as they caught sight of Ethan's beaming face, they knew their gift had been a success.

Ethan thanked them in his little way, holding out his arms for a cuddle and a kiss, his heart overflowing with joy and gratitude.

Shortly after, the phone rang, and Lauren called on Facetime.

"Happy birthday, little man," Lauren shouted.

Ethan told her that he was given a puppy for his birthday.

Ella picked up the puppy and showed it to Lauren, who was thrilled to see the joy on Ethan's and Ella's faces.

"I suppose that has made you extremely happy, too, Ella," Lauren remarked.

"Absolutely," Ella replied with a smile.

"What's its name?" Lauren asked.

"He hasn't been named yet," Ella replied.

After what seemed like a long conversation, it was time to say goodbye to Lauren.

As the evening came to an end and the guests had departed, it left Ella, Tim and birthday boy Ethan playing with the new addition to the family in the conservatory, which overlooked the excellent maintained garden adorned by many different trees.

The lively young puppy, full of energy, dashed joyfully around the cozy room, completely at home in his new environment. Their hearts were filled with overwhelming love and fondness, and even Tim couldn't resist the puppy's irresistible charm. For now, they affectionately called him Mr. Who, but they knew it was only a matter of time before they discovered the perfect name.

And true enough, it didn't take long, the next day, in fact.

Discussing names over breakfast for the adorable puppy, Ella looked up while Ethan was finishing his cereal and said, 'How about calling the pup Willow?'

Ethan was beaming with pure joy as he excitedly clapped his hands in delight.

Tim had just walked back into the room, carrying a steaming pot of coffee, and he couldn't help but share in Ethan's happiness. They had just chosen the perfect name for their new puppy, filling them with a sense of warmth and contentment. They knew that this little puppy would be loved beyond measure by all the family, and they couldn't wait to start this new chapter in their lives together.

Chapter 36

As Christmas approached, the family decided to travel to their newly acquired apartment in Provence for the Christmas festivities, spending quality time together.

To complete the holiday, they decided to take the family car and take with them Willow, who now had a Pet Passport together with the appropriate Health Certificate, that allowed him to travel.

They ensured that all of Willow's injections were up to date, as this was essential for the trip.

It had been arranged that Tim's parents would fly down to the apartment a few days later so they could babysit Ethan and dog-sit Willow while Ella and Tim spent a few days skiing together in the Alps.

The day of the holiday had arrived, and the family was brimming with excitement, especially young Ethan, who was bursting with joy. The scenery changed from peaceful rolling hills and charming villages to majestic, snow-capped mountains and pristine valleys, adding to their thrill.

However, the arduous journey began to take its toll on little Ethan; at two and a half years old, he was visibly exhausted and increasingly fidgety and struggling to keep up with the adventure.

Willow, on the other hand, was a picture of curiosity. Safely secured in his cage at the back of the car, he remained wide-eyed, his gaze flitting back and forth as he observed the ever-changing surroundings. His tail wagged eagerly, and he emitted a soft, contented purr, a testament to his enjoyment of the journey.

Finally, after a long drive, they arrived at their recently acquired apartment well after midnight.

As they shared a loving gaze, Ella and Tim felt a sense of contentment wash over them. They knew they had stumbled upon their happy place, and nothing could taint their joy.

Nevertheless, there was something troubling Ella and Tim had noticed a worried look on her face.

She told him that she wanted to ensure that Attwoods would run effortlessly without them.

After several phone calls, Ella was overjoyed to learn that the team had handled the Christmas reservations and clients with remarkable skill and professionalism, leaving no margin for error.

Despite the bustling ambiance of the restaurant, the staff flawlessly managed every aspect of their responsibilities. Ella found solace in her team's unwavering dedication, allowing her to fully embrace the Christmas holidays without any concerns.

The next day, they set out to find the perfect Christmas tree for Ethan. The little boy had been asking non-stop if Father Christmas would see him while he was away from home. Ella confidently reassured him, "Of course! Father Christmas knows where every child is on Christmas Day."

The holiday became even more special when Tim's parents arrived. The crackling warmth of the log fire and the twinkling lights on the Christmas tree, each adorned with unique decorations, created a cozy and comforting atmosphere for Ethan.

Snuggled peacefully on his soft, plush blanket, Willow curled up into a cozy little fur ball. His eyes gently closed in contentment, and a faint but unmistakable smile appeared.

As Ella and Tim stood together near the window, they were captivated by the sight that greeted them.

Countless twinkling snowflakes descended from the starlit sky, transforming the world outside into a magical, glistening winter wonderland.

Tim and Ella stood facing each other, their eyes locked in deep connection. Tim's gaze shifted downwards to meet Ella's as he tenderly expressed, "In this very moment, I have everything and everyone I hold dear in my life. I couldn't have wished for more."

Feeling herself falling into his arms, Ella knew she finally had everything she wanted. It wasn't just the warmth and comfort of his embrace but the sense of completeness that came with having the love of a family again in her life.

After a wonderful Christmas, with far too much food and wine, the Christmas season began winding down.

It was now time for Ella and Tim to pack their bags for their upcoming mountain trip to Provence-Alpes-Côte d'Azur.

The anticipation of the journey was profound, but at the same time, it was a bittersweet moment for them as this was the first time they would be leaving their darling son, Ethan, behind. Although they knew he would be in good hands and probably showered with love and attention by his grandparents, the thought of being away from him still tugged at their heartstrings.

Meanwhile, Willow was having the time of his life on his holiday. He was in his element with the crisp mountain air and endless walks in the picturesque surroundings. Willow was greeted with adoration and attention from the locals everywhere he went, who couldn't resist his charm.

The villagers were smitten with this soft ball of fur, and Willow was more than happy to oblige them with cuddles and affection.

As Ella and Tim set out on their mountain getaway, emotions engulfed them.

Their hearts brimmed with excitement at the prospect of finally having some time to themselves.

This precious opportunity came after such a busy time, from managing Attwoods to welcoming their new baby, a new puppy, Willow, and moving to their new home.

Amidst the joy, uncertainty lingered as they pondered how best to make the most of their precious time alone.

However, Ella knew the importance of focusing on the present moment and cherishing every minute together. For the next week, they would finally be able to unwind and be a couple again without the distractions of everyday life. It was a much-needed break from the hustle and bustle of their busy lives.

As they said goodbye, Ella could feel Tim's mother's genuine warmth and tender emotions enveloping her. It was as if her mother was not far away, saying, "Take good care of yourselves" through their embrace. This emotional connection left a lasting impression on Ella, and she knew it would stay with her for a long time.

Arriving at their hotel in the mountains, and once unpacked, Ella couldn't wait to show off her skiing expertise to Tim, but it wasn't long before she began falling and sliding about.

"Thought you could ski?" Tim said affectionately.

Ella told him it had been quite some time since she experienced the slopes and that he had to give her time to regain her nerve.

"I'll believe that when I see it, he said flippantly."

Despite enjoying their time together and making new memories, their minds constantly depended on Ethan.

Once it was confirmed that Ethan was enjoying time with his grandparents and Willow too of course, they felt happy and at ease.

As Ella savoured her hot chocolate, she reminisced about her backpacking days in Chamonix with Jo.

The experience had been unforgettable in many ways, but almost one of the best times of her life.

Despite the occasional intrusions of a somewhat cold relationship with Hugo into her thoughts, she found solace in the arms of her husband, Tim, who had given her so much happiness.

The memory of Hugo was quick to fade away as she reflected on the joy that Tim and Ethan had brought into her life. She felt grateful for such a wonderful family, and nothing could replace the warmth and comfort they provided her.

She often found herself lost in deep contemplation, recalling Eric and Marie, the managers of the enchanting ski resort in the stunning Chamonix Valley. The tranquil atmosphere they created, like a soothing balm, lingered in her thoughts. She couldn't help but wonder if they had gradually handed over their responsibilities. Yet, she held onto the belief that they were leading lives filled with contentment and purpose. The memories of their affectionate bond and the tranquillity they exuded as a couple continued to hold a cherished place in her heart.

Under the soft glow of the cafe lights, she cradled her steaming mug of hot chocolate, relishing the way it brought warmth back to her cold cheeks.

Despite the cozy atmosphere, a persistent unease nagged at her thoughts as the vision of a potential snow slide or avalanche loomed in her mind, filling her with an unshakable fear. However, the touch of Tim's hand and his steady presence by her side gradually eased her apprehension.

As she leaned across the table, the gentle clasp of Tim's hand filled her with a sense of security and tenderness, surrounding her in a moment of profound comfort. In that instance, she was overwhelmed with a deep sense of gratitude, a deep appreciation for her continued existence and well-being. She couldn't help but reflect on how vastly different things could have been on that fateful Christmas Day in Chamonix.

She and so many others were lucky to get away with their lives.

Ella believed that her recent trip to the mountains with Tim was not only a chance to enjoy skiing but also an opportunity to reflect on her fears and leave them behind.

She felt safe and secure in her husband's arms, knowing that nothing could come between them.

It was a time to let go of the past and embrace the future.

After a most beautiful and refreshing trip to the mountains, Ella and Tim arrived back at their apartment to find an excited little boy and a lively puppy eagerly awaiting their return.

Tim's parents were excited to share their enjoyable experiences with Ethan and Willow. They cherished every moment spent with their grandchild and the adorable puppy and would be delighted to be the perfect grandparents once again.

Tim's parents had now flown back home and were thankful for the most wonderful Christmas they had spent in Provence.

A few days later, the time had come for the rest of them to bid farewell to the picturesque Provence region, leaving behind the sweet-smelling lavender fields and enchanting villages. They couldn't help but feel sad as they prepared to depart from this captivating and idyllic setting.

They carefully packed their belongings into the car, making sure not to forget any souvenirs they had collected during their stay.

As they drove down the winding roads towards the coast, they discussed their plans to possibly visit Tilly and Maddie before completing the final journey home.

The excitement of surprising their friends with their unexpected visit filled them with anticipation.

They decided to take a considerable detour due to the uncertainty of winter weather and the forecast of more snow in the southwest of France. However, the journey was worth it when they finally arrived and saw the overwhelming joy on Tilly and Maddie's faces as they opened the door and found their beloved friends standing there, brimming with happiness at the sight of them.

As Tilly turned the doorknob and opened the door, her eyes widened, and her face broke into a joyful smile.

"Wow! This is unbelievable!" she gasped, eyes wide with surprise and excitement.

"My wonderful second family is finally here.

Maddie, come quick, you have to see this.

It's Ella, Tim, Ethan, and the most beautiful and lovable dog I have ever laid my eyes on!"

Tilly and Maddie were delighted to meet little Ethan and Willow. They showered them with overwhelming attention and spent hours playing ball and fetch with Willow. The joy and happiness on Ethan's little face was truly priceless.

They were incredibly kind to Ethan, and he cherished every moment spent in their company. "I really like it here, Mummy," exclaimed Ethan, clearly enjoying his time with Tilly and Maddie.

Whilst catching up and sharing a bottle of wine, Maddie revealed that she might have sold two paintings at the recent Art Show held in Milan. It could be a turning point in her career, as it could help her gain some recognition in the Art World.

Ella could sense the excitement in her voice, and it was evident that she had worked hard and was dedicated to achieving this level.

Everyone eagerly awaits the realisation of her dream, and with everything crossed, hopefully, she will achieve her goal.

Ella then inquired about Tilly's current work situation.

It was only last week when Tilly suddenly decided to respond to a job advertised in the local fashion magazine.

A prestigious fashion house preparing for Fashion Week in Paris required an assistant dressmaker for their upcoming collection.

Surprisingly, Tilly found herself talking with one of the designers of the fashion house, who, after a long discussion, promptly offered her the job after hearing all about the qualifications she had gained at university back in England.

With this job, Tilly finally felt like she had found her place in the world and was eager to make the most of it.

Tilly also believed that "Everything comes to those who wait" and spoke with an air of so much confidence.

As Ella reflected on the current situation, she couldn't help but notice Tilly's remarkable transformation.

It seemed that Tilly was ready to embrace the unknown challenges of the outside world despite the hardships she had faced in her life so far.

This new, resilient Tilly was a testament to her strength and determination.

Ella couldn't contain her excitement as she expressed how happy she was for her.

All this great news resulted in a celebratory mood, with champagne bottles popping to mark the occasion.

Tim was savouring a moment of relaxation, thoroughly enjoying Tilly and Maddie's pleasant company.

They all got along fabulously, and Tim felt entirely at home in their company once again.

Although it was still winter, the air was starting to feel warmer even after the recent snowfall during Christmas.

The temperature was certainly rising and rising fast.

The sun was starting to emerge from behind the fluffy clouds, casting a warm, golden light.

The next morning was a glorious day, so they decided to stroll along the tree-lined promenade of the gorgeous coastline, admiring the beautiful landscape and moorings of expensive and luxurious yachts.

This was undoubtedly the place for the rich and famous, remarked Tim.

"Hey, perhaps we should get a boat," Ella suggested playfully.

"Didn't know you were a sailor as well as a skier," Tim replied sarcastically.

"There's more to me than running a restaurant," Ella jokingly replied.

As they strolled along the promenade, they paused to take in the sight of the waves crashing onto the shore. The ocean water, white and foamy, glistened in the bright sunlight, creating a picturesque image that left them speechless.

Walking alongside them was Willow, whose nose twitched with excitement as he sniffed the ground, his long, silky ears fluttering in the breeze.

The waves continued to crash against the shore, creating a soothing sound that filled the air.

The salty ocean air was refreshing, invigorating their senses with its briny scent.

As they walked on, Ethan began to feel sleepy.

His eyes grew heavy, and eventually, he fell asleep snuggled in his buggy whilst the others continued their walk, admiring the scenery around them.

As their time in the picturesque town of Antibes drew to a close, they couldn't help but feel that everything had gone so quickly.

However, the moment of departure was fast approaching, and they knew they had to bid farewell to their beloved friends and the enchanting scenery that had captured their hearts.

As they carefully and thoughtfully loaded their car, they took a moment to ensure that Willow had ample room to stretch out and relax during the long journey ahead.

The air was filled with a bittersweet sensation – yet a tinge of sadness for leaving behind the memories of a beautiful time spent with special friends.

As they exchanged heartfelt hugs and goodbyes, Tilly and Maddie informed Ethan that he could now refer to them as Aunty Tilly and Aunty Maddie.

Puzzled, Ethan asked, "Are you really my Aunties?" To which Tilly and Maddie replied, "Yes, we are now."

The ferry departure was scheduled for the following day, allowing them ample time to cover the 700-mile distance with a planned overnight stop. They cherished every moment of their journey, and their expressions of pure joy and contentment spoke volumes about their unforgettable experiences.

Chapter 37

It's unbelievable that five years have passed since Ella and Tim began their culinary journey together, demonstrating unwavering dedication. They have invested their hearts and souls into their restaurant throughout this time, and the results have been truly remarkable.

While Ella and Tim have taken a step back from their day-to-day operations, they continue actively overseeing their restaurant's thriving progress. They have meticulously assembled a dedicated and reliable team whose invaluable contributions play a critical role in the establishment's ongoing success.

Attwoods has solidified its standing as a leading culinary destination in the region, attracting an ever-expanding base of loyal patrons who value the exceptional menu and top-notch service. Furthermore, the restaurant has recently broadened its offerings to include exquisite wedding ceremonies and receptions in its newly renovated banqueting suite, further establishing its position as a premier event venue.

Ella and Tim are elated by their accomplishments. Their unwavering commitment, relentless hard work, and unbridled passion have allowed them to surpass their expectations. Together, they proudly stand, their journey serving as a testament to the rewards of unwavering commitment and relentless hard work.

In the Henderson household, life is always bustling with activity. The addition of their daughter, Darcy, has brought even more joy and excitement to their family. At just six months old, little Darcy has already captured the heart of her older brother, Ethan.

Lauren's recent announcement about this remarkable man in her life called George has brought overwhelming joy to everyone around her.

Ella now feels that Lauren can move forward with her life, fully engaging in her career while enjoying herself and potentially finding a new romantic connection.

Lauren shared with her sister how she and George first crossed paths at the hospital nearly nine months ago. He works as an Orthopaedic Consultant, and although their differing shift schedules initially posed a challenge, they eventually found time to connect.

Lauren confided in Ella that she believed she now had the one person to settle down with and hoped she would be as happy as both Ella and Tim.

Jo and Ryan now have two wonderful sons, Jack and Liam. Their dream of building a life in Canada has become a remarkable reality that seems almost like a storybook tale. They have firmly established themselves in Banff, renowned for its breathtaking natural beauty and picturesque landscapes, and they have no plans to leave.

Jo's parents make a dedicated effort to visit their beloved grandchildren often. The little ones have brought immense happiness into their lives, ensuring that each visit remains a cherished and unforgettable occasion.

Tim's parents are known for their kind and generous nature, especially when it comes to spoiling their treasured grandchildren.

They are always eager to lend a helping hand with babysitting duties whenever possible.

Ella has developed a deep affection for Tim's Mum, and she often sees a resemblance to her late mother. Not only does she display a natural motherly instinct towards Ella, but her love and support provide comfort and solace, filling the void left by Ella's loss.

The story of Tilly and Maddie is an awe-inspiring testament to the power of perseverance and hope. Despite their challenges and obstacles, Tilly and Maddie exude an infectious aura of happiness, contentment, and, most of all, love.

As Tilly recounted the harrowing details of her abusive childhood, Ella's heart swelled with a mixture of profound sorrow and overwhelming happiness. She felt immense sadness for the unimaginable pain and adversity Tilly had endured during her formative years. Yet, she also showed much happiness knowing Tilly had found a new life filled with peace and fulfilment. Tilly's resilience and a newfound sense of hope served as an inspiration to everyone around her.

Tilly said that Ella and Jo had played pivotal roles in guiding her towards a positive and hopeful outlook on life. Their unwavering support and encouragement had been instrumental in helping Tilly navigate through her difficult past and embrace a brighter future.

Since leaving university, Ella's life has been quite a journey. She has travelled widely to many places, and experiencing its highs and lows with the ability to remain resilient in the face of adversity is truly inspiring.

Dealing with the immense pain of losing her mother and her cherished dog, Sammy, was a tough challenge.

However, she realised that she couldn't navigate the journey of grief alone.

That's when Tim came into her life. His unwavering support and empathy became a symbol of hope for Ella, and she will forever be grateful.

Tim stood by her, offering a listening ear and a shoulder to lean on whenever she needed one. His unwavering empathy and comforting presence helped her through the most challenging times, eventually leading to a deep and meaningful connection between them.

After parting ways with Hugo, Ella believed she had lost everything. However, she soon discovered true love with Tim. The two boldly decided to embark on the challenging adventure of running a restaurant. Through perseverance and unwavering commitment, they overcame numerous obstacles and achieved remarkable success, enriching their lives with boundless happiness and inspiration.

Ella and Tim experienced immeasurable happiness as they blissfully welcomed their two precious children. Their growing family, nurtured by their enduring love and unwavering strength, has deeply moved all those who have witnessed their remarkable journey.

As Ella reflects on her life, she is filled with contentment and gratitude for the experiences and lessons that have enriched her.

However, a part of her will always be tethered to her beloved Yorkshire, no matter where life takes her.

She will forever carry the spirit of a proud Yorkshire lass, a testament to her roots and cherished memories, embracing the rugged landscapes, warm community, and beloved traditions that have shaped her now and forever.